GEORGE
BELLOWS
» Painter of America «

George Bellows by Robert
Aiken, 1908

*The Columbus Gallery of Fine
Arts, Columbus, Ohio*

GEORGE BELLOWS

» *Painter of America* «

CHARLES H. MORGAN

with an introduction by
Daniel Catton Rich

REYNAL & COMPANY   *New York 1965*

CONTENTS

	Preface	*7*
	Introduction	*11*
I.	*The Columbus Years, 1882–1904*	*17*
II.	*The New York School of Art, 1904–1906*	*37*
III.	*Foundations for Fame, 1906–1908*	*63*
IV.	*Recognition, 1908–1910*	*85*
V.	*The Holy Estate, 1910–1911*	*113*
VI.	*Reverberations from an Armory, 1911–1914*	*145*
VII.	*The War Years, 1914–1918*	*183*
VIII.	*Reorientation, 1919–1921*	*223*
IX.	*The House that George Built, 1921–1925*	*251*
X.	*The Aftermath, 1925–*	*287*
	Plates	*303*
	Index	*371*

Preface

In 1925, when George Bellows died at the age of forty-two, the American Art world was pulling itself apart at its seams. On the one hand was the National Academy of Design with its emphasis upon technique and upon an indefinable but delicate ideal of "beauty." Opposing this was the tide of European influences with its exploration of new palettes, new brushwork, new objectives. Between these two extremes Bellows appeared an enigma. He was an Academician, and at the same time a vigorous champion of the best that contemporary France could produce. There was nothing he would not explore if it offered an opportunity to learn.

He refused to be typed as a "Portraitist" or a "Landscapist," insisting that any subject was suitable for painting so long as it provoked the interest of the artist. Despite his reputation as the arch-interpreter of pugilism he painted only four canvases of action in the ring, and today the intimate portraits of his family and friends are considered quite their equal.

Intelligence was his and courage to support his convictions. At a time when it was considered suicidal for an artist to take critics and editors to task he never hesitated to do so if he thought his cause correct. He was born with extraordinary talent but earned the ability to discipline it.

Homer and Eakins to whom he was frequently compared in his lifetime both went abroad. Bellows never did, preferring to ferret out the best European work that came to this country and learn from it what he could. On the other hand no American painter of stature has ever so thoroughly covered his own native land, from Mattinicus and Monhegan off the coast of Maine to Carmel, California, and from Chicago to Santa Fe. Each change of scene gave him a new aspect of light, texture and color, while everywhere his lively personality opened up friendships, and with them ideas.

The title of this book was originally designed as "George Bellows, All American." He could more easily have made a name for himself as a shortstop in the major leagues than as a painter in New York. His contemporaries constantly noted the flavor of Walt Whitman in his pictures. He was completely of his own times yet he transcended them with his selective respect for the past and his clairvoyant view of the future. The study of his life has been a rewarding experience to the author.

A great many persons and institutions have contributed to its composition. First and foremost are Anne Bellows Kearney and Jean Bellows Booth who supplied the letters, manuscripts, photographs and clippings from their parents' estate. Gordon K. Allison has been a constant and invaluable aid through his close relationship with the family and his lifetime study of George Bellows' works. Viette and Leon Kroll knew the painter and his wife from a professional point of view and their recollections and interpretations have been of inestimable importance. These five have all read the manuscript and approved it. A few years ago the late Ethel Clarke wrote a fifty-page summary of her recollections of George and Emma Bellows for their children. This document, amplified by conversations with her, has contributed greatly to the tale.

Others who have aided in one way or another included relatives: Mrs. George K. Brown, Mrs. Frank Barry and Mrs. Howard Monett; artists: Edward R. Keefe and the late Randall Davey; friends: Miss Lucie Bayard and Mrs. Wesley G. France, daughter of Professor Joseph Taylor.

Among the most eager supporters of this enterprise have been Bellows' teammates from Columbus: Fred Cornell, Ralph Hoyer, Wright McCallip, Frank Shannon, and the late Charles Grant and Robert Patterson.

Dealers who knew Bellows and handled his work include H. V. Allison and Company, Hirschl and Adler, and the late Robert McIntyre of the Macbeth Gallery.

Many institutions have contributed generously, among them Ohio State University, The Boston Public Library, The Archives of American Art, The Columbus Gallery of Art, The Ohio State Historical Society, and The Yale University Library.

The staffs of many museums have cooperated with enthusiasm. Especially valuable have been researches of Leon A. Arkus, Miss Louisa Dresser, Henry S. Francis, Sinclair H. Hitchings, Edmund A. Kuehn, Daniel Catton Rich, Frederick A. Sweet and Mahonri S. Young.

Assistance of diverse kinds came from Edward Howard and William Lane of Columbus, Mrs. Horatio Bunker of Mattinicus, Mrs. Virginia Myers Downes of the New York Y.M.C.A., Mrs. Leon Polsky of 146 East 19th Street, and Homer A. Thompson of the Institute for Advanced Study.

The bibliography on George Bellows is small between hard covers, and enormous if it includes magazine articles and newspaper reviews; for during his lifetime, he was forever in the public eye and has been ever since. The major publications were supervised by Emma Bellows, both published by Knopf: "George W. Bellows, His Lithographs," 1927, and "The Paintings of George Bellows," 1929; valuable contributions are contained in the three major exhibition catalogues: "George Bellows Memorial Exhibition," The Metropolitan Museum of Art, 1925; "George Bellows," The Art Institute of Chicago, 1946; and "George Bellows, A Retrospective Exhibition," The National Gallery of Art, 1957. The smaller picture books offer somewhat indifferent illustrations: "George Bellows," by George Eggers in the Whitney Museum series, 1931; and "George Bellows" by Peyton Boswell, Jr. The last of these contains an excellent record of the articles published on Bellows before 1942. After that the "Art Index" completes the tale.

Random notes of importance occur in "Lonely Americans" by Rollo Brown, New York, 1926, and "The Jersey Midlands" by Henry Charlton Beck, Rutgers University Press, 1962.

Note: George Bellows painted his first boxing picture in 1907 and called it "Stag at Sharkey's." In 1909 he painted another which he named "Club Night." When the Cleveland Art Museum purchased the latter in 1922 there occurred a change of titles for reasons no longer clear. To avoid confusion in the text over the identity of one of Bellows' most famous paintings, I have consistently referred to these paintings by their present, not their original, titles.

Introduction

For years George Bellows has remained a puzzle to me. How could the man who painted "Both Members of this Club," "Elinor, Jean and Anna" and the unforgettable "Portrait of his Mother" turn out mannered pictures like "The Crucifixion" and "The Picnic"? Among his lithographs I could admire a number; others seemed thin and lifeless. At times his drawings surged with power. Again they seemed to me disagreeably hard and brittle. To complicate the puzzle was the undeniable fact that almost everything Bellows did before 1913 was infused with spontaneity and executed with a command of paint rare in American art. After that it is the occasional success that holds us.

Now Charles Morgan has furnished part of the solution. He has written a lively, revealing biography of the man—his beginnings, his struggles and achievements. Having access to the family papers and impressions from those who knew him, he has constructed a Bellows we can better understand. He has projected the artist against a skillfully arranged backdrop of the period; social and political as well as artistic.

The result is a biography that reads like a novel. It might have been written by Booth Tarkington (without his irony) and have been called *Portrait of the Artist as an American*. Like many artists who die young, George Bellows was a young man in a hurry. He worked with a stubborn passion, almost unconsciously aware that he must succeed, now and at once. The author shows us the sources of Bellows' vitality and the bigness and sympathy of his understanding. He makes us see the hesitations and problems that surround the painter in America, and particularly those during the first decades of our century. The successful athlete from Ohio, with his narrow background of Methodism and Republicanism, never wavered in his desire to become a major artist. The moment he left Columbus and plunged into New York, he found his way. In the tenements and boxing clubs of the city and soon in the wilds of Monhegan, he discovered his own brand of staunch romanticism.

Twenty years ago during the big Bellows exhibition in Chicago, I suggested that when he came in contact with European modernism in the Armory Show, his confidence was shaken. No one seems to have paid any attention to that observation. It was neither, as far as I know, accepted nor rebutted. But I believe, looking at the later works, that it is still valid. Of course, I do not insist that this sudden outpouring of Cubism and Fauvism was the lone force that upset his painting. Before the First World War we were an affirmative, optimistic nation—with all the optimism of our isolation. During the war and afterwards, things changed, violently and unexpectedly. But though Harold Rosenberg recently defined the Armory Show as a public event with little consequence to our artists, I believe he is mistaken. Take for example the later development of the Eight, those painters with whom Bellows was most closely associated.

Two of them, Prendergast and Lawson, were already converts to Post-Impressionism. They simply went on in the same way. Luks, on the contrary, never met the issue. He now began to turn out weaker versions of a robust early style. Arthur B. Davies, misunderstanding cubist structure, dressed up his slender nudes in a Harlequin-faceted décor. Glackens succumbed completely to the color saturation of the late Renoir. Shinn repeated himself wittily and stylishly. Sloan finally ended with cross-hatched nudes, a late echo of Neo-Impressionism. Henri, the teacher of Bellows and the greatest influence on his art, merely grew flashier and more external.

Only Bellows, younger and more impressionable than these men, tried, with all his will, to redirect his vision. Hence the infatuation with Hambidge's theories of Dynamic Symmetry and disastrous experiments with Maratta's color palette.

It is well to remember that for all its talk of new approaches and the profound values of life, Henri's revolution harked back to an earlier point of view. Twentieth-century social content was expressed in a nineteenth-century technique. It is customary to point out Henri's debt to Manet. Actually he is in the lineage of Duveneck and Chase and his paintings spring from the tonal practices of Munich and Düsseldorf. Now Bellows of Columbus certainly knew Duveneck's portraits in nearby Cincinnati, and he began as a pupil in the Chase School. In New York, he quickly put himself in line with this tradition. It takes nothing away from Bellows to point out that there is a strong academic current in his art. This explains why the National Academy quickly took him in, while excluding true modernists like Maurer, Max Weber and Marin. It goes a long way toward accounting for the rather frightening array of prizes he won in exhibitions.

The only difference was that Bellows was a born painter. He could take an older tradition and make it live. I believe he saw best in relations of light and dark and when he used a rather narrow gamut of rich, striking color. If he attempted to *design* his works according to new formulas and started to heighten his palette artificially, he produced a stylized and often garish result. Bellows' enemy was not the National Academy; it was the new International Academy, toward which he yearned and which—in the long run—would only confuse him.

For the truth is that Bellows was not an intellectual painter. He was a highly intelligent one and brilliantly gifted in the visual and manual aspect. Theories and recipes defeated him. They got in the way of his instinctual feeling for the flowing gesture of brush or pencil. They dried up his emotions. Bellows was never sentimental but they reduced the pitch of his true sentiment.

Again and again during his later years Bellows threw away an attempt to be "modern" and painted with his old insight and exuberance. Here Eakins—seen in a climactic exhibit at the Metropolitan Museum in 1917—helped to free him. Charles Morgan has recorded his enthusiasm for Eakins and especially for the profound portrait of Mrs. Frismuth, "The Collector of Musical Instruments." Without a memory of this monumental canvas he would never, I am convinced, have painted the deeply-felt "Portrait of his Mother," now in Chicago. Another of his heroes was Whistler. This seems surprising, but only for a moment. Like Whistler, Bellows was continually searching for large, simple forms, and beneath vigor lay great delicacy of touch.

Today I do not look to Bellows for social comment. Sloan, our Rowlandson, is far more telling. Even Guy Pène du Bois who turned out artistic versions of the robots of John Held, Jr., reveals more of the mood of the twenties. Contrast his little pictures of Maud and Chester Dale dining out in New York with Bellows' unsuccessful and somewhat "official" portraits of the Dales. I believe the best of Bellows lies in those strong, simple and almost puritanical portraits where a love of painting and the unconscious bond between sitter and painter triumphed. Or in the early, powerful canvases of the prize fights, with their fused excitement of theme and brushwork. Or in a whole series of romantic landscapes, deeply, spontaneously set down with an authority rare in native art.

The best of Bellows lies in his freedom—not in his studied discipline. Twenty years after his death a group of American painters would for the first time in our history throw off their final shackles to create Abstract Expressionism. There is a tenuous tie between the expressiveness of Bellows and their revolution. And in his later works with their near-neon color and hard shiny surfaces, there appears a link with today's art of Pop. Perhaps, years ago, I underrated this side of Bellows' art. Either time has toned it or I have grown more liberal. For through the artist's work, as Charles Morgan portrays him, runs a consistent force that made it all possible.

Daniel Catton Rich

GEORGE
BELLOWS
» *Painter of America* «

Sunday, Going to Church; *lithograph, 1921.*

THE COLUMBUS YEARS

» *1882 - 1904* «

» I «   *"I arose surrounded by Methodists and Republi-cans."* George Bellows

Anna Smith Bellows sat in her rocking chair as her pains came and went, and the Ohio sun of August 12, 1882, blistered the paint on the iron fence around the lawn. She was a good-natured woman, tall, black-haired and bulky who, at the age of forty-two, had forsaken her spinsterhood and her home in Sag Harbor, Long Island, for a short slight widower nine years older than herself. It is doubtful if either had considered the possibility of their elderly union producing children; but at this moment, two years later, a child was very much on the way, although certainly in no hurry to arrive. Finally, after seventy-two hours of labor, she bore a son. "I could have had him right there in the rocking chair if the doctor hadn't been so fussy," she was fond of saying later. She named him George, after his father, but she tucked in the middle name of Wesley because she was sure he was destined to be a Methodist bishop.

The boy's father, at fifty-three, was a ginger-whiskered contractor and builder who held fine materials, sound craftsmanship, the Republican party, and the First Methodist Church in high esteem. In a nation-wide atmosphere of padded contracts and unscrupulous gains, his meticulous standards earned him the name of "Honest George." He asked only a modest profit for his work, and this made him an anachronism in Columbus, Ohio; but by spending an absolute minimum of his income, he was, like the rest of the world he lived in, building up a small but tidy fortune.

The family circle was soon enlarged to include Anna's sister Eleanor, always called "Aunt Fanny," who had come from Sag Harbor to add her own inexperience to the raising of her sister's son. A middle-aged wisp of a woman, Fanny Smith moved briskly about the house always attended by a Victorian aura of romance. She had been in love for years, but because the man of her choice was already married she sedulously refused him. That her suitor's wife was a hopeless lunatic made no difference at all, because Fanny would not countenance divorce. The Lord had made the marriage in the first place, and only the Lord could dissolve it. There was nothing to do but be patient.

The sole element of youth in the Bellows household was the baby's eighteen-year-old half sister. When pretty Laura Bellows married Benjamin Monett, a rising realtor, in 1884, her two-year-old brother's life was encircled by advancing middle-age.

There is a painting representing Shakespeare in his cradle watched over by all the immortal characters he would one day create. Except for some occasional earthy phrases murmured by his mother and his aunt, daughters of a long line of whaling captains, no hint of the social extremes or the vast spaces of the continent that he would one day immortalize attended George Wesley Bellows in his infancy.

At first the walls of the small brick house his father had built at unfashionable 265 East Rich Street bounded his existence. The porch looked out on a quiet, shady thoroughfare whose dusty surface echoed none of the incessant clangor from the iron-shod cart wheels rolling over the cobbles on East Broad Street, a few blocks away. When he could toddle, his world expanded to match his mother's. East Rich Street terminated at one end in a market, shaped like a rectangular cornucopia bursting with fruits and vegetables, meat and cheese. Here Anna Bellows, a formidable trencherwoman, spent many happy hours picking over the produce of the farms and the gossip of her neighbors. Just beyond the other end of the street was the First Methodist Church, the second pole of her existence. East Rich Street gave her all the bodily and spiritual sustenance that she, and for a time her son, required.

The larger world unfolded slowly, always under hen-like chaperonage. When the boy was three, the cornerstone of his father's Franklin County Courthouse was laid with great ceremony; a skinny child with lank, brown hair mercilessly parted and plastered down on his high sallow forehead, he sat between his mother and his aunt. His blue eyes sparkled at the flags and the uniforms, his large ears absorbed the efforts of the band. Sometimes he was escorted to the banks of the Olentangy River to watch the endless freight trains clanking their way through town, led by a snorting engine and terminating in a jouncy caboose that might, in cold weather, put out a little plume of smoke of its own. On Memorial Day and again on the Fourth of July, the G.A.R. veterans marched vigorously amid a swirl of brass and banners; and the circus parades were replete with spangled equestriennes, clowns, menageries, and horses bolting at the smell of elephants and lions, the steam calliope always shrieking a gaudy exit through the crowds. Such days were more exciting than Sundays.

The Sabbath Day was regimented in every respectable Columbus household. Mornings began with preparation for church, scrubbing, polishing, brushing, and the constriction into uncomfortable garments for the Lord—and the congregation—to see. The horse harnessed, the family drove decorously down East Rich Street to the First Methodist Church and entered wholeheartedly into the service. With the indiscriminate capacity of childhood, George ingested enormous quantities of Biblical lore and quickly learned to enjoy singing along with the hearty choir. The sermons atoned in part for their length with their liveliness, and the fervor of the congregation joining in the hymns, the "Amens" and the "Hallelujahs" made Sunday mornings of some interest.

Sunday afternoons were more tedious. After an enormous dinner, George's father took a nap, while his mother settled into her rocking chair and read aloud by the hour from the Bible or Longfellow or Scott, or anything else that came comfortably to hand. George sat quietly beside her and drew.

Nothing that she read to him found a place in his pictures. Instead, he chose the realities he knew, the parades and the freight trains, admirably suited to the long, narrow trimmings from his father's drafting board that served as drawing paper. One exception in his factual repertory was the Battle of Gettysburg, still a lively topic of conversation when two or more veterans gathered together and relived the Civil War.

It is conceivable that, given other outlets for Sunday afternoons, George Bellows might well have turned his talents to some other field than art. His first drawings show no special gifts at all. But as month succeeded month, his long slender fingers unconsciously received their first discipline. Aunt Fanny thought the drawings wonderful, treasured them, and encouraged him. While still a small boy he made up his mind to be an artist; thus Aunt Fanny, who had joined her sister primarily to keep her nephew washed and groomed almost beyond endurance, unconsciously opened the way to his career.

A few years later the Lord freed Aunt Fanny to follow the devices of her own heart. Her widowed suitor, Mr. Daggett of San Diego, came to Columbus to claim his new bride, and Aunt Fanny moved to the West Coast taking with her some of George's drawings and the only spark of imagination that graced the elderly Bellows household.

It was a scared, rather aloof small boy, dressed all in white, who faced new problems at the Sullivant School on State Street where Principal Susan McLaughlin and her aides dispensed the three R's to an assortment of boys and girls ranging in age from five to fifteen. A gangling, poorly coordinated, long-nosed child, George had none of the easy give-and-take that came so naturally to youngsters brought up in big families by young parents. His outlook on life was a long generation's older than his contemporaries. His clothes looked odd. He was clumsy at games, and this ineptitude hurt his pride, while his schoolmates' ridicule sharpened his temper. Worst of all, he called himself an "artist." When his fellows reminded him that art was sissy stuff in Columbus, combat ensued, and in the heat of these clumsy scuffles his stubbornness congealed his determination to become a real artist. Anna Bellows viewed her son's torn and bloodied white suits with dismay, but she was obstinate, too, and kept George in them until he was eight, a conspicuous target for the scorn of his contemporaries.

His intelligence spared him the onus of chores around the house. Told to weed the plantain out of the lawn, he did it so thoroughly that all the grass came with it. Sent out to the stable to groom the horse, he returned covered from head to foot with the groomings. After a few such experiences he found himself liberated to spend his time as he chose with a state ward named Charlie who had been taken in by George's parents and now provided him with noncombatant companionship. Charlie's life ambition was to become an undertaker, and he created a miniature cemetery in the backyard while George designed and executed the tombstones. If the boys of the neighborhood wanted no part of the "artist," the little girls adored his drawings, and he spent many hours on their front stoops turning out the pictures he knew best while they hung over him breathlessly and fed him dates and figs. His lively imagination made him a good storyteller, and he dabbled in poetry as well. One of these verses has survived, beginning:

> "HOW I LIVE
> "I live in a tent way out in the wood
> "And the shy foxes taste very good . . . "

On the fourth of May, 1891, the "Haymarket Bombing" in Chicago introduced dynamite into the growing tangle of American labor disputes. The Anarchists were blamed for the outrage, and although the conservative sage of American letters William Dean Howells, and the rising young dramatist George Bernard Shaw sided with the seven men accused, the Knights of Labor and most of the liberals hastily dissociated themselves from the movement. In later years Anarchism was to be of major interest to George Bellows, but at the age of nine it is doubtful if this incident had any impact on him. His elders' opinions can be guessed with certainty—the Bellows' home was a Gibraltar of conservatism.

At ten, George was a lonely, proud, bewildered boy. He had abandoned his long panoramas in favor of copying pictures of sailing ships, and his graphic skill was now such that his teachers encouraged him to decorate the blackboards with festive designs at Thanksgiving and Christmas. His less gifted schoolmates envied this distinction and made life so miserable for the "artist" outside the classroom that he remembered: "I was faced by a continual need of self-defence, and in those days either the street was too dangerous or my face and fists were wounded with the penalties of adventure. It was very good for my muscles."

One summer day in 1892, George Wesley Bellows came to an unlikely but momentous decision. From a vacant lot several blocks down the street drifted the familiar yips and yells of the "East Richers" playing a scrub baseball game. Everything he wanted and did not have was represented in those raucous sounds—friendship, participation, a chance of success in the one field that every one, old or young, would respect, not only in Columbus but in a whole nation seized with excitement over baseball. Such aspirations could invite only anguish at the start, promise disappointment thereafter, and hardly suggest the faintest hope of success at the end. To George Wesley Bellows, aged ten, some of these hazards were clear; yet he had courage, optimism, and an extraordinary mind. With no thought of abandoning his career in art and without considering his own dismally inadequate physique, he determined to become an athlete.

This resolution was at once a declaration of independence from his mother and a declaration of war on his contemporaries. These facts became evident immediately, but it took two decades to reveal the end result: the National Game would equip George to become the painter of the nation.

On the decisive afternoon the aspirant to future stardom evaded his doting mother and the family coachman she had imposed on him as a bodyguard, drifted as casually as he could onto the makeshift ball park, bided his time, and then politely asked the captain, Bob Patterson, if he might keep score for the team—provided, of course, that he got reports of the game into the local journals. Derisive howls echoed down East Rich Street at the mere suggestion that the "artist" might tag along with the "regulars," but the bait of publicity was too great to ignore. George was admitted on sufferance to a humble place in the local gang. He had won the first skirmish, but he still had no idea of how to handle a baseball.

For the next five years he watched every play in every game. He threw and caught with anybody he could find, often dragging Charlie from his graveyard to practice until either twilight or his mother's commands to supper put an end to the day's absorption. With the same extraordinary power of concentration that would later enable him to turn a six-foot canvas into a masterpiece, he trained as best he might, and he trained hard. When his vicarious first baseball season was over he joined the Y.M.C.A. where a newly invented game, basketball, was being played. His father approved of this association because it put his son into properly Christian hands, wholly unaware that the only hands that mattered to his heir were the ones he was trying to teach by himself. Year after year he romped like a crippled colt down the boards of the basketball court. Summer after summer he disciplined his glove to meet unlikely balls and to throw them fast and accurately on one improvised baseball field after another. The time inevitably came when a regular member of the team was down with the chicken pox or indentured to a lawn mower; the players were hastily reshuffled, and George found himself ignominiously holding down right field, for better or for worse, as well as he could. He was improving, slowly.

At the end of five years George's arms and legs were beginning to work in unison. He had moved one short step forward from right to center field. When a ball caromed off a tree branch in erratic descent he knew exactly how to catch and field it. He was, and always would be, a poor batter, so he set his sights on the infield as offering him the likeliest chance to star. There was a skill in his eyes and in his hands that made him ambitious to play shortstop, a position where a fraction of a second can differentiate between winning or losing. Slowly, very slowly, this objective became a fixation. Two arms, two legs, with the separate trunk that united them must be taught to respond to the instantaneous command from the excellent head with which he had been born.

He learned the pains and joys of management as he went along. From the start it was plain that scrub ball was small time, and the only road to fame was won through organization. In 1893 the "East Richers" became the "Brownies," and Bellows played a vital part in organizing a schedule of regular games with other teams of their own size. In their first season the Brownies won all but three of their twenty-seven contests, so extraordinary a feat that the Columbus papers finally acceded to George's plea and began to print accounts of the games. The Brownies were news.

In 1897, Central High School, designed and built by George Bellows' father, absorbed the architect's son along with the other Brownies and the greater part of his East Rich Street acquaintances. High school, academically, troubled George not at all. He acquired a lifelong interest in geometry and failed only one course, botany, a possible explanation of the odd fact that as a painter of renown he never essayed the still life pictures that brought many of his professional friends both reputation and money.

His athletic prowess developed less rapidly than his personality. While many of his schoolmates sneered at his new masthead for the *Kero,* Central High's monthly publication, and wanted no part of the "artist" in their midst, the serious hard-core Brownies stood solidly behind him. Support like this was a new sensation, the "experience" he had hunted for so hard and so long, and gave him the confidence to join the boys' glee club, for his voice had grown into a fine deep baritone and he knew how to use it well. Although he was definitely not a ladies' man, he dutifully squired damsels to the dances and discovered a new outlet for his comic talent in the school's dramatic productions.

The social and academic orbit still left him time to draw, and he left off copying pictures of ships under sail to try the more immediate rage in illustration, pen-and-ink drawings in the manner of Charles Dana Gibson. At this point he foresook his familiar pencil and began to master the exacting brilliance of a medium which offers no chance of correction. Each stroke must be executed as planned, each erasure a sign of ineptitude.

This new facility in his chosen field began to repay the artist. During the winter of 1900, following the national election of that year, he helped to popularize an amateur vaudeville show with quick drawings of McKinley, Mark Hanna, Teddy Roosevelt, and the Principal of the high school, all hilariously interspersed between a magician, a quartette, a base soloist, and a clog dancer. George Bellows, a genius in semi-suspension, was growing into a man.

He now developed more rapidly on the playing field than in the studio. The years at the Y.M.C.A. made him a star on the basketball court and also earned him a derisive athletic nickname he ultimately made respected beyond the borders of Ohio. Despite his progress with the Brownies, a majority of his fellows knew him slightly if at all. During a tight game between Central High and its arch-rival, East High School, when the play became intense and

George raced down the floor for a basket, the stands rose in a mighty cheer of "Bellows! Ho!" Then, when the tumult had subsided a little, one wag thought that to shout "Belly" instead of "Bellows" and "Hole" for "Ho" was more fun, and the next time George, dribbling swiftly and adeptly, drove across the boards the chant went up: "Belly Hole." It was great fun for the stands, but older spectators considered the epithet improper and thereafter the exhortation was solely "Ho."

For all his success during the winter months George's heart was still set on the spring and on baseball. Gradually, his six foot two inches of malcoordinated bones and muscles had drawn themselves together, and during his final spring at Central High he played shortstop, the core of the infield, his every move predicated on every possible drive of the ball. He was reported to have made a double play unassisted, and although his hitting was still poor, he could be counted on to steal an extra base if he could manage to reach first. Such skill attracted more than local notice, for the baseball scouts were viewing him with appraising eyes, and before long the Indianapolis team of the Western League was urging him to "plug the hole at short." Word of this offer spread like crab grass over the high school campus, and for a time his Brownie teammates proudly called him "Colonel Watkins," after the owner of the Indianapolis nine.

In 1901 he graduated from Central High, and the long summer days began before the opening of Ohio State University. The Bellows family spent its summers in various ways determined largely by father George and his cautious view of the family pocketbook. Always his son spent a part of his time in learning the trades the father himself could teach—basic carpentry, brick laying, cabinet work, drafting—but two or three weeks of every year were devoted to "vacation," a change of scene if not necessarily a change of personalities. Every so often they made a pilgrimage back to Sag Harbor, the Long Island nest of both the Bellows and Smith families that bristled with relatives on every side. The trip east was an expensive one, not to be indulged in often, and more frequently the family gravitated north, in the company of its many friends and neighbors from Columbus to Lakeside on the shores of Lake Erie. It was, and still is, a Methodist Camp Meeting Ground, its cottages arranged cheek-by-jowl on a gridiron pattern so that every mother in her rocking chair can chat with her neighbor while keeping track of her child's voice as he tests the world around him. Divine services brought everyone together on frequent occasions and so did the enormous meals that followed every ceremony of devotion. There were choirs, sailing, tennis, and the beach for the young. On special occasions Japanese lanterns turned the grove into a jeweled paradise.

When the vacation was over, the Bellows family boarded the train and covered the hundred miles between holiday and home oblivious to the rich farm lands they knew so well, the broad, Dutch-roofed barns and narrow, steep gabled farmhouses each set in its own cluster of trees, every whirling windmill shooting up over acres of blue-banded wheat and arching corn. Presently the city closed them in, and life took on its normal routine. Anna resumed her eternal rocking on the front porch. Her husband inspected the progress on the new First Methodist Church now raising its handsome Richardsonian Romanesque walls and windows to the sky. Their son returned to his accustomed place between second and third base on the Brownie team, picked up occasional pocket money by playing on local semiprofessional nines, swam in the muddy waters of the Olentangy, and drew and drew and drew.

At his graduation from Central High, his art teacher prophesied that Bellows would become a great artist, but Columbus could offer him little to advance his technical skill. By contrast, its baseball teams provided him with a rich and varied assortment of personalities and associations, and these in turn developed in him an extroverted wit and a remarkable alertness. Few professional art schools can provide such training, yet it is essential in the process of turning a craftsman into a master. Of less importance to his art was his acquisition of a vocabulary too profane for use in his own home, but later to become an indelible part of his mature personality.

The summer of 1901 came to an end and with it a sudden reversal of fortune. Freshman "Beanie" in his pocket, George Bellows strode confidently down the street one morning to meet Charlie Grant, board a street car, and enroll at "the School in the Cornfield," Ohio State University, whose broad oval campus cut across the northern suburbs of the city to the banks of the Olentangy. Upper-class veterans lounged under the elms, observing the new students swarming up the steps of towering University Hall, gauging potential fraternity material from all the superficial rules of thumb that adolescents believe to be important. To Bellows, community life in College appeared far more interesting than academic exposure. He had slaved for a whole decade to earn the recognition of his fellows. His closest friends were "going Beta." He wanted Beta. Beta failed to bid him, and his nineteen-year-old world disintegrated about him.

The success he had won over incredible obstacles at Central High seemed wiped away. Despite the bold façade he assumed to his disappointment, he was inwardly a lonely and dejected figure throughout the greater part of his freshman year, ranging alone across the campus, keenly resenting the title of "Barbarian" derisively bestowed on all "non-Greek" undergraduates. He tried out for football, only to be told that his lanky seventy-four inches were too light for the game. Basketball found uses for his talent and gave him some outlet for his energy. The *Makio*, yearbook of the University, accepted several of his cartoons. His *bête noire* in the curriculum was required Military Training, but after some weeks of drill his ingenuity found an escape. If he must march, he might as well have some fun out of it, so he joined the band, learned drumming, and became so proficient that the following summer he was invited to perform with the professional musicians on the bandstand in the park.

George's studies, in general, interested him little. Since all the university's courses in art were barred to freshmen, he managed to elect one in physiology that gave him a good knowledge of the human skeleton. Yet far more important to him than this was his course in English literature, less for the material it offered than for young Professor Joseph Taylor who taught it. He turned the contents of Palgrave's "Golden Treasury" into a growing garden of ideas, and before the year was out Bellows found himself more and more often at the hospitable Taylor fireside, analyzing, debating, and reading or listening for pure enjoyment. Together the two men explored the radical genius of Walt Whitman and the impudence of the young Irish dramatist George Bernard Shaw, condemning heartily the work of Clyde Fitch, the then-fashionable *couturier* of dramas for female stars. Taylor was something of a poet himself and a good amateur watercolorist as well. Lively minds and shared experience cement the most enduring friendships, and this one, needed so desperately by George during his dismal first year in College, lasted a lifetime.

His hopes were pinned on the baseball team, but as the winter gave way to spring he faced the almost insoluble barrier of a nine composed largely of seniors who had been playing together for years and had no intention of giving up berths to freshmen, irrespective of their abilities. The regular shortstop, no match for George, retained his place through sheer seniority, yet Bellows managed to make the squad as a general utility infielder and was privileged to take all the trips with the team.

With this foothold in the familiar fold, his gloom began to dispel. He loved nothing more than active companionship, the tenseness of a close contest, the free give-and-take between players. Once, when ordered back to the sidelines, he promptly took off his pants and put them on backwards, explaining to the bewildered coach that if he had to warm the bench, he might as well have his padding where it would do the most good. Waiting for a chance to play he amused himself and his fellow substitutes by drawing everything in sight—and out of it for that matter. He had become adept at heckling and once, when the dignified president of Ohio Wesleyan was exhorting his team and George roared at him, "That's right! Give 'em hell, Doc!" the visiting team from Columbus required a police escort to the railroad station. At the end of the season the coach was so impressed with his ability that he gave him a regular post at shortstop on the semiprofessional team he was managing for the summer.

Sophomore year proved a complete reversal of his freshman experience. His Brownie friends in Beta had kept the Bellows image large before the brethren who could no longer overlook his obvious promise as an athlete even if he was also an "artist." They bid him promptly, and he accepted with alacrity, endured the indignities of hazing, confounded his superiors by reciting verbatim the entire fraternal ritual after hearing it only once, and became a perfect nuisance around the house as his unexpended energies and his delight in horseplay found the release it needed so badly.

As a sophomore he was admitted to the hallowed courses in art. A Mr. Martin introduced him to "color standards, color theory, color harmony, color appearance, tone and gradation" through a series of lantern slides in an age barely acquainted with black-and-white projection. He was also given some instruction in watercolor, an art he had already explored by himself and with Professor Taylor to the point where he was the equal of most of the major practitioners in New York, Winslow Homer excepted. He took a required course in economics that presumably reflected the conservatism of the state of Ohio and may account for his later violent opinions on labor, management, and wages. At least he learned the language of the discipline so well that he could subsequently hold his own technically in adult debate when he espoused socialist and anarchist theories in the intellectual climate of New York.

The *Makio* asked for more drawings, while Kenyon College engaged him to help illustrate its yearbook. His mastery of the swift, sure strokes of the pen, the elegance of his ladies, and the smartness of his gentlemen owed their all to Howard Chandler Christie and to his own tireless exercise in a lesser medium that approximated in the brisk suavity displayed expensively in oils by John Singer Sargent and Anders Zorn. The "artist" was reaching a wider public, he was more respected at home, yet he still was only the echo of skilled performers with nothing to say for himself in his chosen field of art.

Sports had saved his self-respect in his freshman year and had indeed become an indispensable part of his life. His performance on the basketball floor commanded notices in the press all winter. Then, in the spring, the baseball squad turned out. The entrenched seniors of the year before were battling their independent careers to fame and fortune in the great outside world, and in their places stood seven of the original nine Brownies equipped and ready to take over the diamond for Ohio State. They had no need of coaching. Each man's personal standard of excellence was determined by the rest, and it was high. Every one of them responded, not to signals from the bench, but to his own anticipation of his team's reaction in any kind of a situation. Each member knew how the next would behave, instinctively moving in advance of every play. Their speed and brilliance packed the stands at every game and Ralph Hoyer, a football star, remembers vividly the way Bellows walked onto the field "easily, almost proudly, as though he owned the place." He also remembers Bellows' long-armed, lean, perfectly coordinated figure stepping out to meet a fast grounder and then, with an indescribably beautiful gesture, throwing the ball squarely into the first baseman's glove. Sophomore year at Ohio State saw the culmination of George Bellows' career as an undergraduate.

The summer of 1903 differed little in pattern from the ones that had gone before, but there were odd undertones within it. At commencement, for example, the Reverend David Gregg, a conscious replica of William Jennings Bryan, tossed back his abundant locks and launched forth on the topic of "Brains, their value and their use." Supporting his stand that "there is no discount on brains!" he cited six passages from the Old Testament. Then he committed himself: "In a certain sense brains are everything . . . Viewed from the lowest standpoint, brains are money!" Sentiments such as these had a sound appeal to George Bellows, Sr. His son took particular delight in the example that followed the speaker's initial apothegm: "The brains of Millet, the artist, are an illustration. Millet bought a yard of canvas for one franc. He then paid two francs for a hair brush and some colors, sixty cents in all. Upon this canvas he set his genius to work and produced his famous picture, 'The Angelus.' . . . His brains took sixty cents of the raw material and raised it to the sum of one hundred and five thousand dollars, for that was what 'The Angelus' sold for."

On the Fourth of July, 1903, Barney Oldfield came to Columbus to break his world record of fifty-nine and three-fifths seconds in a racing automobile. He did not disappoint his audience of ten thousand in the Driving Park: "The 'Red Devil' swung onto the track . . . at a speed that reminded one of the speed of a skyrocket . . . The deeper barking exhaust of the four big unmuffled cylinders sounded like the explosion of a string of Chinese firecrackers . . . The crowd watched in breathless amazement, expecting to see him at every minute dashed to eternity." Barney Oldfield took less than a minute to show his audience that he was still alive and that it had witnessed the breaking of his own record by three and one-fifths seconds.

The summer was also marked by an epidemic of lynchings so numerous that the local journals reviewed the record of these outrages over the last ten years, broke them down by areas, causes, and races, and opened a powerful inquiry into the scope of the law. One especially horrifying episode concerned the abduction and burning of a Negro, described by the Columbus *Dispatch* in such vivid terms that they seared themselves into George Bellows' memory and many years later inspired one of his most powerful lithographs. Justice was always to be one of his major concerns.

Change, new horizons, re-evaluations were in the air. The "artist's" sophomore year had turned adversity into a triumph that his junior year could not hope to repeat. Columbus and its university offered him no more in prospect than they had in the past to fructify his talents. The larger part of the old Brownies' team was scattering to other schools, to professions, to individual careers. Bellows' future stared at him squarely and demanded a decision.

The summer months of 1903, of play and leisure, passed in an atmosphere of romantic mourning. As the Brownies fell apart at its team's collective seams, the survivors met constantly at each other's homes, spinning out every tense and happy moment of the past—singing, playing impromptu games. George's mother loved these gatherings and could always be counted on to speak hilariously ahead of her thought as when she asked eagerly, "How many boys on a baseball nine?" Her son adored her, usually addressed her as "The Fair Anna," and teased her unmercifully all the time, one day announcing that the laundry had sent back one of her wrappers with a note: "We don't do up tents."

Anna accepted her son's maturity, but his father did not. At seventy-four the patriarch of the Bellows family tried to deal with the problems of a young adult in the home as his elders would have done. Hampered by increasing deafness, stubbornly set in his lifetime habits of caution and frugality, the prospect of his only son adopting a painter's career sent a trickle of ice through his aging arteries. The boy should stay in Columbus, become an architect-contractor like himself, live his life surrounded by security, morality, and thrift. The old man had perhaps forgotten his own journey into that unknown land behind the Appalachians more than a half century before, or resented his son's vitality and romantic restiveness that was splitting the well-ordered Bellows house asunder.

Junior year, 1903–1904, opened with the usual academic routine of registration and the introduction to new disciplines. George Wesley Bellows chose his program of studies with his usual eye for experiment. He took a course in Greek art because he could copy the lantern slides assiduously as they passed across the screen, picking a back seat to avoid any chance of academic detection. Like many before him, he avoided philosophy by choosing elementary psychology instead. Unlike most of his fellows he selected a course in law and thereby gained a vocabulary that he would use and misuse to the end of his days.

Everything that Ohio State University could still offer him in art was on his schedule, including one course that promised some acquaintance with the oil technique. The only surviving example of his early style in this medium is a dreary, dark-brown copy of a landscape acknowledged as such by his honest signature "Bellows after Hasbroek" in the lower right-hand corner. Educationally, Ohio State had offered him its best. It was not enough.

The *Makio* gave him an unprecedented chance to keep his hands in practice: he was asked to make all of its dozens of drawings for the issue of 1904. He paid his debt to Beta with a series of sketches in pen-and-ink and wash. One of these, a football scene in which he implied a forward pass through the action of the players without showing the ball, frankly acknowledged its source in the signature: "Bellows after Gibson." Charles Dana Gibson was the reigning hero of illustrators in America. Gibson observed the elegant Edwardian world around him and set it down so crisply and so desirably that all his contemporaries in every walk of life understood and adored him. It was a graceful world, punctuated with arch conventions and scented with aloof romance—a decorous, mildly provocative environment that exacted a modicum of tender understanding from its audience and extreme facility from its imitators.

The Bellows drawings for Beta brought the atmosphere of Edward VII's court to Ohio State University in terms that its students could enjoy: a couple out for the evening in top hat and tails, the football hero modestly displaying his immodest "O" above a manly chest. Only once did the artist lower the high standards of his formula by depicting "The Pledge" as an uncomfortable little freshman crouched in a chair while three upper classmen discussed his desirability as a brother-in-the-bonds. There could have been personal bitterness in this design, but his experience at Ohio State had already taught George Bellows the blessings of an objective mind.

"Musical Organizations," drawings for the *Makio,* 1903.

Photographs remain of his final year in college: in basketball uniform, baseball uniform, ascot and cutaway, business suit with high collar, and full-dress for the Glee Club. With this latter organization he went on tour during Christmas vacation with "When She is Gone," "Monk of the Mountains," "Reveries," and "Old Black Joe" as the staple repertoire. The group was entertained at every appearance, and George learned the villainy of alcohol one evening when his too generous host spiked the punch and the songsters rose to a throbbing morning of hangovers.

During the winter of 1903–1904 Bellows blossomed a little in the social sphere. He was listed among the dancers at college affairs and as a guest at one card party that ended "in a dainty lunch, the table made the more beautiful by a Japanese lantern hanging under the light." More often the newspapers described him on the basketball court as: "The phenomenon of Ohio State." His reputation as a star spilled out into the eastern states under the name of "Ho Bellows." Yet there was a staleness about the whole triumph. He had enjoyed it at Central High School, and if his scope was now larger, so was his outlook on life. The inevitable consequence followed him onto the baseball diamond. As early as January, the College's *Lantern* commented: "Among the older men . . . Bellows, of course, will show up at shortstop . . ." Routine, familiar and mastered, hemmed him in on every side, yet even this had changed. The old familiar teammates at first and third and home had gone off in search of their fortunes, and here was "the old man," George Bellows, with his heart set on a career in painting making perfect throws to youngsters who could not even catch a ball.

The Ohio State faculty had no more to teach him. Baseball scouts including the Cincinnati "Reds" were breathing down his neck offering him the money he needed but a career he did not want. His evenings at 265 East Rich Street swelled with arguments too violent for the small brick house to contain. Anna Bellows was miserable, her big-nosed face usually so ready for laughter now more often lined with tears. She minded less her shattered image of a Methodist bishop than the sight of her husband and her son locked in angry opposition. It was no help that Laura Bellows Monett and her husband sided with George in his frantic desire to escape Columbus and become a painter, for the head of the family was adamant. Michelangelo, in his opinion, was a good artist, but art was no profession for a young man. After these sessions the son would fling himself noisily out the door and stride or cycle the long distance to the home of Professor Joseph Taylor where he found a more sympathetic, but equally sage, reception.

The Columbus years collapsed like a child's castle of blocks when final examinations came and went—without benefit of

George Bellows. There was only one way to end his torment, and he took it in a reckless mood with the finality of Alexander the Great dealing with the Gordion Knot. Not taking the examinations meant that he could not return to Ohio State. All thought of careers in the Methodist ministry or of architecture or of contracting were sliced off cleanly from his own and his family's consideration. His life was now his own to shape as best he might.

Semiprofessional baseball and cartooning earned him a nest egg during the summer months while he made such peace as he could with his parents. Then, in early September, he quietly put his savings in his pocket. Without fanfare and with only a dutiful blessing from his disappointed father he swung his bag aboard an east-bound train.

The Life Class; *etching, 1st State; ca. 1916.*

THE NEW YORK SCHOOL OF ART

» 1904 - 1906 «

» II «

"Arrived in New York I found myself in my first art school under Robert Henri having never heard of him before . . . My life begins at this point."
George Bellows

The new, handsomely-rusticated façade of the West Side Y.M.C.A. at West Fifty-Seventh Street and Broadway turned its back on the baking sun as George Bellows passed through its arched portal tugging with him his bags and his ambitions. He had his savings of $500 and his father's promise of $50 a month for the next year. Father and son had both readily agreed that the cheapness of accommodations at the "Y" was a good thing, that full board per week to members at only $4 meant about 60 cents a day for sound nourishment and was a real bargain. His mother was comforted by the thought that his room would be not only inexpensive, but clean and wholesome as well.

His parents were delighted that their son, a stranger in a wicked city, would find himself in a proper moral environment. George was untroubled on this score, but he did recognize the opportunity of playing on the Y.M.C.A. teams. Sports had become a necessity to him almost as compelling as art, and although the Association's basketball teams were simon-pure, many of the players picked up handy small change in semiprofessional teams in and around New York. Five dollars a game plus expenses would be useful to a young man who had to pay not only for food and shelter, but also for instruction, materials, clothes, and an occasional taste of extra-curricular fun.

For the moment, he put aside all visions of stardom and profit, dumped his modest luggage in his room, and strode out in quest of his immediate and ultimate goal, the academy where he could find instruction in painting. The New York School of Art lay only two blocks to the east at Fifty-Seventh Street and Sixth Avenue. Its proximity to the "Y" was one reason for his choice, perhaps the only one, although he had certainly heard of its presiding genius, William Merritt Chase, whose international fame as a portrait painter was so great that it had spread back to the Ohio Valley whence master and pupil both came. George paid his registration fee, purchased the necessary supplies of canvas, paint, pencil, paper, charcoal, and erasers and climbed the single flight of stairs to the studios, barn-like in their roominess, their floors cluttered with stools and easels, their walls encrusted with palette scrapings. Permanent features were purely utilitarian—pot-bellied stoves and model stands.

New York was somewhat less prim than Philadelphia about the use of nude models, but still thought it well to separate the male from the female students at life classes so that the only contact of the two groups during school hours was in the long connecting corridor where they lounged uncomfortably, smoked, and engaged in long, often loud, discussions of the latest plays, books, political philosophies, and sex. All these sounded exciting and radical to Middle Western Methodist ears. Ibsen, Tolstoi, and Shaw were much in debate, and the proprieties of "Mrs. Warren's Profession" and the implications of "The People" were bandied about with as much enthusiasm as the paint administered in the studios.

Over the whole establishment, so thoroughly identified with it that it was often known by his name, presided the portly figure of William Merritt Chase. His flowing mustache and imperial outdid even those of the late Napoleon III in their luxuriance and their grooming. He dressed with care and elegance, always careful to reflect the precise image of the portrait that Whistler had painted of him. He exacted enormous technical skill from his brush, and could depict a fashionable dowager or a pile of dead fish with equal brilliancy. His students were urged to paint so well that their dexterity would not be apparent. Despising overt sentimentality, he professed to be at odds with the prevailing cult of the dainty and "the beautiful." He commanded a certain wit.

Once, when a student protested that it might be his eyes that caused his poor performance, Chase said, "I think not. I think not, sir! In your case the trouble is a little higher up." Or, in another round of criticisms: "If it looks like that in the park, I don't want to go there." His real love in painting was the subtlety of Whistler spiced with a decorous dash of Sargent's fluency.

A few days after Bellows' formal entry into the mysteries of art in the metropolis, the door to the studio was opened firmly and a tall rangy man with a small mustache strode into the space between the easels and looked about him with slanting, penetrating eyes. Robert Henri, late as usual, had a reputation much younger and less broadly established than that of Chase, but rumor, which he did nothing to deny, persisted that the Luxembourg Museum in Paris had bought one of his paintings. His lack of orthodoxy and his teaching made him the idol of the younger artists and art students along the North Atlantic seaboard.

Like Chase, Henri had had training in Europe, but he retained none of its Old World courtliness nor academic prejudices. The Academie Julien had given him little but dissatisfaction, and he had found his own milieu in the Old Masters of the Louvre—Hals, Rembrandt, Goya, and Velásquez. Of all the recent French painters only Manet had struck a responsive chord; but Henri would not follow that master, nor Renoir whom he also admired, into the atmospheric kaleidoscope of Impressionism. He agreed with Chase's observation that "the old Dutch painters were fortunate in having such ugly subjects," but he would say it with passionate affirmation rather than as a witty aside. He was the apostle of the universality of subject matter: "Anything that strikes you as real is worthy to be painted." In this radical doctrine he opposed not only Chase but the whole genteel selectivity that then dominated the "official" art of both academic painters and American collectors.

When Henri entered the Men's Life Class at the Chase School in the fall of 1904 he greeted his former students warmly and began chatting with the new recruits. To Bellows, only a shade taller than himself, he said: "Where are you from?" "The West." "What part of the West?" "Columbus, Ohio." "That's not *The* West, that's the Middle West! Let's see some of your work." The facile drawings for the *Makio* were carefully at hand. Henri riffled through them quickly, noting their unusual imitative skill and the real and potential discipline that had produced them; but all he said was: "Haven't I seen these before?" He talked to the group for a while in his eager, quietly compelling voice: "An artist who doesn't use his imagination is a mechanic. . . . Don't belong to any school. . . . Don't tie up with any technique. . . . Art has relations to science, religions and philosophies. . . . The artist must be a student. . . . If one could only know better when he has touched the truth."

That night George Bellows returned to the Y.M.C.A., his head swimming with ideas that had never occurred to him in such concrete form. He liked them and the man who advanced them, and he then and there became Henri's disciple. The Gibsonesque drawings were put away carefully, for they represented something precious from the past, but he never looked at them again except to evoke a bitter-sweet nostalgia. In his turn, Robert Henri walked home to his studio on the East River turning over in his mind thoughts of his new student. There was talent there, he thought, and facility—a dangerous thing, facility. It had to be rigidly contained or it could ruin the finest painter in the world.

Every time Henri came into the Chase School he delivered another flood of maxims: "Develop your visual memory. Draw everything you have drawn from the model from memory as well. A drawing is not a copy but an invention." To the recent semiprofessional cartoonist from Columbus this was very good advice and not hard to follow. Bellows already had an extraordinary visual memory, and Henri's exhortations kept it fresh. "Draw your material from the life around you, from all of it. There is beauty in everything if it looks beautiful to your eyes. You can find it anywhere, everywhere."

To the conventional artists of the National Academy of Design, even to William Merritt Chase, the greater part of New York City, its life and most of its inhabitants, looked anything but beautiful. To Bellows the whole setting differed from Columbus only in that it was undeniably much bigger and was a good deal taller. Both cities were expanding at prodigious rates in the first decade of the twentieth century, but whereas the capital of Ohio could extend out over the flat plain at will, Manhattan, squeezed between the

Hudson and East rivers could only grow northward. Thus the area just south of Central Park was rapidly losing its residential character, although only a few blocks east of the "Y" the palaces of the Vanderbilts and Goulds haughtily surveyed each other's costly façades. Merchandizing was crowding in around them, yet not very far to the west lay the slum area known as Hell's Kitchen, where big-time gambling flourished, and minor and major crimes were daily affairs. To the south, acres of dismal tenements somehow absorbed, for a time at least, the hundreds of thousands of immigrants that annually poured in by way of Ellis Island, while to the east and west miles of docks disgorged passengers and cargo to the shore and tugs and scows and ocean liners into the bustling river traffic. The air was charged with hurry and worry and dynamic drive.

Through the huge network of the city's streets Bellows ranged in all directions. The Flatiron Building's lofty wedge of pseudo-masonry was the talk of the town, and every one who could spare the time paused to watch the final touches being applied to that latest miracle of steel construction, the new home of the New York *Times.* More often George's bent took him to the slum districts and the teeming docks. Henri believed that there was more likely to be character among the poor and underprivileged than elsewhere, and George found himself looking for it in the quaint patched clothes of the immigrant children, in their pinched little faces, in the grinding clatter of iron-shod Percherons dragging their heavy drays across the crowded cobblestones. He made quick sketches on the spot, and many more from memory when he returned to his room.

Henri pounded away at the artist's need to develop an individual style and advised his students to take advantage of any and all means to achieve it. "Know what the old masters did—but don't fall into their conventions. They made their language. You make yours. But all the past can help you," he would remind his students. On occasion he would stride into the studio with a brisk: "Put away your paints and get your hats—we're going to the Metropolitan." He urged them to read and to go to the theater to find inspiration for expressing the essence of man and nature. He adored Whitman, Emerson, the Russians, and Wagner, but he had a lighter side as well for he rarely missed one of Harry Lauder's concerts.

Henri had small patience with the professional "aesthete." This problem did not exist in his present group of students who were extraordinarily promising: Edward Hopper, shy and retiring; Rockwell Kent, fresh from a start in architecture at Columbia and fully aware of his unusual gifts; Glenn O. Coleman, who would one day rival the masters of city genre until the Armory Show undermined his confidence in his own abilities; lively Edward Keefe, who had escaped his father's pressure to make him into an architect in New London.

Keefe especially attracted George, also an ardent sports fan and an accomplished basketball player. They played together on the "Y" team, strictly amateur, that winter but, with their three teammates, played elsewhere as "The Colonials," picking up $5 fees in Northern New Jersey and Southern New England as far east as Newport. Henri liked games of all kinds, tolerated horseplay in the studio when he was not in it, and encouraged his class to form their own baseball team when spring came along. Bellows and Keefe threw themselves into its organization with enthusiasm and played vital roles in its victories over such equally patchwork opponents as the students at the School of the National Academy of Design and the Art Students' League.

There were dances at the school, too, although of necessity simple affairs. Cheap, imaginative decoration usually consisted of burlap applied over the paint-smeared walls, and on this drawings were carefully pinned. If funds permitted, the students brought in a two- or three-piece band, but there was always talent enough among themselves to provide a passable musical background. For all their primitive settings, these dances were conducted with a long-forgotten formality. Every one was provided with a card, printed or improvised, with a number and a partner for each dance. On such occasions the big sliding doors between the men's and the women's studios were opened as they were for William Merritt Chase's criticisms.

It was on such an evening that George Bellows, squiring a Miss Skilly Hillsdale, met her friend Emma Story from Upper Montclair, New Jersey, also a student at the school. Emma would ulti-

mately fashion much of his life, but at the time he seems to have
been aware of her existence only as another student at the Chase
School and a handsome young woman as well. It was significant
that at this first formal meeting George escorted the girls from
Miss Hillsdale's Greenwich Village flat to the dance by trolley car,
and Emma tactfully seated herself as far away from the other two
as she could. Later, in the spring, she consented to at least one
walk with him in Central Park, and they agreed to correspond
during the summer when she would be visiting in Nova Scotia.
She was more interested at the time in Edward Hopper, with
whom she often crossed on the New Jersey ferry, and in Rockwell
Kent, who quite fascinated her with his learning and who lectured
to her on St. Gaudens' statue of General Sherman.

Social life, thoroughly neglected during George's first months in
New York, had reasserted itself in the need of close human companionship. Living at the Y.M.C.A. was cheap and hygienic, but
the roomers and boarders had hardly heard of Chekhov or Balzac
even as names and looked upon the classic nudes of Bougoureau as
racy subjects for locker room conversation. Ed Keefe from New
London was lonely, too. The two aspiring artists decided to find
a place of their own, near enough to the "Y" to take advantage of
its $3-a-week dinners, but some haven that was entirely theirs.
An artist, they reasoned, does not live in an institution.

Their first essay in independence, only a few blocks away from
the "Y," was within their means and lively enough, but it immediately proved lacking in the intellectual pretensions they sought,
since the building was largely peopled with call girls. Shortly
thereafter they located another spot at 352 West Fifty-Eighth
Street, in a house owned by a doctor whose one relaxation after
office hours was to play lugubriously on the organ. He had let
another room to two homely young women who shared with the
artists the sole substandard "retiring room" which did, however,
contain the amenity of a gas ring. For all their plainness, the girls
turned out to be part of a musical comedy chorus, and supplied
their fellow lodgers with free tickets for many a theater evening.

Although the room was small and rather shabby, it was home.
They set up their cots and easels, messed around with paint, and
enjoyed to the full the illusion of being professionals. George's
share of the modest rent, $7.50 per week, proved to be beyond his

budget, so they set up a third cot and formed a triumvirate with Fred Cornell, George's long-time teammate from Columbus who was seeking fortune, if not fame, in New York with Western Union.

The heat of 1905 closed down on the city. The New York School of Art recessed for three months. The great Henri departed for Spain, and Ed Keefe returned to New London to spend his summer sweating over a drafting board in an architect's office as part of his agreement with his father. This temporarily made more room in the "studio" at West Fifty-Eighth Street, and with Cornell on his job all day Bellows had space and quiet to devote to painting on his own. He worked on at least two canvases, one of which he recorded—a "Night Scene" of three girls in Central Park looking at the moon—and another which he later forgot, also done in the park, that ultimately found its way into the Faculty Club of Ohio State University. It is a revealing piece, conceived in alternating light and dark green planes across which move the almost black shapes of carriages and trees, the sky between the branches overpainted thickly to catch a luminous effect, and tiny, block-like figures touched with red and white and violet, all in the Henri manner but curiously recalling the style of Glackens whose work George hardly knew at this time.

Walking in the park cost nothing, but it paid nothing either. Playing sandlot ball meant the open air, exercise, and enough money per game to pay for a week's meals, so he played it. Between times he roamed the streets and docksides or rambled around the river banks, still free from the encroachment of the city, always observing sharply and storing up impressions and incidents for development later in his room. He was finishing his first twelve months in New York with almost nothing but experience to show for it—rich and varied experience.

Ed Keefe returned in September, his aspirations undimmed by three months of architectural drafting. The Chase School opened without benefit of Robert Henri who lingered on in Spain for some extra weeks and had persuaded his friend John Sloan to stand in for him during his absence. George viewed with interest this handsome, volatile illustrator, recently arrived from Philadelphia, whose etchings had already commanded praise from liberal critics and condemnation from Anthony Comstock's "League of Decency."

Sloan the teacher proved a new and interesting experience. The words of Henri's texts remained the same, as did their context, but the emphases were different. When Sloan stated that: "Contemporary success means failure," he was bolstering his own ego. He could hardly conceal his bitterness that he, thirty-six years' old, had never sold an oil, while Henri was already represented in the Luxembourg in Paris and was about to receive the Harris Prize in Chicago. He could never drain his own frustration out of his warning against "facility," a "dangerous thing," always wondering in the back of his mind if his own facility had not been his terrible handicap. He demolished the generations-old threat leveled at art by the camera by observing that because of it "few artists know today the difference between the aspect and the concept of the thing," while his own mind recalled how photography had outdated the graphic reporting from which he had made an early living and how soon it might replace the magazine illustrations that were his daily bread. But his nerves lent timbre to his vocal chords, and while he scolded when Henri might have urged, and fussed when Henri might have complimented, the weeks under Sloan's criticisms were valuable for every one in the studio.

When Henri resumed his duties at the school again he was delighted with Bellows' progress and his seemingly limitless capacity for absorbing new ideas, for work, and for growth. Before long the rangy Ohioan became a frequent guest at Henri's "Tuesday Evenings" when he held open house for his close friends and his more promising pupils. In his big studio, bright with the latest Henri canvases, perfumed by coffee, beer, and tobacco, George found himself surrounded by the veterans of the Master's Philadelphia days, the inner circle. There was short, bluff George Luks who supported himself by drawing a daily comic strip for the New York *World,* perhaps one reason why he was never at a loss for a tall tale; Sloan, whom he had already encountered at the school; debonair Everett Shinn, the one member of the group attracted by the glitter of the footlights and the world of the demi-monde; William Glackens, as gentle as Luks was gruff, as tactful as Sloan was blunt, a sound craftsman already experimenting with the palette and mannerisms of the French Impressionists.

These men were all a decade or more older than Bellows, all but Henri still struggling for recognition, more or less bitter about their lack of success. It was Henri who led the discussions, channeling them into the basic points at issue, prodding, probing, hunting for a solution to the current throttling of their efforts to create a truly American art. The "issues" always simmered down to two.

The first could be properly laid at the door of the American collector, whose passion for French painting, especially of the Barbizon group—the rage of the moment—had led many American painters into the web of imitation. This sort of parasitic fad was anathema to Henri, whose permanent crusade was the development of native talent, using its own raw materials in its own independent way. He saw no sense whatever in trying to turn the mighty Hudson into a pretty reflection of the Seine. Only a fraction of America inhabited elegant drawing rooms, wore gowns from Paris, and drove English carriages in the park; Henri regarded these as bloodless mannekins in costume. There was a mighty pulse beating in America that could be felt nowhere else on earth—that of a rapidly growing nation, as powerful and as vital as youth itself. Henri wanted his associates to catch this rhythm— Bellows already had it. What he needed was the means to express it.

It was conceivable that the American collector might be educated away from foreign and imitative models, but the only way to accomplish this, Henri thought, was to expose him to the work of the American "Realists" as they were beginning to be called. This brought into focus the second issue, finding suitable exhibition space for their works. The New York dealers, with high rent to pay and reputations to maintain, were chary of giving over any of their elegant and expensive walls to so speculative and unpopular a cause. The cost of hiring an independent hall was prohibitive. Only two organizations, the National Academy of Design and the Society of American Artists, had showrooms of their own and regularly invited artists to submit their work for possible exhibition. At this moment the Society had agreed to merge with the Academy and to relinquish its galleries along with its identity. This meant that the National Academy of Design, which mounted only two exhibitions a year and was notoriously conservative in its selections, offered the sole chance for most American artists to show their wares, not a promising prospect at all.

Henri himself was the hopeful bulwark. He was not only a member of the Society of American Artists, but also belonged to the committee arranging for its absorption into the Academy. He had recently been elected an associate academician, and by the terms of the merger he would automatically become a full member of the Academy. His would be almost a lone voice, but a persistent and powerful one in the promotion of liberality. Consistently he championed the paintings of his friends. As a member of the jury at Pittsburgh's Carnegie International Exhibition that fall, he had been instrumental in awarding Honorable Mentions to pictures by Glackens and Sloan. One thing was quite clear in the not too pleasant view of the future: if the new American Realism was to have a chance of public favor, Henri, and only he, could achieve it.

When talk on this major problem dwindled, Henri's friends on the "Tuesday Evenings" could always debate about politics, hinging usually on the virtues of Socialism as opposed to Intellectual Anarchy, or let themselves indulge in execration of the latest fashionable European portraitist to invade the American scene. Impromptu skits leavened the more serious discussion, and at these Bellows' innate skill at improvisation and clowning excelled. There were bouts of drawing each other or choosing some scene from memory, anything that would send the pencil excitedly racing over the drawing board. After one of these evenings there was little sleep for any one in the crowded little room on Fifty-Eighth Street as George reported everything to Keefe while Fred Cornell clamored for quiet. Western Union was not paying $13.50 a week to employees too sleepy to work.

During the fall and winter of 1905 George painted only one street scene in the Henri manner, but he concentrated almost all his efforts on heads. Fellow students cost him nothing as models. He rendered Ed Keefe in full face, one Preziossi in profile, and still another of an engaging newcomer to the school nicknamed Robin. Robin was his frequent companion that winter, especially on social excursions. George gave Ed his portrait, and gave Preziossi's to the School. Decades later, one of the major Hollywood studios bought the picture of Robin and presented it to the sitter who had long since achieved fame, not with the brush, but as the actor Clifton Webb.

In October, Miss Emma Story who had abandoned painting for music, paid a chance visit to the Chase School. George saw her as for the first time and fell immediately and hopelessly in love.

The American male at the turn of the century had a single vision of ideal American womanhood—The Gibson girl. Tall and handsome, magnificently modeling her shapely, sweeping garments, her pompadoured small head perched with a delicious touch of haughtiness on a graceful neck, she was as improbable as she was remote and utterly desirable. George had drawn her likeness many times at Ohio State, but he had never encountered the model personified as now he did as he looked upon Miss Emma Story. This was not the smocked, slightly grubby fellow student of last spring, but a radiant, self-confident young woman. From this moment Emma Louise Story was, in his mind, destined to be his wife; and being accustomed to having his own way and getting it as quickly as possible, he wasted no time in beginning his campaign. His impetuosity reckoned without Emma.

Thomas Beer has described the ideal American woman of this time as "The Titaness." She was beautiful, of course, and bursting with moral character, more and more inclined to take the center of the stage away from the men because it was her duty to her sex to do so. She liked to be broad-minded—within limits—and she patronized rather daring plays which she interspersed with the latest social nothing by Clyde Fitch and the sentimentality of "The Empty Chair." She bowed in a friendly way to the arts in general. With poise and determination, when she thought about it, she was planning to make the world a better place for its own sake and for women. She listened politely to her father and her uncles and her brothers, but she also read and approved of Lucy Stone's demand for female individuality and of Carrie Chapman Catt's campaign: "Votes for Women."

Emma had all the qualifications to develop into a full-grown Titaness. She was born in New York, in 1884, the third and considerably the youngest child of William E. Story, a well-to-do businessman who perpetually wore a high hat and gloves and whose short vision and good nature never faltered with his fortunes. Her mother was a quiet, immensely kind woman firmly dedicated to her husband, her children, and to Christian Science. Shortly after Emma's birth, Mr. Story's prosperity waned a little and he moved to Montclair, New Jersey, a less fashionable locale better suited to his earnings. By the time Emma was eight his fortunes had ebbed further and the family moved to Upper Montclair. Their first child, Lillian, grew up as the perfect Titaness, an ardent feminist who found herself a pliant husband. She accepted his name in defiance of Lucy Stone, but substituted for the earthly and confining chore of rearing children a degree in jurisprudence and the active practice of the Law. Brother Edward, two years her junior, early discovered that life was pleasanter if he allowed Lillian to dominate him entirely, and chose to defer to her in everything.

As Emma grew up it was her sister who set the pattern for her life. From her father she acquired dignity, and from her mother, the patience and devotion to Christian Science that lasted all her life. But it was Lillian who early developed Emma's pride in her sex, her desire for an independent career, and an attitude that men were all very well in their place. God had given her the perfect face and figure, and she herself developed a cool self-control, an inner containment that was entirely her own. Thus she emerged at twenty-one the living Gibson girl, a fortress worthy to be stormed. George, who loved a challenge of any kind, learned from his siege of her powerful defences the full measure of their worth.

The chance encounter in the studio which had moved him so profoundly called forth no answering response in Emma. To her he was something of a curiosity. During his first year in New York he had deliberately cultivated his Mid-Western drawl and made something of a fetish of his untidy dress. He loved to clown, to use archaic elegancies of phrase, and to derogate in loud and positive statements anything that he considered conservative or trivial. But his height and athletic grace made him a suitable escort, and his dynamic personality, especially when he was in good humor, overshadowed what she considered his raffish mannerisms. Besides, she was human enough to like young men who liked her. She had enjoyed the stimulating company of the artists she had met the year before, and George's obvious interest in her provided one more excuse to leave the rather stodgy atmosphere of Upper Montclair for the excitements of Manhattan.

During that fall he would write to her to come in to a dance or the theater (when he was in funds), or to visit the Metropolitan Museum, which was free. Sometimes she accepted and sometimes she did not; and because the telephone had not yet changed one of the basic habits of the nineteenth century, they made all their arrangements by mail. On one occasion she turned down his invitation to a football game, pleading as an excuse that she had to play the piano for a dancing class, and ending her note with the following: "Having read this letter you'll say *out* upon girls in general and this one in particular." He replied: "Why not come right out like a dandy little lady and say mama wouldn't let you go. *Out* upon you. Well, I saved my money, although I came near to having my trousers pressed, but your letter reached me in time."

In December a touch of charity toward the male, wholly unworthy of a Titaness, overcame her. She knew he had no money for a holiday trip to Columbus and being mischievously eager to see how her mercantile father would react to her admirer from the West, she invited him to Christmas dinner. Since he had never met her parents, an essential step for any suitor with honorable intentions, he accepted with alacrity.

The Story house, bulging with hospitable Victorian bay windows, stood a good mile from the Upper Montclair station. The Storys kept no horses, and Emma, partly to test the humor of her unpredictable guest, tramped through new-fallen snow to meet the train. George arrived, scrubbed (as best he could remember his mother's and Aunt Fanny's disciplines) and edgy with anticipation. Emma saw the look of adoration in his face, recognized it without sharing it, and covered her uneasiness by walking him a good dozen unnecessary blocks, slogging along in her drenched, ankle-length skirt already soggy with the wet snow. She rather envied his pleasure in meeting the challenge of the weather with his long firm strides.

At last, when she was sure the gigantic porterhouse steak was about ready to be served, she led him up the slope and the steps to her home, and with little respect for the image of sister Lillian, presented her unusual swain to her parents. Mr. Story received him with tolerance, Mrs. Story with less interest than for what was on and in her stove. This was by no means Emma's first beau, and Mrs. Story was apparently convinced that he would not be the last.

Mrs. Story's Christmas dinner met every requirement of a middle-class feast; but George, who was trying his best to charm with his half-forgotten Columbus manners, failed to do justice to his plate. When dinner was over Emma departed upstairs to "make herself beautiful," while Mrs. Story disappeared into the kitchen. Mr. Story found himself settled in front of a great log fire with this strange young man obviously bent on making a good impression. As a proper host he tried to put his guest at ease by bringing up the subject of art. He explained to him that although he had been a neighbor of George Inness in Montclair, he held a rather low opinion of his work. Now, there was another painter who could out-do nature in the painting of a duck's feather! Bellows, all of Henri's dislike of imitation rising to his throat, launched into a heated discourse on what *was* the true nature of art. As he warmed to the task, a radiant Emma descended the stairs and Mrs. Story returned from her duties to prod and protect and protest a little in the argument. They all enjoyed themselves hugely and invited George Bellows back for New Year's.

He was so excited over the day that when he and Emma walked down Park Street through the slushy snow to the Upper Montclair Station he could remember neither the title nor the artist of Giorgione's Castelfranco Madonna which Henri had taught him to admire. On her part, she was a little annoyed with him for taking her father to task on art and at the same time proud of him for having done so. She said good-bye. The Erie clickety-clacked its way to the east, the ferry tootled its departure, George Bellows martialed his feet for the nickel-saving walk back to his lodgings; and arriving there, sat down to reaffirm his acceptance for January 1, 1906.

The transition from the warm fire of the Story's living room to his cramped quarters, the challenging and delightful company, the obvious approval which Emma's parents had accorded him all contrasted sharply with his lodgings on Fifty-Eighth Street from whence Ed Keefe and Fred Cornell had fled back to their homes and a Happy New Year. Even the homely chorus girls across the corridor were on tour, and he was left alone with nothing but the strains of the doctor's dolorous organ on the other side of the partition for company. "When I think of the unholy loneliness of this place . . . ," he wrote. He would come for New Year's, but assured Emma that after the holidays were over she could tell her mother that he must "settle down and dig."

He did just that in the early winter of 1906, laying the foundation for his whole career.

Henri's wife died that winter and the "Master" abruptly left the school for a change of scene in North Carolina. Empathy for Henri's teaching? The expected thrust of genius? George tossed off a drawing of basketball that he thought worthy of record, and then produced in the crowded confines of his triply shared room a large canvas which he named "Kids."

"Kids" sums up in embryo the unique qualities of Bellows' best paintings. He had a gift for titles. Certainly no one could improve on this one. The subject, while thoroughly Henri's in its insistence on the vernacular, shows a breadth that Henri never tackled: in their odd foreign dress, George presented two groups of immigrant children, the larger one happy in a childish game, the smaller shrunk into childhood's miserable insecurity. The composition was based on Hogarth's "line of beauty" with its strong "S" curve down the center. The artist would use it again three years later in his most famous picture, "Stag at Sharkey's." But the essence of this painting is contained in the sheer joy of anticipation on the face of the little girl about to be jerked upward by friendly playmates, her feet planted flatly in mock protest, her tiny features suffused with delight. Yellows and pinks enliven the somber Henri palette, a touch that would later become Bellows' declaration of independence from his master.

Henri viewed the painting and ensured its showing at the final exhibition of the Society of American Artists in March, 1906. He had always encouraged his students to face the "dispraise or blame" of critical opinion, and in this case his principle was well rewarded by the press which had a good word to say for "Kids" and bracketed it with Henri's own entry. After only eighteen months at the Chase School the work of George Bellows was already news.

His courtship of Miss Story moved much too slowly to suit his impatient disposition. It was inevitable that their two positive personalities should clash, the more frequently that spring when he was avowedly her suitor and sometimes signed his letters to her as such, while she imagined herself in love with a handsome and eligible young doctor. That the latter's profession and her religion were utterly incompatible was an irritant she compensated for by making George as miserable as possible without losing his attention. On one occasion, when she surrounded herself with admirers at a party, he responded by ignoring her presence. This infuriated her, but she had already invited him to her house again before receiving his cool explanation that "six is company, seven a crowd." Early in June he came close to losing her entirely.

He suggested an excursion to Staten Island with another couple on a Wednesday afternoon (he would be playing baseball all weekend), returning to Upper Montclair by early evening. The moon, he was careful to point out, would look better there. The trip was made as planned, but the magic of the moon and the excitement of a delightful day combined to prove his undoing, and he returned to New York a thoroughly chastened young man. Victorian codes of behavior were ignored by the upper class except when the Prince of Wales stepped far enough out of line to be called into court, and the lower class went its own way as it always had, immune through its own vitality. It was the middle class that supplied the victims to the rules, and here George and Emma were caught up in the conventions that had surrounded their birth and their upbringing. It is likely that George overstepped the critical mark by attempting to kiss Emma. Such a contravention in those days was so severe that William Glackens' future mother-in-law, when she accused her daughter of kissing her fiancé and received a positive answer, stated firmly: "I should *think* you would leave *something* until *after* marriage."

Emma, firmly in the saddle, took her own time and wrote George two days later: "Strange as it may seem I really don't hate you as you think I ought to. Everyone has impulses now and then

. . . I *was* rather cross that night because I didn't think you thought me that kind of a girl but now that you know I'm not, don't let's say any more about it." Immediately she asked him to Upper Montclair, but postponed the date for more than a week and, in a postscript, added: "You're not a fool and I hope this letter doesn't sound like a Sunday School book . . ."

George, conscience-stricken, had played wretched ball for the Brooklyn "Howards" over the weekend. He had taken a long gamble and lost. Whether the defeat was final or not he did not know, but he had broken the conventions they both knew and shared. The magnate who owned the "Howards" took his team for a brief cruise over Saturday and Sunday, and the players gorged fully, swam, and acquired sunburns, painful but not rigorous enough to allay the remorse of their star shortstop. When Bellows finally reached his room on Sunday night and found his reprieve his relief overwhelmed him. Careful to write on the outside flap of the envelope: "Steady! This is mostly Third Class Matter," he began,

"YOU YOUNG FASCINATOR:

I confess to being on edge three days or so waiting for the letter I feared might not come at all, but which I was waiting for just the same . . . I don't like to say anything and then 'have to renig' so the book hath it. So I guess I'm not sorry . . ."

He recounted the weekend in sophomoric terms, and ended up with the valedictory: "Yours as usual . . ."

At least each now knew where the other stood, and the clarification benefited both. Perhaps this devastating contretemps of theirs fell into perspective a few days later when the whole nation let its morning cup of coffee grow cold as it read about the extremes to which love can drive a man.

On June 25, 1906, plutocrat playboy Harry K. Thaw willfully shot and killed the eminent architect Stanford White at his table on the roof restaurant of Madison Square Garden. The murder alone would have caused the stir, but with Thaw's wife as the stated cause of it even the ultrarespectable New York *Times* could not play it down. Mrs. Thaw, the former Evelyn Nesbit, had been a chief attraction in the chorus of "Floradora" and "The Wild Rose." Handsome John Barrymore had been her frequent escort.

Known as the most beautiful artist's model in America it was rumored that she had posed for Charles Dana Gibson's famous drawing, "The Eternal Question." She was the reason, or the excuse, for the death of Stanford White, America's most expensive and best-loved architect.

At the time there could have been very little debate about the proprieties of the case in Upper Montclair. White was a ranking artist. Evelyn Nesbit was "no better than she should have been," and Thaw should have known it after traveling around Europe with her for months before they were married. Middle-class Vic-

Newspaper cartoon of "Forty-two Kids."

torian circles made up their minds about the case long before the jury and the judge saw it. Oddly enough, John Sloan, the unpredictable, rather cottoned to Thaw, largely because he admired his mother at the trial.

When the Thaw-White case was sparkling conversation, Miss Ethel Clarke, a childhood friend of Emma's, paid her annual visit to the Storys and met George for the first time. Decades later she put down her first impressions for the benefit of his children. Having been posted as a lookout by Emma she suddenly "heard musical rumbling from afar, growing louder and louder as song developed—'Rolling down to Rio'—his current favorite . . . Emma had said George was as big as all out doors, and when he came plunging up the front steps he seemed to fill the whole horizon."

Sunday dinner with George had become a normal event in the Story home, but to Ethel Clarke it was an experience. He and Mr. Story roared each other down between mouthfuls, and Republican versus Socialist politics were kept in check only by Emma's perpetual protests of, "Oh, George!" and Mrs. Story's second helpings.

Miss Clarke described him as follows: "Rumpled as to clothes, paint specks on coat, necktie askew, fingernails far from clean, and one cheek half-shaven, due to nicks and scratches from a dull razor. Violent and argumentative about almost everything. Lacking in all small courtesies. Different from anyone I'd ever met. He irritated and shocked me."

Yet later that same day when Emma beat him five times in a row at croquet and he called it a "damn silly game," she riposted, "Not when you win." When the young of the neighborhood, immaculately groomed in bear's grease and white ducks, dropped in George looked like an "unmade bed." Then Emma swept to the piano to tinkle such popular rag-time as "Hello, My Baby," until George yelled "That's not music!" Emma's hands were still and her eyes flashed a challenge. He picked up with "Mandalay," "Jeanie with the Light Brown Hair," and "Hills of Home." Miss Clarke considered his voice quite beautiful, and apparently the rest of the company, indoctrinated, agreed with her. When all the guests had gone at last and Emma and Ethel were combing their waist-length hair against another day, Ethel remarked cautiously: "He sings well." To which Emma agreed: "He does a lot of things well. You'd be surprised. I often am."

Summer pressed its sticky fingers on New York. Ed Keefe bent over his drafting board in New London. Fred Cornell checked in and out on a schedule entirely befitting a rising Western Union executive. The hospitable and homely chorus girls were on tour. George Bellows became a painter.

His first essay of the season was a small canvas of swans in the park. Then, early in July, he persuaded a grubby little rag-gamuffin, one Thomas McGlannigan, to pose for him. The resultant picture was not only his first great portrait, but it established his emancipation from Robert Henri.

The urchin type and the energetic brushwork were still the master's, but with this painting the pupil lifted himself to a secure plane of his own. It might be called his graduation piece. One sees at once in the typical Henri waif the grin or the frown—and passes on. The Bellows guttersnipe catches attention and holds it firmly, telling a story of poverty without asking alms, reserved yet rebellious, self-confident yet inquiring, the crossed eyes turned, like the pock marks on Houdon's bust of Mirabeau, into a defiant strength rather than a deformity—a transient glimpse transformed into a lasting personality.

The inevitable Henri background of black remains, but the grays and blues surpass the usual pyrotechnics of the master. The portrait at once closes a respectful curtain on the prelude of a student and swings wide to disclose a full-fledged artist.

He did innumerable drawings, three of which were later recorded in his book. "Street Marathon" and "The Watermelon Man" belong strictly to the Henri formula of noting down interesting but not necessarily important incidents. "Struggle with a Drunk" struck a different note. The title was normal for the American Realists, but he gave it a different twist, the whole of his Methodist upbringing surging to the fore. Never in his life could he persuade his genre drawings to assume a "social consciousness," but on adolescent grounds he could be a willing propagandist. His treatment was as obvious as that of an Anti-Saloon League reformer, but the result was saved by his sense of scale.

Mindful of John Sloan's income from prints he tried a single etching, much in the manner of both Sloan and Hopper, who was trying out the same increment to income at this time. He chose provocatively the title of "Nude Woman Entering a Bed," but the subject was foreign to his Victorian nature, the medium too fussy for his impatient disposition. Although badly in need of funds, he then and there abandoned the idea of print-making for a decade, and when he resumed it again it was in the more direct and congenial form of lithography.

In August, when his duties with the baseball semipros spared his afternoons he ranged the river banks, to the Hudson or the East River where the cool air of the sea relentlessly pursued the heat. As he passed along groves of trees, shanty-Irish hovels, and along weather-beaten docks on the up-stream side his well-trained eyes and ears were as sharp as a hunting lion's, honed by Henri's doctrines, "quick perception, and visual memory."

Sloan, Glackens, and Shinn had been brought up on reportorial jobs for newspapers, illustrating in a matter of hours an accurate and vivid reproduction of a fire or a murder or a riot. These subjects could not possibly be done in the confusion of the spot, but still had to meet the early morning edition deadlines. George had the instinct, a little experience, and an extraordinary capacity to learn. During his incessant rambles along the riverside watching the Palisades and the bridges and the shipping, he was constantly aware of the swarms of little boys infesting every delapidated pier like grubs, stripping off their summer rags and plunging gleefully into the river. The glint of their small bodies, like a school of flying fish, caught his eye and held it, a vivid contrast to the scarred earth banks and the drab tenements lurking over the urchins. One day a dozen such casual scenes came into focus in his mind and "River Rats" was born.

Years before, Thomas Eakins had treated a similar subject in his "Swimming Hole." Bellows had almost certainly never seen that painting, although he may have heard about it from Henri or his Philadelphia friends. Except for the basic ingredient of bathers it is hard to imagine two less similar concepts, Eakins with his solidly-knit human triangle in the foreground, Bellows brushing in his tiny actors like shimmering spindrift far away from the river's edge.

The Bellows family passed through briefly on their way to Sag Harbor—father, mother, sister Laura Monett, and her son Howard. George painted the latter's portrait, showed the old people some of the sights, and promised to spend a few days in Sag Harbor with them before the summer was over. Such an excursion would present financial problems, for in two years his allowance had not been increased and he had run through the better part of his savings. His mother and sister doubtless slipped him a little money on their visit, but his dependable sources of income were singing in the Broadway Tabernacle and playing ball with the "Howards." If the Sunday service at the Tabernacle happened to be a long one, there could be anxious moments over his conflict of responsibilities. On one occasion the sermon was so eloquent that Fred Cornell, waiting to join him outside, suffered agonies of apprehension. When George finally emerged Fred seized him by the arm and whirled him into a dead run for the Long Island ferry. They barely made it and then played a memorable game on a dragged over dump studded with empty cans and broken glass from the adjacent saloon. At one point George, attempting to steal third, slid for the base and ripped a deep gash in his leg on a jagged bottle neck. First aid was in order and the bartender, to whom this was no new experience, dashed out with a bottle of uncut whiskey, lathering the wound so liberally that his patient howled in anguish and one of his teammates quipped: "That's more likker than George ever saw in all his life." This was probably true.

The Brooklyn "Howards" solved part of his problem of getting to Sag Harbor. The team played a couple of games on the eastern part of Long Island, and this paid George's expenses out. It was eight years since he had been in his mother's birthplace, a tidy little town that had once been an important whaling center. The Bellows family always stayed with a relative, Captain Davis, whose formidable, capacious house on Amity Street boarded schoolteachers in the winter and summer folk in season. It was only a step down the street to the four-square Methodist Church, a half-step further to the village center, and no distance at all to the piers where the breezes off Long Island Sound met the visitor more than half way. He swam, crabbed, sailed, played tennis, and enjoyed himself so much that he picked up a low-grade infection of the sort to which he seems to have been prone. This hampered his playing with the "Howards" on his return, although he reported to Emma, once more enjoying herself in Nova Scotia, on one highly satisfactory game. Notoriously a weak hitter, he had "garnered three beautiful swats two of which went beautifully safe. There's no music as beautiful as the ring of a good bat meeting the ball on its dear little cheek—when you play the tune yourself. This kind of music like all great music is essentially personal."

Emma reported a carefree holiday. Her doctor admirer was in attendance, and she used this circumstance to tease George mercilessly as she recounted driving handome horses, learning to steer a motorboat, and picnicking on the sand in the moonlight. Generally he could needle her in turn, but at this point his poverty and obscurity and his resentment thereof overtook him and he wrote: "I wish I owned a horse and a motor boat and a mountain and a sunset and beach to build bonfires on. I'd let you play with them. The only thing I seem to have at present is a 'line of talk' and of course you're welcome to that."

Symbolically, the most important event of the summer of 1906 was a change of quarters. He and Ed Keefe had long since discovered that their room was too small. After two years at the Chase School they needed more space in which to work, to store their growing stack of canvases, to supply a more professional atmosphere. When Ed left for New London in June it was agreed that George should find a real studio; so between painting, singing, playing shortstop, and dating Emma before she went away, he read the advertisements and listened to the gossip, climbed miles of steep, dark stairways to inspect made-over lofts and attics, and finally found just what he wanted in Studio 616 on the top floor of the Lincoln Arcade Building at 1947 Broadway. It was bleak but airy, had a splendid high skylight on the north, and the rent of $40 a month he and Ed could swing with the help of Fred Cornell who wanted to go in on the venture with them. There was an alcove for a stove and a wash basin, while curtains strung along the south end could cut off ample sleeping space for three, and cots in the main part of the room could accommodate any overflow of roomers.

When Ed returned early in September the great eruption of moving day from West Fifty-Eighth Street took place. Actually, the change of locale was more of emotional than physical importance. None of the three had much to transport—a few assorted coats and trousers, a little linen, some books, stretchers and drawings, three cots, assorted chairs, and tables. George tacked up the "Cross-eyed Boy" and "River Rats" and reproductions of the masters he revered—Velásquez, Manet, Henri. Ed contributed a scene of Columbus Circle in the snow. Just as a small boy putting on a policeman's helmet can feel like an officer of the law, so the skylight seemed to bestow professional status on two aspiring artists, neither of whom had yet sold a picture.

On the East Side, *drawing*.

FOUNDATIONS FOR FAME

» 1906 - 1908 «

» III «   *"To be a student is to have an eternal aptitude of
mind for the assimilation of understanding, impressions, and knowledge."* George Bellows

Studio 616 in the Lincoln Arcade Building was duly given a house
warming, whose pattern was repeated on a smaller scale many
times in the next four years. The ingredients were always the
same. Up the five steep flights of stairs trudged a wildly assorted
troupe of young men—actors, artists, writers of every kind,
reporters—and a sprinkling of girls, each bringing along whatever
he or she thought appropriate or happened to have on hand in the
way of food and drink. Crackers, cheese, and salami were the staple
solids, coffee and beer were the liquids with not very much of the
latter. Hosts and guests generated their own excitement, conversation waxed long and loud on every imaginable topic, and sometimes the festivities lasted the better part of the night.

Before long the occupants acquired an ancient upright piano
and an equally venerable and unreliable victrola. Emma and others could operate the one, and any one could put a scratchy record
on the other. George led and dominated the singing and dancing
at which he was an impetuous performer, inventing new steps in
accurate rhythm, but often with no logical sequence. And there
was always the latest joke or catchy ditty or wild embroidery of an
escapade.

The loosely knit firm of Bellows, Keefe, and Cornell luxuriated
in the space of their new quarters; but in Upper Montclair, New

Jersey, William E. Story, dealer in fine linens and laces, regarded it with increasing disfavor. He had never been able to understand George Bellows. Mr. Story himself always dressed immaculately right up to and including his inevitable silk hat, while Emma's odd beau might appear publicly in almost anything. The Westerner's manners were uncouth, his speech unorthodox, and his vitality utterly bewildering. Mr. Story had well-considered opinions on everything with which the young man never agreed. Worst of all, Mr. Story prided himself on using words worthy of H. G. Wells' immortal Mr. Polly, but when he would carefully interject a "surbounding" here and an "extineordinary" there, George would retort with: "It is extineordinary that you have amassed such a surbounding vocabulary," and poor Mr. Story was not sure whether this was said in praise or in fun. Young Lochinvar was confusing at best and so probably unsound; and as Emma's visits to the studio continued Mr. Story was frequently overheard to refer to it under his walrus moustache as "that den of iniquity!"

George's parents, with his sister and nephew, came and viewed his new splendor. No record remains of their opinions but they certainly braved the studio and met Emma who must have shared their astonishment at the confrontation. To her they must have seemed antediluvian in their age, costume, and method of speech, while to them she appeared as the properly dressed young lady they had always hoped their peculiar son might meet. One serious misadventure attended their trip, for Anna Bellows succumbed to overcaloric entertainment and, as George explained to Emma: "She went wrong the evening we planned to have Sunday tea with the Bells." Anna's amazing constitution came to her rescue, however, and she and her husband moved leisurely westward once more.

Laura Monett and Nephew Howard lingered somewhat longer, time at least for George to paint his portrait. Then the last of the family hegira with its attendant duties was over and Studio 616 could resume its normal operations. George promptly established his lifelong method of painting. Studio 616 gave him the space he had always needed. In the classroom the easels crowded so closely in on each other that he had been hard put to move his right arm from his palette to the canvas—it was a long and energetic arm.

The doctor's room on Fifty-Eighth Street had been almost as bad, what with his friends and Ed's wandering in and taking up space and with Fred Cornell's desperate exhortations to put out the light and let a working man sleep. Now there was real room for an easel, for a palette placed several feet away, for a model stand. His legs could adapt themselves to the distances with the gravity of a pavan or the piquancy of a polka. He would place himself before the easel studying the sitter, decide just which tone to use, move back to his palette with time enough to review his decision as to color, confirm it with a glance at the model, and on the return journey to the canvas reconsider exactly what stroke he had intended. And as he placed the right pigment on the right spot with precisely the right gesture his eye was already measuring the next problem of color, of light, of intensity of tone.

This ritualistic cadence served as a safety valve for his intentness. If he were working on a remembered scene without a model he often kept at it for hours until the painting was done. Then he collapsed onto the nearest seat available. With a portrait or a nude he had the further focus of the model stand and often broke his cycle of action by flopping into a rocking chair and allowing its relaxing motion to shift his focus from the model to the canvas to the model again until he had discovered exactly what he had been looking for.

Such unorthodox technique was aided and abetted by the life work of a color devotee named Hardesty S. Maratta, paint manufacturer, chemist, and artist. The degree of red or blue or yellow is, after all, only a question of its purity of tone and this, according to Maratta and almost all the painters of his time, was produced by adding white or black in varying amounts. Artists were accustomed to squeezing their favorite basic colors plus a generous dab of white and a more modest blob of black onto an oval wooden palette and mixing them as they went along. Not Maratta. He produced paints in tubes already mixed to a set formula of purity and degree of dark. The difficulty with his method was the need for more palette space than the old-fashioned, thumb-through-a-hole bit of wood allowed. A good-sized tray, with a compartment for every tone was his substitute, and this George provided for at his own studio and at the School. Henri thoroughly approved. He used the method himself.

Bellows took fewer classes at the school that fall. William Merritt Chase, gracious and urbane as usual, had recognized his unusual talent, and even paid him the honor of dropping in unannounced at Studio 616. George recounted this august descent to Emma somewhat casually: "Wm. M. Chase just stepped into *my* studio this evening with his daughters. Ed and I came down from playing basket ball at Columbia and found our place filled with beauties. I had on my old clothes but stepped into some one else's and did things."

There was no sense in being an artist with a real studio without using it in a really professional way, and early in the fall of 1906 George stretched a monumental canvas, hired a model, and began to work on his first independent nude. Henri was his idol, and Henri's nudes were indescribably his own. His "Nude with a Parrot" is a lusciously sensual piece and his "Figure in Motion" which was exhibited at the Armory Show flaunts its cheerful lack of inhibition. Compared to these, Bellows' first essay in the field is academic in its dedication to anatomy and puritanic in its stark realism. It possesses a homeliness worthy of Eakins, although with so much attention to anatomy that none of the inner personality of the model appears at all. When it was done he approved it, hung it prominently in the studio, but rarely exhibited it. It was characteristic of him to record it as "Nude, Miss Bentham." There was no "artists and models" nonsense about George.

Along with his labors on Miss Bentham's physique George continued his drawing. Remembering the whole long summer of throwing to first and sliding perilously to stolen bases on semiprofessional fields, he sketched two versions of "Kill the Umpire," one in ink and the other in a combination of crayon and wash, odd as a mixture of media but mild compared to some of the ones he would later concoct when he had become well known as an illustrator.

As fall gave way to winter, indoor entertainment expanded. George and Emma with another couple or a friend as a chaperon followed the bright lights as often as they could afford them. In one extravagant gesture he squired her to see William Gillette, whom she vastly preferred to John Drew, but more often they settled for vaudeville which was much less expensive. As in all things George felt free to express his frank opinions. Once, Ethel Clarke wangled three free passes to a highly sentimental hit. She and Emma were joyously crying their eyes out when George jumped furiously to his feet, oblivious to the enraptured house and growled, "Can't stand any more of this silly slush. I'll come back later for you idiots," and shouldered his way out. Emma took him to task for this. "If you want to let off surplus energy please choose places that are not public like Theatres and Restaurants," she wrote; but there was no curing him, and she always forgave him in the end.

At Christmastime he suddenly felt homesick for Columbus. Cash was in short supply as usual and it remains a mystery where he found the necessary railroad fare. He did save the cost of a telegram and walked in on his family quite unheralded, to the consternation of his mother who had to be persuaded that this sudden apparition was really her son. After more than two years he was back again, loaded not with honors but with paint box, canvas, and a ripening skill. He proceeded to demonstrate this by painting his father's portrait, reading into the frail old man all the strength and wisdom that had once been his which the camera could not show. His son's vigorous brushwork could.

Most of the original Brownie team either had settled in Columbus or were back for the holidays. His Christmas gift of Tolstoi's *Twenty-three Tales* to third baseman Bud McCallip indicates one of the directions his voluminous reading was taking at the time. He had long chats with Joe Taylor and other members of the Pen and Pencil Club which proudly exhibited one of his paintings all through his stay. His relatives and his parents' friends came to inspect him as an oddity from the metropolis who was still determined to be an artist. His mother fairly burst with pride when he took his accustomed place in the choir of the First Methodist Church. It was a grand reunion.

O'Henry wrote in "The Duel": "Every man Jack when he first sets foot on Manhattan has got to fight. . . . There is no resting between rounds for there are no rounds. It is slugging from the first." The restless energy of the city caught Bellows up at once on his return, yet his first production of 1907, "Dance in a Madhouse," was a fantastic recollection of the Ohio State Mental Hospital in Columbus he had known so well as a youth and revisited at Christmas to see his friend Sox Raymond.

Henri had given George a fondness for Goya, and he suffused the big drawing with an eerie feeling for motion which he heightened with telling, unnatural effects of light and dark. Throughout the design the ghostly motion of the dancers contrasts with the apathy or despair of their audience so intimately that it brings a shudder of embarrassment and an uneasy sense of violence on the verge of eruption. What might, in less skillful hands, have become a cruel caricature remains a powerful and penetrating masterpiece.

In 1907, the most spectacular manifestation of the city's dynamic growth was the huge hole being gouged out of the island's back to receive the Pennsylvania Station. Entire blocks on the West Side were uprooted and from them two long tunnels relentlessly pushed their way under the Hudson to the Jersey shore. Almost daily George joined the sidewalk superintendents watching men and machines assault the virgin rock, storing up impressions to work over in his studio. His first canvas that year, painted in February, was entitled appropriately enough "Pennsylvania Excavation," and he returned to this theme again and again during the next two years.

In the late winter and spring he produced a number of drawings in the Henri vein: "Dogs, Early Morning," two sketches of Ma Thun's boarding house where he took a good many of his meals, "San Juan Hill" (which he subtitled "Niggers Having a Tin Can Battle"). That he achieved this much was a credit to his powers of concentration. Studio 616 was in a constant turmoil of transient tenants such as Glenn O. Coleman and Rockwell Kent, fellow students at the school, and Lloyd Grisby who taught Latin at Manlius. Kent had just returned from spending the better part of the winter on Monhegan, a rockbound outpost off the frigid coast of Maine, bringing back with him pictures that were as cold and dark and primitively simple as the island itself. He had captured and disciplined the beetling cliffs and the lawless glitter of the surf around them in a majestic way that made the pretty meadows and elegant elms of the fashionable academicians look wan and undernourished. Kent's grays and blacks added power to the starkness of his designs. Bellows never warmed to Kent the individual, but he feasted his eyes long and enviously on these pictures, vowing that some day he would go to Monhegan himself and do better ones.

In addition to the four or five who regularly slept in the studio, a steady stream of friends and acquaintances of all sorts drifted in and out at all hours of the night or day. Among these appeared a picturesque ex-schoolmate of Ed's in New London, one Moses King, the lightweight champion of Connecticut, who was picking up bouts at various clubs in and around town. Public boxing was illegal in New York at the time, but there was nothing to prevent its taking place in private clubs. One such was operated by Tom Sharkey almost across the street from the studio. Sharkey, who had once almost taken the heavyweight title from Jim Jeffries, now followed the usual pattern of the retired pugilist by setting up a bar where, at intervals, he staged bouts for the edification of his customers. To insure that he would retain their patronage, his bar became a "club," tickets to the fights became "dues," and the boxers themselves were announced from the ring as "both members of this club," thus giving the ensuing mayhem a certain legality.

Moses King had a match coming up at Sharkey's and suggested that Ed see it—and bring along his friend. Sharkey's small backroom—large enough only for the ring and a handful of spectators, wreathed in blue cigar smoke and the aroma of cheap, stale beer, the hot concentration of light in the center, the hum of excitement rising to a roar—provided the setting for the primitive violence of the bouts themselves and for the uninhibited reactions of the toughs and bums that were the charter and sustaining members of the club. George, with his passion for sports of all kinds and the need to release his own elemental energies, found here an intriguing environment that frequently drew him back and from which he memorized actions and episodes for later inspiration.

He exhibited whenever he had a chance, encouraged by the reception of "Kids" at the Society of American Artists' finale. To Philadelphia, in the fall of 1906, he had offered three contributions, and his drawings of "Basket Ball" and "Struggle with a Drunk" had been shown. In March of 1907 he valiantly sent an entry to the haughty National Academy of Design for its spring exhibition. The odds were all against its acceptance. Chase may have said a good word for it, and Henri's presence on the committee of selection certainly did it no harm. At any rate, before his twenty-fifth birthday, the "Wild Man from Ohio" had a painting, "River Rats," hanging obscurely in one of the exhibition galleries of the academy.

There the reporter for the *Nation*, Frank Fowler, noticed it and between his observations on J. Francis Murphy's "The Golden Wood" and Childe Hassam's "Church at Old Lyme" he found a number of good things to say about it: "So sordid a theme proves afresh that the artist and not the subject makes the work . . . the painter has created a work of art . . ." He likened it to "some delicate conception of Cellini, in which his dainty figures appear more chaste because of their rough setting."

There was a celebration in Studio 616. George had "arrived."

A month later honors were more evenly drawn. A dozen students from the Chase School mounted an exhibition in a gallery at Eightieth Street and Broadway. George entered "River Rats" again as well as "Pennsylvania Excavation" and his drawing "Dance in a Madhouse." Despite the relatively remote location of the show, the reviewers nosed out both the place and the Bellows entries. The *Telegram* was kind. It noted the strong imprint of Henri's personality on all the contributors, found "George Bellows perhaps the strongest of the lot," and saw in "River Rats" some "passages that the masters might envy." The critic for the *Globe* was far less charitable: "A more dreary and unhealthy lot we have seldom seen." He pleaded for "a bit of beauty, of hope, of optimism," and left "with a sense of oppression," for the exhibition had seemed "like some depressing dream, best forgotten." The *Times* benignly took away some of the sting. It lauded the general quality of the show and singled out "Pennsylvania Excavation" for especial praise, commenting on it as a "slice of New York keenly observed, keenly transcribed." It added that, while the subject was not very alluring, "When you paint a crab apple you don't give us a luscious peach (but the idealists always clamor for a peach)."

These exhibitions had been gratifying to George, but quite apart from his own success, the Spring Academy had sparked the beginning of a revolution. Robert Henri had left the jury of selection on March 3 in a quiet, long-drawn rage. Pointed nose quivering, long narrow eyes at the broil, he stalked home furiously as his mind ran over the smug efficiency of his fellow jurors. The jury's session of elimination had resulted in the polite but virtually unanimous rejection of almost all the works of his friends: Glackens, Luks, Shinn, and Sloan. He had not even been able to persuade those moribund jurors to fill up a vacant wall space with one of their works. "What do you want?" one of these overfed, overpublicized, overrated patricians had had the gall to ask, "The appearance of the wall or of a name?" Faugh! The whole performance had not only been a disgusting exhibition of ingrown intolerance, it was a personal affront as well. Henri had played the academy's game long enough. From now on he would use all his energies, persuasiveness, and prestige to establish some rules of his own. His long legs swung to a rhythm worthy of the Marseillaise as they cadenced his momentous decision.

The National Academy of Design had grown out of a rebellion, nearly a century before, when Samuel F. B. Morse could take no more of the crusty despotism of old John Trumbull's New York Academy. But although Morse was the most gifted painter of his time, he found the profession unprofitable and turned his interest entirely to science, thereby depriving the young institution of his revolutionary services. Successive captains of the Academy and their crews contented themselves with trimming sail for their own comfort and a fine disregard for any other interests. They welcomed aboard new members from time to time, for even the best die off sooner or later, and in these elections they were careful to see to it that only thoroughly compatible persons of impeccable aesthetic standards (their own) were admitted. When unavoidable compromises had to be made, such as when the Academy absorbed the Society of American Artists, and nonpliable personalities such as Henri thus automatically became academicians, there was nothing to do but put them in their places politely but firmly. With utter correctness of speech and manner, and with expert manipulation of their rules, the "regulars" could slit newcomers' throats with a deftness that would make a hungry mink look clumsy. "Beauty" was theirs to interpret and protect for the nation, and they did their best to be worthy of this self-arrogated trust.

Their definition of "beauty" was easy to comprehend if one was a true academician. "Grace" there must be, "good breeding," a nice "sentiment," a fine technique, a good deal of the Old World with some seasoning from the New—only a little from the latter. Not that everything European was admirable, of course. There was something to be said for the Impressionists who were attracting American patronage, but certainly not their rabid successors such as the Pointillists and Cézanne. There was definitely a place for Bouguereau (really a splendid technician), for American morality could be counted on not to let the influence of his nudes "go too far," and his models were obviously "of good character." Beauty and American taste were quite safe in the hands of the academy, and no radical doctrine such as Henri's *universal* beauty could budge them an inch. After all, anybody who was anybody knew that the essence of beauty must be aristocratic.

All during the spring of 1907 Henri nurtured his grievances and planned his campaign of frightening or enlightening the Academy into a broader point of view. If he could not, unaided, infiltrate its stronghold he would invest it from without. All he needed was a handful of liberally minded and able artists to join with him and, above all, a place to show their wares. The first concomitant was no problem. Sloan and the rest of the ex-Philadelphians were delighted to join. Two or three other artists, not of their group but of their caliber, could be persuaded. Finding the place was the problem, a big one. To hire a hall, light it, and decorate it suitably for the occasion would be far too expensive. The dealers were, almost to a man, too concerned with their own stables of painters, the disapprobation and possible boycott by the academy and the critics, and too worried about sales to welcome a motley group of relatively unknown artists, however big the reputation of their leader might be. Henri found the exception in their ranks, one William Macbeth.

The Macbeth Gallery had consistently been friendly to American painters of all kinds, and its owner gladly offered his walls to Henri, quite enjoying the prospect of a little change of pace, but he could not do it for charity. Henri talked enthusiastically of prospective sales; would a percentage on these be satisfactory? William Macbeth was inclined to think not. His overhead for a month was considerable, and if the show proved as successful as Henri predicted, sales from his own stock were sure to suffer. He must have a guarantee of $500 plus 25 per cent to cover his costs.

To this proposition Henri assented readily enough. In his excited imagination the sales from the show would much more than cover the basic figure. His next move was to round out his complement of painters. The ex-Philadelphians would make a fairly homogeneous core, but he wanted to avoid any charges of nepotism, needed variety for contrast, and believed that other "un-Academic" individuals should have a hearing too.

As the least radical of these independents, Henri invited Ernest Lawson, an objective disciple of French Impressionism who concentrated on landscape and greatly admired Cézanne's experiments in three dimensions achieved through color. Lawson preferred the still masses of hills and bridges, the shimmer of foliage and moonlight, the simple organization of forms in space. But he was a reasonably gregarious soul who could on occasion forsake the grandeur of the Hudson for the gaiety of Coney Island and so, although rarely, take on Henri's favorite subject matter.

Maurice Prendergast, a Bostonian partly transplanted to New York, also used an Impressionist technique, but in a highly personal way. He cared nothing for mass but delighted in surfaces and especially in the shapes upon the surfaces. A parasol, a broad-brimmed hat, or a carriage wheel repeated itself like an amoebic cell over his canvas or his water color pad in such profusion that these became virtually mosaics in paint. He used units much larger than the niggling dots of Seurat and the other neo-Impressionists, but with much the same effect of glowing, ordered design. A park, the Rialto Bridge in Venice, a street fair—he approached them all with so specialized a vision that each bears a startling family resemblance to the others.

Arthur B. Davies who completed Henri's roster lived in a dream world quite divorced from his upstate New York origins and his Boston Brahmin admirers. His pictorial Shangri-la was usually located in utopian Greece, a site he shared with Bryson Burroughs and Howard Pyle. He peopled it with high-breasted, long-limbed nudes moving in a trance-like state between manicured trees and unicorns standing at attention. A slight, rather secretive man, he managed his domestic double life so deftly as to escape all suspicion, while his light-minded mysticism could never be confused with the raffish gusto of Henri and his "gang." Nor could anyone

have guessed his quiet ability to raise and handle money or his
very great ambition.

Place and personnel for the exhibition now in order, the press
was early alerted, and on May 15 the *Sun* gave long advance warning of a revolution in art scheduled to explode the following
February, 1908. Referring to the painters as among those pilloried
because they dared to paint on their own, the reporter stressed the
independent character of the group: no leader, no president, no
formal organization. The notice pleased Henri who did not want
the papers to invent some story of a deliberate attack on the
Academy. He was out to demonstrate the artist's right to show his
wares, and that was all.

This localized squabble over liberty of expression in the arts was
only a tympanum in Henri's ear from which he picked up the
larger echoes from the area of politics and social thinking at the
start of the twentieth century. "Big Bill" Haywood and two other
Anarcho-Socialists were to stand trial early in May for allegedly
engineering the murder of mining bosses in Colorado, Idaho, and
other states. Socialism in every phase was furious. Eugene Debs
frothed. Maxim Gorky, by sending the prisoners a note of sympathy, called down upon himself such a glare of publicity that his
irregular private life came under review and was pilloried by no
less august a liberal than Mark Twain. President Roosevelt, by
coming to a public verdict before the court had sat on the case,
found the accused "guilty of incitement to, or apology for blood-
shed and violence," and thereby gave thousands of excited liberals
a chance to blossom with buttons reading "I AM AN UNDESIR-
ABLE CITIZEN." On the evening of May 4, a procession of
Socialists clogged Fifth Avenue for hours with a lantern and flag-
spangled procession sparked by the "Marseillaise," while a companion demonstration held up all traffic on Lexington Avenue. It
is inconceivable that twenty-four-year old George Bellows did not
fill in marching space in one or the other column. Ideologies
apart, he could never be a simple spectator in such a show of color,
excitement, and mass vitality.

Against this stimulating surge of a new interest there always
stood the powerful ghost of the Bellows background. His parents

wrote frequently, and what remains of their letters speaks eloquently for a generation already wholly removed from his own. His mother reported: "Father and I are well as usual. I have a cold in my head . . . Laura went downtown with me to select my new *head gear* which I hope will be satisfactory as usual . . ." Her description of a church reception "in the palatial home of Mr. Edward Johnson" invites a comparison to the parties in Studio 616. "Mr. Shawan was President. He made a few remarks, then Miss Brent sang two solos, then Father made a speech . . . then Miss Conis sang twice which was followed by a few remarks by our Pastor, then Mrs. Pletsch sang twice which closed the evening's program, after which refreshments were served, sandwiches, coffee, ice cream and cake, and then we returned to our respective homes . . ." (Monroe Avenue, Columbus, to Broadway, New York.)

A transcript of his father's speech was sent to him. Young ambition keeps no time clock, but age inclines to reflection. Asked to make "a few remarks" as the oldest member of his church, George Bellows senior could only ask: "How was I to put sixty years into a few words or a short talk—Sixty years—why not ask someone to build the State House in a week, or jump on a flying ship and visit the Moon, and return tomorrow morning?" The airplane was then less than four years old.

It may have been such diversity of loyalties that was responsible for the extraordinary variety of Bellows' work that summer. For once he was in tune with the thunderous weather. He began in typically Henri fashion with a series of drawings of the slums including a street fight and portraits of two urchins, "Jimmy Flanagan Laughing," and "Frankie the Organ Boy." Immediately thereafter he found a fresh and tender subject, little Queenie Burnet who brought him his laundry. He changed the title of this picture several times: "The Laundry Girl," "Little Girl in White," but it was the painting not the caption that brought him laurels later on.

In this big canvas he tackled a new theme. He had already shown that he could equal and surpass Henri in his penetrating study of the street Arab type; the opposite sex at the same age presented a very different problem. His approach to it reveals an unconscious synthesis of influences, for it has the blunt contrasts of Henri without his grace and the brilliance of Sargent without his suavity. Yet the result could never be confused with either of these masters, for it establishes the empathy with the sitter that he had achieved in his "Cross-Eyed Boy," shyness and an awkward charm here replacing rebellious pugnacity.

The paint on these portraits was hardly dry when he picked up his crayon and charged fist first into a thoroughly unfashionable theme which had haunted him ever since he paid his membership dues at Sharkey's. "A Knockout," his first prize-ring picture, represents the instant of culmination. Thousands of casual enthusiasts today sit in their easy chairs at home, highball in hand, and watch a bout on television, hoping to see it end in a knockout. At Sharkey's, in 1907, the crowd was so small and so compact that it bred an instant intimacy and partisanship over the beer mugs and the smell of resin and cigars. Each clout and grunt from the ring rallied boos and cheers demanding a dramatic finish. Science went by the board in the excitement. No one wanted a decision, only a comatose body on the canvas and a blood-stained, hysterical victor standing above him in the ring, held back by the referee to prevent sheer murder.

In "A Knockout" the loser extends a strong horizontal line, his shoulders heaving into a flattened triangle as he struggles to push himself up. Above him the referee, grappling with the winner, forms a sharper triangle and brings violence to a simmering halt. The howling crowd with fists and shoulders surges into the ring. In the foreground one face turns outward with a dreadful grin.

Then, in an almost automatic change of pace, Bellows left the aromas of Sharkey's Club and returned to the open air. "Forty-two Kids" reverts to the theme of "River Rats," but brings his actors closer into focus as a theme and then projects them into timelessness. Here the bathers, instead of serving as froth at the edge of a large comber, become the components of a small wave in themselves, building up in tension from static figures in the foreground to a crest that breaks in a spraddle of knobby knees and a pair of small splayed feet as one little starveling flops into the placid river. The setting happens to be the Hudson, but might as well be the Olentangy of Columbus or any American swimming hole at the turn of the century.

Sharkey's, however, was still very much in his mind. He switched back to it in a large canvas now known as "Club Night."

In contrast to "A Knockout" he chose a moment of suspense. The fighters are sparring, closing in, looking for a lethal opening. Their legs, shoulders, and arms weave in rhythmic pattern under the glare of the lights. The crowd follows their savage dance with heads moving hypnotically in time, except for one rubicund devotee who claps his hands and jeers at the pause before a violent collision.

The fighters' bodies form a great feline curve, their gloves poised like the paws of cats feinting with their prey, but the angles of arms and knees and elbows strike staccato notes through the hard sharp play of light and shadow that permeates the whole.

This picture was done from memory as Bellows did all of his figure compositions at this time. Later on at least, he would make a quick sketch and then verify some of the points from a posed model. But in general he was not particular about detail; it was the design and the essence of the action that mattered. When one expert pointed out that fighters never worked their hands and feet in some of the combinations he gave them, he retorted: "I don't know anything about boxing. I am just painting two men trying to kill each other"; and, to another critic: "Who cares what a prize fighter looks like? It's his muscles that count."

Fame is a fickle commodity. In the spring of 1907 George Bellows' name had dominated the reviews of young painters and their work. Yet in October one Eugene Speicher, a squarely built, spectacled basketball player from Buffalo, newly enrolled at the Art Students' League, dropped in to see a game at the West Side Y.M.C.A. Watching it he had no idea who was the "tall vigorous young fellow, unquestionably the best player." When they were introduced he immediately identified the name with that of Ohio State's star performer of four years before. The two talked about the game and athletics in general for a while in the locker room and went on to a restaurant for dinner, still on the same subject. It was not until they walked up Broadway to George's studio that it became inescapably clear that "Ho" Bellows was also an art student. "We talked into the morning about art," Speicher remembered. "That evening was the beginning of a rare friendship."

The fall term put an end to much independent painting. George turned out one fine portrait of a fellow student, Prosper

Ivernizzi; he studied the new exhibitions, continued his intermittent quarrels and reconciliations with Emma, and vastly enjoyed the rising controversy in the press as it anticipated Henri's forthcoming group show. Determined to stress his lack of conflict with the Academy, Henri urged all of his confederates to send in contributions to its winter exhibition in December, only to learn that his flag of truce had been ignored. His, alone of all the offerings, was accepted, and this was an automatic gesture, since every member of the Academy was entitled to show one picture. It is difficult, however, to understand how—with the conservative tide within the Academy in full flood—George Bellows' two entries of "Pennsylvania Excavation" and "Club Night" were both hung, if not in posts of honor, at least where they could be seen. The reviewers, on the whole, approved highly of these particular selections.

The *Times* spoke of both as presenting "passing phases of the town in a manly, uncompromising manner" and went on to regret how little opportunity there was for the public to see the work of these younger men, "the leaven of today and the hope of the future." The *Sun* pronounced "Pennsylvania Excavation" to be "a picture to make rosewater idealism shiver and evaporate. But it is real. It is truthfully painted"; and although the reviewer found "Club Night" neither pleasing nor edifying as a subject, he admitted that "for the artist and amateur the play of muscles and the various attitudes and gestures are positively exciting." TAD of the *Journal* decided to spoof the Academy, the show, and everything in it. "They have everything there," he wrote, "from flower pots to paintings of invisible moons . . . No. 383 ["Club Night"] by George Bellows, is a wonder except that the ring is very shy of light . . . It would be a pipe for the losing man to run in the dark corner and hide there . . . I didn't notice any bartenders in the front row either. Why not a little color there, Bellows?"

With notices such as these in his pocket, George journeyed for another Christmas in Columbus. His family and the community had a warm welcome for him and a seat in the choir. ("But you're not to rock," his mother warned him, "you are the first and only one I ever observed take that position . . .") He had brought some paint with him and essayed another portrait of his father and one of a member of the Pen and Pencil Club named Lundberg. But he was anxious to get away. The envelopment of Columbus bade well to destroy his image of it, a sentimental concept which he had already transferred to the person of Miss Emma Louise Story of Upper Montclair, New Jersey. She had the conservatism, the healthy simplicity, sometimes the downright dullness which was an essential part of his Ohio background.

Illness struck him and delayed his departure for weeks. Emma received the news with vexation. The violets he had sent her at Christmas were a gesture that touched her pleasantly, but she had no patience with physical ailments of any kind. She wrote that she was sorry he was not "in his usual cheerful happy spirits. This last is sarcasm. I thought I had better tell you as you might not realize it. Your poor mother has my sincerest sympathy as I know exactly what you are like when you look like a funeral . . ."

This hurt; but in any case he had the honesty to admit its truth. His normal mood was one of abnormally optimistic gusto. When it failed, the gloom that rushed in to take its place was no doubt equally intense. This exaggeration of his temperamental poles was one of the marks of his genius, but not an easy one with which to live.

George's normal good health returned in plenty of time to indite Emma a valentine from New York, headed "The Occasion of Feb. 14, 1908," complete with colored frontispiece, and bursting with forty-two lines of verse which begin:

"If I were gifted with the tinkling tongue
"Or note of rythmic melody were mine;
"Could I but dream the eternal music of the world,
"With sun-born words create a soaring symphony . . ."

Clearly, his talents did not run in the direction of "sun-born words." For all their tribute to Professor Joe Taylor's grounding in Milton, Keats, and Shelley, the poem remains a romantic grab bag from which the reader emerges relieved that George Bellows generally preferred to express himself in paint rather than in poetry.

By the time this epic was delivered, the great event of the year in the art world had already taken place. On the third of February the exhibition of "The Eight" opened at the Macbeth Gallery, 450 Fifth Avenue. Because Sloan refused to hire appropriate dress for the event, only seven of the artists greeted their guests at the private inauguration of Henri's venture. These braved the congratulations of the invited guests, complimented each other, and ultimately departed for a party at the Sherwood given by May Wilson Preston, all according to schedule. The unexpected followed when the public reacted to the show like children at a carnival and poured in, sometimes at the rate of three hundred an hour, for a look at the freaks. Many remained to praise, some even

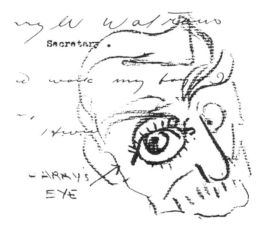

"Harry's Eye," addition to National Academy's Letter, 1908.

to buy, including the generous patroness and artist Gertrude Vanderbilt Whitney. The press was gratifyingly mixed in its opinions. Those in favor applauded it more for its demand of freer exhibition space than for the quality of the paintings themselves.

The opinion of the expert for *Town Topics* could be anticipated: "Vulgarity smites one in the face . . . Is it fine art to exhibit

our sores?" He was horrified at the idea of hanging Luks' "pos-
teriors of pigs" or even Glackens' "Chez Mouquin's" in his living
room. To him the work of Prendergast and Shinn was "unadulter-
ated slop," that of Arthur B. Davies was a kind of limbo between
"genius and insanity," that of Henri was "a streak of coarseness . . .
Bah! The whole thing creates a distinct feeling of nausea."

The *Sun,* however, shone benignly on Luks' repellent swine:
"They are genuine porkers, pink, dirty and black." And the
World defended the general choice of subject by observing that
seven of the Eight, "believing that character, too, has beauty . . .
have sought it out in the highways and by-ways of New York. They
invest the commonest attitudes and gestures of life with the dignity of earnest art . . ."

Although the *Sun* made it plain that the exhibition was no
revolution from the academy or a stunt to call attention to unknown artists, the visitors continued to pour in, and when the
show was over they had bought nearly $4,000 worth of pictures.
All the artists except Prendergast, Sloan, and Glackens had sold
something. The Gallery guessed that if the stock market had recovered from the panic of 1907 the sales might have reached
twenty-five thousand. Although entrenched opinion in academic
art hurled epithets such as "Revolutionary Black Gang" and
"Apostles of Ugliness," the idea that an exhibition could be exciting even if not chic became fixed in the public mind, providing an
atmosphere for future controversial exhibitions.

Henri's students were fired with excitement over the success of
"The Eight." Scraping the money together, they hired the top
floor of the Harmonie Club overlooking the construction of the
new Public Library in Bryant Park. So busy was Bellows in helping with the hall's redecoration that he found time for only one
picture that February, "North River," which would become the
cornerstone of his reputation. Out of this medium-sized canvas he
fashioned a masterpiece. A snow-dappled foreground containing a
few spindly trees and a deserted iron bench funnels down to the
shore where slender piers and a pair of smoking small craft thrust
out into the white-flecked river. Behind, the Palisades run firm
and level under a narrow strip of sky. When Henri criticized it in
the studio several other students had versions of the same theme.

The master observed the use of line, of light, of shapes in each painting, holding his audience breathless with interest, as usual, and then swung dramatically to "North River." "You have all observed," he said, "that ships go up and down stream. This is the only one that shows they cross it as well."

The picture was not ready for the pupils' show on Forty-Second Street which firebrand Rockwell Kent, losing all restraint, was advertising as "the death warrant" of the academy. In this ultimatum he was disappointed, for the Academy and the greater part of the press virtually ignored the insurgents. Very few people attended, and such critics as did were sour. The *Evening Mail* headlined it as "The Eight Out-Eighted" and continued: "Having had 'The Eight' we now have their direful consequences . . . This exhibition is being held, incongruously, in the 'antique store' at 43 West 42nd Street. These youths are not 'antiques.' They are so far from it that most of them belong to a future that is never going to happen at all.

"George Bellows, the headliner of the group, is a coming man all right. His pictures come alive; his 'Jimmy Flannigan' here is a pearl of the gutter . . . but the work and attitude of most of the others of the group [is astonishingly] like the work of Robert Henri. These young men [in] copying only the eccentricities of their masters [are] eating the shucks and throwing the corn away."

After three weeks the hopeful student show closed down, unmourned by any but its exhibitors. Ed Keefe and Glenn O. Coleman were among these, also Edward Hopper, one of the present giants of twentieth-century American painting.

Henri's independent exhibition had had one intended effect. The success of "The Eight" shook the Academy, if not to its foundations, at least to the ground floor. When its spring exhibition opened, the New York *Times* ran the headline: "New Spirit Seen at the Academy" and commented that the show deserved "more than passing notice. It is by far the best that that institution has held in many years . . . The Henri, Glackens, Lawson group have been given a wall to themselves . . . ." Then it found Winslow Homer's "West Wind" to have "force and freshness driven home in an unexpectedly exhilarating fashion" and linked with this painting "the rugged and almost startling reality [of] the amazingly clever canvas by George Bellows called 'North River' . . . In its truthfulness of observation and in its painter-like qualities, this is the best piece of work produced by this young man so far."

The New York *Herald* commended "Forty-Two Kids," calling it "one of the most original and vivacious canvases in the show . . . An artist need never leave Manhattan Island if it yields him pictures like this."

Another critic, although he called "Forty-Two Kids" a "tour de force in absurdity" and found the boys "more like maggots than humans," unconsciously paid George the greatest compliment of them all in his biting final observation: "Very few artists could have painted it and perhaps no other would."

The flow of these reviews was heady wine for the young artist from Columbus. His name had been linked with the Eight and with Winslow Homer. To fill his cup to overflowing he received the following letter:

"National Academy of Design

March 23rd, 1908

Mr. George Bellows
1947 Broadway
Dear Sir:

It gives me great pleasure to inform you that the Jury of Selection for the 83rd Annual Exhibition of the National Academy of Design have awarded the Second Hallgarten Prize to your picture No. 164, 'North River.' The amount of this prize, Two Hundred Dollars, ($200) will be sent you in due course by the Treasurer of the Academy. Offering you my personal congratulations I remain

Yours very truly

Harry W. Watrous
Secretary

P.S. [handwritten] Keep up the good work my boy. I have my eye on you. H.W.W."

Artists Judging Works of Art; *lithograph, 1916.*

RECOGNITION

» 1908 - 1910 «

» IV «   *"Every student must become at once editor and judge of who and what is for him worthwhile."*
George Bellows

In March, 1908, George Bellows set out to emulate the Eight and in the process quite literally "out-Eighted" them. "Steaming Streets" takes a trivial moment in city life, not unlike John Sloan's "Dust Storm, Fifth Avenue," which may have inspired it. On a dismal thoroughfare covered with slush and filled with the vapors of melting snow a team of horses, partly braked by a furious driver, plunges toward an oncoming team and a halted trolley. At one side a fascinated crowd leans out from under sign-studded shop buildings; at the other the end of a huge crane moves inexorably behind a barrier of boards. In concept and force the painting is magnificent, yet it embodies the basic weakness of Henri's (and Bellows') belief that any subject is worthy of painting. The moment chosen for "Steaming Streets" is trivial, temporary, melodramatic. The canvas leaves one with a sense of extravagance, a topic better dashed off in crayon or pencil, not one to be made monumental on canvas and in oil. George may have realized this, for he never tried a similar theme again except in illustration.

The success of "North River" at the Academy sent him back to virtually the same site in April for his setting of "Up the Hudson." Here the focal tug puffs smokily upstream as a diagonal bar linking a catboat tied up at a foreground pier with the flatly slanting ridge above the Palisades on the farther shore. Bellows was dissatisfied with the proportions of this canvas, and he and Ed Keefe restretched it several times until the composition exactly suited them. The result was a painting subtler yet more majestic than "North River."

The effort drained him of inspiration. He became, as always in this mood, restless and irritable. In late April, Emma Story found him poor company: "I am coming up to the Studio on Friday and please have it c-l-e-a-n . . . Don't you get another grouch or I'll never speak to you *again*"; and, in May: "I am getting displeased with you and no wonder I scowl . . ."

Classes ended in June, and Henri sailed for a summer in Spain with a troupe of young female students who were looking forward to a season of Iberian sunshine, Velázquez, Goya, and the company of that incomparable and eligible widower, Robert Henri. Not until the ship was at sea did he disclose that the beautiful red-headed girl, Marjorie Organ, who shared his cabin was also his wife of several weeks' standing.

Long before this news reached New York, Bellows had recovered his spirits, and hastened to make amends to Emma. There were boating parties on the lake in Central Park, trips to Coney Island that gave him an idea for a painting, visits to the theater, to galleries, games of tennis and, no doubt, croquet. Once Emma wanted him to escort her to a party in Upper Montclair and baited him with the assurance: "A dress suit isn't really necessary as this is only an informal summer dance. Please come."

For all his better humor, George's restlessness continued. Except for his one picture of Coney Island, which he liked at the time and then later reworked, he found it impossible to paint, and when the offer of a teaching job at the University of Virginia's summer session came his way he bade farewell to Emma and the Brooklyn "Howards," packed up his materials, and hurried southward. The change of scene, however, failed to work wonders; the heat was much worse than New York's, and after six weeks he returned with $5 in his pocket, one undistinguished oil, one excellent, vulgar drawing inspired by the Virginia Horse Show, and a careful copy of Daumier's grim murder scene: "Rue Trans-nounain, 15 Avril 1834."

Another drawing, "Raising Hell," perhaps reflected his momentary humor so starkly that he later destroyed it.

All through the steaming weeks in Charlottesville he had missed Emma badly and had craved the coolness of the sea breezes at Sag Harbor. Why not combine the two? She rather liked the idea although, of course, she could not possibly go with him alone. "Are you really in earnest," she wrote, "because I might be able to go if Jessie can." At the same time she could not resist teasing him. Another beau had left with her a copy of a new magazine, the "Red Book." "It has a long article entitled 'Should Artists Marry?' or something of the sort. I have just been poring over it and will save it for you. You may get some valuable hints from it." Then she reported the engagement of a mutual friend. "Every one seems to be doing it and I am just waiting to hear you are (engaged, I mean) any minute."

Jessie let her down; and Emma protested that she could not possibly stay with George's sister, Laura Monett, who was "living in a boarding house [Captain Davis']." "It would be different if she had a house. Oh! if you only knew how I was dying for a sail . . ."

Furious with disappointment he seized on the first companion he could find, Bud McCallip, the Brownie third baseman who happened to be staying at the studio, and dashed down to Sag Harbor. They stayed in Captain Davis' big, solid mansion long enough for McCallip to fall in love with the captain's daughter; but George's heart was in New York, and he was back there again in a few days with his cousin Howard. Emma kept him at arms length for a time, fending off offers of tennis and Howard's companionship, but she finally relented on the evening before she left for a visit to Ethel Clarke. In a desperate gesture of devotion he brought with him "The Cross-eyed Boy" which she had always admired and made her a present of it. She was touched by this gift, for she knew George prized it highly. Later the painting took on something of a symbolic meaning between them, and on the rare occasions when it was exhibited they put such an outrageous price on it that possible buyers let it alone. Then she was off on her visit to Ethel Clarke, and George ranged moodily and fruitlessly about his stifling studio and the tar-scented pavements of New York.

In the fall he was still fumbling about in search of a subject. New ideas escaped him and he settled down to his most Henriesque manner. Jimmy Flannigan was always available, an Irish imp on his doorstep; for nothing better to do he propped him up on the model stand again and painted "Red-Faced Boy Laughing." A little later Jimmy's cousin, Paddy, obliged and was painted with a cocky tilt of his head and a smile revealing his large incisors. His ragged shirt, worn with an almost regal air, gave the picture its name: "Boy with Bare Chest." On this canvas Henri's slashing stroke is everywhere apparent, as is his swift capture of a fleeting expression. Deeper than these effects the pictures do not go. But even if his brush was moving to another's rhythm, at least George was painting again.

Suddenly, in December, he recovered his peculiar tempo and produced two fine pictures unmistakably his own. Both themes reverted to ones he had used several times, but now he developed them further. "Excavation at Night" took him back to the site of the Pennsylvania Station. He saw it in rich, vivid contrasts of light and dark, the workmen's fire flowing hotly across grey, blue, and black shadows. Only the houses in the background and the dimly seen outlines of the laborers keep the design from being pure abstraction. He said of it later: "That picture is the best attempt I have made to locate the center of interest by strong light. Those tenement houses behind the excavation always give me the creeps. They're just ordinary houses—but there is something about them that gets me."

Then he went back to the Upper Manhattan area that had inspired "North River" and "Up the Hudson" and painted "Rain on the River." This time he looked squarely downstream into the light and caught the sweep of rocks and trees, the railroad. Farther back, the solid blocks of city buildings form a dark triangle cut off by the steam from a locomotive. The wet roofs of a freight train tie a balancing triangle of the river, the Palisades, and the sky into one sheet of sullen gray. No picture of his ever expressed more forcibly the surge of the city toward its water-bound limits.

The Christmas holidays were approaching, and his parents'

eagerness to see him was reflected in a letter that came by registered mail. This could only mean one thing—money. He opened
the letter with extra enthusiasm, pocketed the bills, and perused
the texts. His father's hand was remarkably firm for an octoge-
narian:

"This morning I bought the turkey for Thanksgiving and how
we wish you were here to help eat it. I think it would taste very
much better if that were so . . . But if you cannot be here we can
do the next best thing and I enclose you $25.00 to get a good
square meal with and help out on something else . . . We are all
very anxious that you should have things coming your way . . . Are
things shaping up somewhat to your liking? We hope so at least
and cannot help thinking that they will, only try and not get
weary. You shall yet reap in due time if you faint not. For as
Longfellow says:

> " 'Fear not each sudden sound and shock
> Tis of the wave and not the rock
> Tis but the flapping of the sail . . .' "

His mother enclosed her own addenda, chatting along in her
pleasant, dull way about family comings and goings, entertain-
ments, trips: "Ben [Monett] and family will be here for dinner
Thanksgiving, should have sent you a lot of good things as usual
which I am sure you would have enjoyed but came to the conclusion that the money would be as acceptable if not more so. Will
try to feed you well when you come home . . ."

He was ready for the Christmas trip in every way except financially. With Charlie Grant, his former schoolmate and now a roving sports reporter, he cooked up a scheme to attract a new market. Grant had picked up an assignment in Cleveland, had just
joined its Athletic Club, and was headed there. What better home
for "Club Night" at a very reasonable purchase price than the
Cleveland A.C.? The canvas was a big one, four and a half feet
long, which meant considerable shipping costs, but Bellows solved
this problem by making Grant its temporary owner, and as his
personal luggage Charlie took it with him free.

Grant arranged for the picture to be displayed in the Club's
dining room where the *Cleveland Press* cautiously noted that it

was "a remarkable specimen of the realist school." Its "brutality," however, had an unfortunate effect on the lady guests who found it impossible to enjoy their peach melbas anywhere near it. In the interests of domestic harmony the governing board elected not to buy it, and George picked it up on his way to Christmas in Columbus.

During his holiday he talked hopefully with Professor Joe Taylor about two possible commissions. Portrait painting has made many an artist rich and famous. Early in the twentieth century Sargent, Chase, and Zorn were in constant demand and charged very high fees. For Bellows to gain a reputation in this lucrative field would make sense to his father, whose practicality his son shared in a considerable degree. More than this, George had already found excitement in the portraits he had done for nothing whether Thomas McGlannigan's, Clifton Webb's, or those of his fellow students. Just as he loved to capture the personality of a city or a river, so he was fascinated by the problem of keeping that delicate balance between the subject's individuality and its representative type. During the fall of 1908 the Alumni Association of Ohio State had set up a committee to secure portraits of two members of the faculty. Joe Taylor, a member, hoped to swing its choice to his young protégé. When George Bellows left Columbus he had no specific promise, but he did have some reason to hope for at least one order by spring.

During his absence from New York there had been a minor explosion in the world of art education. Robert Henri was setting up his own school just down the corridor from Studio 616. All fall in 1908 there had been trouble at the New York School of Art. Henri had returned late as usual from abroad. Chase had exploded with wrath, thus bringing his long-smouldering jealousy into the open. The school's finances were in wretched shape, and back bills had assumed enormous proportions. Almost no one had been paid for a long time, including Henri. Up to December he had nobly stood by the sinking ship with Kenneth Hayes Miller, a charter member of the staff. Miss Bissell, the secretary-treasurer was, as quoted in the press, "in a most agitated state of mind when questioned." The janitor had not been paid, the telephone bill was unsettled, and there were a number of suits pending "including at least three by former instructors." By Christmastime Henri had finally given up the struggle; and before the end of the first week of 1909 he had installed himself on the sixth floor of the Lincoln Arcade Building with eleven assorted female students. When interviewed, Henri stated his aims: not to rob other institutions but to complete his enrollment, organize life, portrait, and composition classes, and another life class in the evening for young men who worked by day and wanted to paint pale pictures by night.

Bellows and Keefe were now painting largely on their own, but the proximity of Henri's evening life class down the hall was an unexpected blessing, as was also the daily association with Henri himself.

Studio 616 had now a new semipermanent resident, another of Keefe's odd schoolmates from New London. The father of this short, slight, handsome young man of the world was James O'Neill who stood in every one's mind with William Gillette as the symbol of success on the American stage. His son Eugene was already acquiring a romantic aura of his own in youthful New York circles. Although only twenty he had spent, or misspent, a year at Princeton, and his female conquests, dating back to preparatory school days, numbered in the hundreds as he was delighted to tell any listener. "While most boys my age were in love with a pure girl," he recalled, "or shivering into a fit of embarrassment at the mere thought of a show girl, I really was a Broadway wise guy."

O'Neill's arrival at the studio one afternoon in the fall of 1908 was quite unannounced. His father had just thrown him out of the house for coming home drunk once too often. He had no place to go. He had somehow remembered that Ed Keefe lived in a studio somewhere. Charlie Grant of Columbus was moving out, leaving an empty cot behind him, and Eugene O'Neill moved in, unpacked his belongings—two shirts, a few other assorted garments and a great number of books—and settled down as a regular occupant.

Eugene O'Neill, brilliant, nervous, and energetic, had at this moment in his life absolutely no motivation and thus appeared as an enigma to Bellows who, between art and athletics, had never experienced a time when he had known nothing compelling to do. O'Neill, with a plethora of talents, was drifting along in a job his father had manufactured for him, selling a kind of junk jewelry whose chief attraction was the flimsy gramophone record that went with every sale. An engaging young wastrel, he found in George's dedication and in his puritanical morality an equal phenomenon. On their common anvil of the arts they would strike out sparks of argument well into the night until one or the other, sometimes both, fell asleep with the light still burning.

George had returned to this environment from the staid Victorianism of Columbus in a restless mood. Emma refused to come near the studio unless he or Ed Keefe were there, since she was disapproving and rather frightened of O'Neill. Her dramatics, dinners, and bridge games, lengthily described to annoy her suitor, left her very little time to entertain him in Upper Montclair. He ranged the banks of the Hudson moodily for a fortnight, painted only one picture, and assented readily when his new roommate proposed a change of scene that would cost them nothing.

James O'Neill, actor-producer extraordinary, owned a summer cottage with a wide porch, a garden, and a waterfall in the long-lost hamlet of Zion, New Jersey. At best the house had never been more than a weekend refuge from Manhattan, and in the winter it was cold, bleak, and terribly empty. Still, all of them, Keefe, Bellows, and O'Neill, had problems of one kind or another. Why not brave the January chill of the country and look at their troubles?

The three occupants of Studio 616 journeyed to Zion where rolling, wooded hills were bright with patches of unsmudged snow. When they reached the cottage, they bothered not at all with sweeping, dusting, or airing, but matched pennies for the two beds (George lost). They lugged water and wood, stoked fires, talked from dusk to dawn, and settled down for a prolonged stay.

O'Neill's friends had been urging him for some time to marry a "pure" girl in the hope that she would get him to settle down. George, whose ambition to succeed in his profession was equalled only by his determination to lead Emma to the altar, took up the theme with gusto. They battled over it nightly; and by day, while the one worked as though he had never put paint on canvas before, the future playwright tramped the hillsides or sat by the stove until the fire had burned entirely to ash, scribbling poetry and brooding over his destiny.

They were remembered in Zion principally because of the senior O'Neill's fame in the community, but no one there forgot the long, angular frame of George Bellows in road or thicket or stream, "painting the crookedest trees you ever saw. But that was a painter's license, just like a poet's."

Emma, addressing her letters to "Decadence Manor," kept George abreast of her activities. She had been to see a large loan exhibition of contemporary German painters at the Metropolitan: "I like 'The Sheep' and 'The Boy Driving the Oxen through the Forest' and the Lenbachs." She had taken some extra time to "imbibe" the Old Masters. She was going to a Damrosch concert: "It is a Wagner evening." She twitted him gaily with: "Give my love to Edward and tell him I'm looking up a post card worthy of the one he sent me. I think he is very attractive . . ." Ever since the unfortunate evening in Upper Montclair, when the moon had nearly proved George's undoing, she taunted him with it. "Did you see the new moon tonight? I should have liked to walk and walk forever—that is, with some one I liked."

By mid-February Bellows was back in New York, but his brief spurt at the easel induced by his change of locale failed to maintain headway. In March he went back to the familiar crater intended to hold the Pennsylvania Station and painted two more versions of it. One of these he ultimately gave to Keefe. The other, "Blue Morning," is now in the Chester Dale Collection in the National Gallery. But in this month he would be rewarded in a significant and unexpected way. He had sent his prize-winning picture, "North River," to the Pennsylvania Academy's annual show. Press and public admired it there as they had in New York. The trustees of the Academy were impressed and offered him $250 for it. He accepted with alacrity. At one stroke he had sold his first painting and was now represented in one of the outstanding museums in America.

This sale proved to be merely the curtain-raiser to a momentous season. He had chosen his entries for the Academy's spring show with care, "Paddy Flannigan" and "Rain on the River." This time he won no prize and found no buyers, but on the morning of April 16 he received a letter on expensive stationery with an awesome heading and address:

"NATIONAL ACADEMY OF DESIGN

Amsterdam Avenue and 109th Street

Sir:

I have the pleasure to inform you that you have been elected an

ASSOCIATE MEMBER

of the

NATIONAL ACADEMY OF DESIGN

Before your election can be confirmed (should you be pleased to accept it), it will be necessary to comply with the requirements of Article 4, Section 5, of the Constitution, a copy of which accompanies this note.

Awaiting your reply, I remain,

Yours very truly

/S/ Harry W. Watrous

Corresponding Secretary"

Harry's eye had indeed been on him. Before his twenty-seventh birthday Bellows had become the youngest associate member the Academy had ever elected. Whatever criticism he may have made of the institution in the past, this signal honor sent a thrill of pride through him, his friends, and his relatives. To them all, the recent discovery of the North Pole was second-page news.

The provisions of Article 4, Section 5, of the Academy's constitution required the presentation of his portrait to the institution. Henri was delighted to supply the likeness since George, his pupil and already a younger friend, had done him honor.

Cecilia Beaux, the most distinguished female portraitist of her generation, took a considerable interest in Bellows that winter. She had invited him to teas, to receptions, and once to share a box at a performance of "Aida." Miss Beaux, who to Emma's professed relief was fifty, had brushed her way to the title of "the Sargent of her sex." Some of her admirers believed that she not only outmatched her male rival's gorgeous sweeps of white, but that she penetrated more warmly and more thoroughly into the characters of her adult sitters. Sargent, all agreed, was masterly with children;

Miss Beaux challenged him in all other types. Her company was pleasant, and for George it provided a splendid opportunity to learn more about the special problems of portraiture. He had received one of the hoped-for commissions from Ohio State University and was determined to make the painting a success.

His sitter, Professor James Canfield, arrived in the midst of the excitement over the academy election. To interpret his big, vibrant, rather florid head onto canvas proved a stimulating experience; but the real challenge came when, shortly after the second sitting, the good professor dropped dead of a coronary and the painting had to be completed without benefit of model. Here Bellows' remarkable visual memory came to his aid and helped him put on the final decisive strokes. When the finished painting was presented to the university, Professor Joe Taylor made the address, concluding: "So great things are painted. It is lighted in Rembrandt's daring manner, achieved with something of Velás-quez' just balance of color." The extravagance of this peroration may have startled George, but there can be no doubt that it pleased him.

Henri's school in the Lincoln Arcade Building flourished that spring, and one of its new recruits, Randall Davey, recalls the night life class when the older "graduates" sauntered in from Studio 616 down the hall: Bellows, Keefe, and a brilliant young Californian, Rex Slinkhard, who was O'Neill's current replacement. George would enter the studio noisily, clap the first man he saw on the back and crack a joke. Then he would move on to the next to pass the time of day, and finally take his own place. In a matter of minutes he would turn out a complete sketch. After this he would go the fraternal rounds again totally oblivious to the havoc he was creating among the plodding beginners and hypersensitive aesthetes while they all waited for the model to take her next pose. Many of the students resented such familiarity from an Associate of the National Academy and much preferred Rex Slinkhard who moved and spoke quietly and preserved what they considered to be a fitting distance from themselves. Besides, Rex could execute drawings they considered just as good as Bellows', and in as short a time.

George painted his new roommate's portrait, typically a Henri concept in the strong emphasis on face and hands, although with a reflective depth in the eyes that Henri rarely achieved. A strong suggestion of Cézanne lurks in the long, prominent line of shoulder and sleeve; and there are quite arbitrary vital dashes of vermillion on the cheeks and hands.

Exhibitions supply the artist with lifelines to the public. There were several in the late spring, and George took full advantage of them. Locally, the New York Water Color Society mounted a show of drawings in the Central Gallery, and to this he sent some entries that the *Times* rewarded by bracketing him with one of the Eight: "Mr. Glackens and Mr. Bellows are also enamored of the ugly truths of which the city streets furnish an ample number . . . Ugliness has a tonic quality in their hands, because it is vigorous, not debased anaemic ugliness . . . Occasionally they see the charming and tender side of their motley subject . . ."

Venice, sitting placidly in the glow of its lagoons, roused itself from its perpetual "Barcarolle" to sponsor an exhibition of contemporary art. To George's delight he was included among the fifty Americans asked to show. He sent them "North River," a conservative subject that he hoped would have more appeal than "River Rats" had enjoyed at the Victoria and Albert Museum the year before. Perhaps his present selection was a little too ordinary for Venice, for some months later the Boston *Transcript* observed: "In general, the American exhibits are pitched in too low a key to catch the general visitor." Yet the critic went on to observe: "The American thing begins to define itself. Hassam and Tarbell, among others, mean a very definite accomplishment, Dougherty and Bellows a splendid promise . . . The foundation is being laid upon which men of commanding genius may readily build if they will first consent to be born."

Bellows sent two paintings to the Carnegie International in Pittsburgh. One was rejected; but the other, "Forty-two Kids," received the plaudits of the jury and of the public as well. A witty reporter protested that all the characters of the "Old Swimming Hole" were there, including Slim, Sliver, Slats, Spike, and Skinny. Only Fatty was missing. He also insisted that the artist should complete the realism of his scene with a blue-clad minion of the law. Nevertheless, he viewed the show as a great one, and concluded: "It is a credit to the dwellers of this no mean city that it has been so largely attended and appreciated."

George was vastly pleased by the reception given his work. More than this he rejoiced in receiving his full price of $300 for "Forty-two Kids." Thus the painting entered private hands before becoming a major ornament of the Corcoran Gallery in Washington.

The original partnership of Bellows and Keefe, now four years old, dissolved in June when Ed threw in the sponge and returned permanently to New London where he was destined to enjoy a prosperous career in architecture. George missed his gay companionship. He grew restless, fretful, and was unable to settle down and work. Emma was petulant too: "Your letter was very interesting but rather peevish and critical . . . I think you are getting awfully conceited and high-handed and I'm sure it is because you haven't seen enough of me lately." They had quarreled when he impetuously decided to visit his family at Sag Harbor; she wrote, semipenitently: "I think you are very mean to go off to Sag Harbor without a murmur but suit yourself. I'm not mentioning what you said about your state of mind but I do not think it is at all a pretty way to talk. Those things are only temporary anyway so by the time you receive this you will probably be beaming on the world at large and I hope me in particular."

One real source of worry was the Bellows family. George's sister and brother-in-law had both been ill, and for some time it had seemed likely that they could not make the proposed trip to Long Island. His mother, reporting on this, added an unconscious expression of her basic medical belief that health and appetite are synonymous: "Father is not feeling very well and is quite blue over the prospect of losing some money through a friend that has lied to him most outrageously . . . Such things affect his appetite and his strength must be kept up . . ."

In spite of all these complications the entire Columbus contingent of the Bellows family, somewhat improved in body, were on hand to welcome George at Sag Harbor when he entered the stout capaciousness of Captain Davis' mansion. There, he found at last the relaxation he so badly needed. He had long talks with his sister Laura, teased his good-natured mother mercilessly, played ball with the local team, and went crabbing with a number of pretty Sag Harbor girls. He hiked, swam, argued, sang, and slept with an insatiable zest. By mail he needled Emma, who retorted: "I wish you would spell 'also' with one 'l' and not like this 'all-so.' " Her life was full of golf and tennis as usual. She had been to the Follies of 1909 and liked them. A beau had squired her to the Waldorf where the orchestra played "The Tales of Hoffman." "Oh! I love that thing . . . I was there again for lunch and they played the 'Peer Gynt Suite' . . . Every time I have whirled past 66th Street Station I have felt a mad impulse to get off. I hear that Mr. Slaymaker [her name for Rex] is living in the Studio . . ."

Rested by his sojourn in Sag Harbor, Bellows plunged into work with all his heart. During August, he painted two of his most famous pictures, "Stag at Sharkey's" and "Summer Night." He seems to have worked on them simultaneously, yet no two of his paintings were more dissimilar in handling and in mood.

"Stag at Sharkey's" has become Bellows' synonym. It has been reproduced hundreds if not thousands of times in this country and in Europe, and has excited more comment than any other picture of its day. Into it he compressed the tension and violence of dozens of bouts, oblivious to detail, concentrating on the fury of the combat. The central figure arches in a dynamic curve of flood-lit muscle that suggests the ferocity of a Barye jaguar. His opponent lunges against him in a sharp diagonal streak, turning abruptly into a vertical as he meets the full force of the other's charge to slip in a right under the opposing upraised guard. The referee's white shirt and extended arm inconspicuously pull the composition into balance. Around the ring is gathered as fine a collection of thugs and touts and hangers-on as Goya or Hogarth could have imagined. The murky blues around the hot central pool of light fairly reek of stale beer, sweat, and nicotine. One can almost hear the rising roar of the spectators sparked with hoarse cheers of encouragement and sharp yips of emotion about to explode. It is the epic of the squared circle.

In contrast, "Summer Night" appears to be a quiet synthesis of his many walks with Emma on Riverside Drive as he escorted her to or from her sister Lillian's apartment. Whistler might have called it "Nocturne in strong greens and blues," a scene wherein isolated patches of yellow light stress by contrast the vastness and silence of the dark. The great vertical bank of trees is almost black, the broad surface of the Hudson a muted Prussian blue. Small figures in the middle distance are sharply defined under the lamp, while those in the foreground are mere ghostly outlines. There is both the plenitude of space and the calm intimacy of a warm evening in the painting.

That he executed it from memory is quite plain, for the full moon, masked by the foliage and reflected in the river, is setting in the west which it can only do just before dawn.

While he was working on these paintings he was also doing odd jobs. One of these was as delivery boy for a dry cleaner who offered to press his trousers free instead of paying him. Since the money from "Forty-Two Kids" had evaporated the artist insisted on cash, for he wanted to spend a weekend at Point Pleasant, New Jersey, where Emma was visiting Ethel Clarke. Emma wrote him detailed instructions about trains, boats, and meal hours at the boarding house. "The price of board per day here is $1.50 . . . There is a barber shop so calm yourself. *Please* see that your hands and fingernails are immaculate because if you sit next to me at table I do not want my appetite taken away looking at them . . . I can't swim yet but still live in hope."

While awaiting his arrival Emma busied herself with other beaux. One of these distinguished himself by eating a huge dinner and then disgorging it after a ride on the merry-go-round. "Imagine *George* being such a sissy," sniffed Emma heartlessly. Yet when she met George a few days later at the station she was confronted with a wildly untidy apparition, collar in folds, no necktie, and a three days' growth of beard. She started toward him crossly only to be disarmed by his infectious grin and his "See! I had my pants pressed just like you asked me to." He redeemed himself at supper time by appearing clean-shaven and almost spotless. The summer boarders immediately felt his charm, especially when, after adjourning to the parlor, he sat Emma down at the piano and sang to them all evening long.

Ethel Clarke's small niece rather fancied her drawing; and next morning George found her perched under a tree copying a picture in a magazine. He snatched her up, gave her a friendly shake and roared: "Never copy *anything* if you want to be an artist. Make your own pictures and don't forget *that,* kid!" He himself had forgotten the years he had spent on the technical discipline of copying prints of ships and the pen-and-ink elegancies of Charles Dana Gibson. Now only Henri's doctrine remained in his mind.

The weekend passed all too quickly. On Sunday, just before packing, he took a final plunge in the surf, in his exuberance diving so deep that he forced water into his inner ear. He emerged from the water roaring with pain and returned to New York in the crowded, sweaty evening train nursing an earache that was to plague him for the rest of the summer.

Something happened that weekend to disturb Emma's emotional tranquility, some trifling incident that revealed her most persistent suitor in a more serious light. Bellows still behaved at times like a raffish clown. At other times he resembled a noisy small boy who could be charming one moment and a nuisance the next. But most of the time he was an aggravating, exaggeratedly independent male. In spite of these serious defects he began to appear more and more to her as an unusually gifted personality with a rare attractiveness. When he was not around Emma found that life lost something of its luster. Her gay mood became more reflective.

The annual migration of the Bellows family moved from Sag Harbor through the metropolis and departed for Columbus. Only sister Laura Monett lingered, long enough for George to attempt her portrait. In the end he was not satisfied with it. He entertained her as expensively as he could, so generously in fact that Laura, once safely in Columbus, sent him a hundred dollar bill:

"Dear Brother:

Now don't mistake the enclosed for a ten. I hope it will cover the expense you had while we were there. When you get a million I won't be sending you any . . . Did you scrape out the picture? We'll try again some day. My love to the little girl [Emma], Slink and yourself."

Change was the order of the day in Studio 616. Rex Slinkhard, a relative new-comer, had established himself, but Ed Keefe's empty cot was still unfilled. So they welcomed another aspiring artist from Columbus, Ohio, one Ted Ireland. (It was Ted who later assisted O'Neill through the disagreeable intricacies of his divorce from the "pure" girl he had married. Later, Ireland became a successful commercial artist.) Much in evidence at the studio was lively and talented Ben Ali Haggin, a young man with a considerable assurance, springing as much from his confidence in his own ability as from the fact that he was being handsomely supported by his uncle, a successful broker. Ben Ali added charm and vitality to any gathering, and his mother became fond of George, seeing in him the same qualities that so delighted her in her son. She was sometimes astonished by his impetuousness and odd informality. Once she asked him for an address, and George, finding no handy table for his paper, dropped suddenly to his knees and used the floor instead. In Bellows' own turn he repaid the Haggins' hospitality with consistent encouragement of Ben Ali's work. Evenings at the Haggins' were gay, often brilliant, affairs. George and, ultimately, Emma found themselves entirely at home with this family.

In September, Emma began to show a certain petulance toward him. She would consent to go with him to a band concert in the park, but only if he bought tickets in the grandstand. Later, she might agree to watch a parade with him, but again only if he could afford to put her into the stands. "If you care about taking me to the Metropolitan you might come back in time from Mr. Ben Ali Haggin to do so . . . I want to see the pictures very much and would rather go with you than any one else . . . I'm awfully sorry you didn't have a good time last night. But you are very, very sweet and I give just one rap about you."

This was her first written word of encouragement—for what it was worth—in four years of courtship. Perhaps the surge of hope it raised in him inspired a sequel to "Stag at Sharkey's," a big canvas that he first called "A Nigger and a White Man" and then renamed "Both Members of This Club" as a wry commentary on what "membership" meant at Sharkey's.

In 1909 Minstrel shows flourished, with black-face as a popular vehicle for comedy. Bellows showed his two antagonists locked in a pyramid of frustrated equality, while his customary ringside characters went through their ruthless (and ageless) pantomime below. The title was derisive, but the immediate action spelled out an even conflict between ivory and bronze, magnificent against the thick blue haze, pilloried in a hot strong glow of light.

This was his next-to-last painting of action in the ring. Later, he made many drawings on the same theme, some of them superior in their sense of action in space. Fifteen years would roll by before he returned to the subject again with his climactic record of the Dempsey-Firpo fight.

He had the exciting experience of being asked to contribute to the *Craftsman*. This forward-looking magazine believed that pictures in themselves could be as elevating and instructive as articles and took pride in reproducing a number of fine drawings in every issue. George sent in one of his Virginia sketches, as vulgar as Coney Island, and as natural. The December issue reproduced it in a section headed "Foremost American Illustrators—Vital Significance of Their Work," and bracketed it with work by three members of the Eight—Glackens, Sloan, and Shinn—as "the group of men who are practically historians of modern conditions."

In November, Bellows essayed a rather academic nude; in December, he turned to a new type of subject. While tunnels were linking the shores of the Hudson, a succession of great bridges arched over the East River to tie the island of New York firmly to Brooklyn. The Manhattan Bridge had been open for a few months, the Queensborough was almost complete. In his big, stark "The Bridge, Blackwell's Island," the structure seems to launch itself in space from its supporting piers. He followed this immediately with "The Lone Tenement," a grim building that had been overlooked when the area around it was razed, standing bathed in a warm light under a great dark bridge span, while children play in the snow and a tug puffs importantly by in the background. Whatever surplus energy he had he applied to finishing up his "Beach at Coney Island," begun eighteen months before.

Henri was perpetually arguing against the jury system of selecting pictures for exhibitions. There ought to be some way, he reasoned, by which every artist could be assured of showing his work and showing the pictures he himself chose. The MacDowell Club of which he was a member possessed a seventy-foot long gallery and was amenable to his proposal that it be made available to self-formed groups of painters who would, in rotation, mount two-to three-week exhibitions. George was flattered to be asked to show with the Henri group and was pleased to find his "Laughing Boy" and "Rain on the River" hanging close by the master's works and pictures by Glackens, Sloan, and Luks. Before Christmas the Club staged a costume party for members and their guests. Dinner was excellent, but the real entertainment was provided by the diners, each of whom in turn stepped behind a huge, empty frame and assumed the pose he considered most appropriate for his costume. Since George wore a huge blond wig and long flowing dress, ludicrously overpadded, it is amusing to guess what attitude he struck.

A little of this gaiety of mood remained with him for the holidays. Before leaving New York, he turned in the blond wig and rented a bald one. Now that his pursuit of Emma seemed to be gaining ground he had studied with alarm the thinning of his lank black forelock. When he embraced his mother in Columbus she gave a shriek of dismay at the sight of a hairless son and would not be comforted until he swept the wig off and put it in his pocket.

But he was all business during much of his visit. He arranged for a showing of his own and some of the Henri group's paintings in the new Carnegie Library, on the condition that something be done about the lighting. The hanging wall of the exhibition room faced the windows, a situation that was murderous to the murky backgrounds he had learned from Henri. He insisted that artificial lights be put in. The directress finally agreed to consider them, but he left town with an uneasy feeling that she would do nothing about it. He was a full-fledged artist now, and while a single bad or poorly lit exhibition would not break him, it could do him real harm.

He returned to New York to encounter one Hugo Reisinger. This fabulous German immigrant had made a fortune in America and was now spending it on art. He was particularly concerned with cementing the ties between the land of his birth and the land of his adoption. The year before, he had organized the exhibition of Contemporary Germans, which Emma had mentioned as having seen at the Metropolitan. He now proposed to reverse the process and send an American show to Germany. Would George contribute?

Here was an opportunity Bellows could not overlook, but what should he send? He already had paintings out on exhibition in the winter show of the National Academy and others in Philadelphia. He feared that the foreign public would consider his scenes of New York life to be odd. It might be that the vagaries of dress or the vulgarity of subject would bring the kind of laughter that the uncomprehending always lavish on that which is new. As for "Kids" or "River Rats" or "Laughing Boy," the denizens of the New York slums could never be appreciated in the countries whence the subjects came. In the end, he chose exceedingly well. "Summer Night" might have pictured a stroll down the Siegers-allée from the point of view of subject, while "The Bridge" represented a spectacle of contemporary engineering quite as familiar abroad as at home.

Meanwhile the Pennsylvania Academy exhibited five of his paintings, a selection calculated to match the realism of Eakins and Anshutz on their home ground. Reviewing the show, the New York *Evening Mail* called his "Girl in White" a "flat failure, looking as if it were cut out of wooden blocks"; but thought " 'Both Members of this Club' a powerful piece of work . . . a marvel of portrayal." The *Post* approved of "River Rats" and then shook an admonitory finger: "To persuade Mr. George Bellows that the demonic energy and reality of his ring fights are excesses of a good thing . . . would be a public service, but he will doubtless find it out for himself without the assistance of any literary fellows." The *Sun* disagreed: "As for Mr. Bellows he is in a class by himself. He has two of his boxing pictures, and call them brutal if you will, they hit you between the eyes with a vigor that few living artists known to us can command. Take any of these Parisian chaps, beginning with Henri Matisse, who make a specialty of movement—well, their work is ladylike in comparison with the red blood of Bellows."

The Carnegie Library in Columbus did nothing about improving its lights, so George flatly refused to send anything there. He wrote Joe Taylor: "I suppose I am in bad with the Columbus Art Association as I have informed my New York friends about the conditions and they are in accord with my stand . . . I went to no pains however to look anybody up . . . The damned ignorance about this light gets me. Mrs. Derby [the directress] wrote to Henri saying that she preferred paintings indifferently lighted by daylight to any artificial light possible. Can you beat it?"

Early in February, the National Arts Club opened its gallery to some of the younger and less traditional painters of New York. The hanging committee grouped together the work of such unorthodox artists as Prendergast, Marin, Hartley, and Maurer, including with them pictures by Glackens, already considered to be an Impressionist, who thus shared the obloquy that poured down upon them from the press. The *Telegraph,* under the headline "Extreme Impressionism at the National Arts Club," found this group "the craziest lot we have ever seen outside the Photo Secession rooms. It may be that it is we who are crazy." The *Globe* had nothing kind to offer to "those who may be said to be in the 'new movement,' which in particular is that departure along the lines formulated by the Frenchman Matisse, who, it is said, has all Paris at his feet; which, if these paintings fairly represent his ideas, would seem to argue little for the sanity and poise of the art-loving public in that somewhat hysterical town."

Bellows' offerings, on the other hand, came in for universal praise. The *Telegraph* was shocked that "so strong a painting as George W. Bellows' 'Winter Afternoon' has been pitchforked into a place over the doorway." The *Sun* was ecstatic: "Mr. Bellows' performance in 'Morning Snow' is altogether delightful, spontaneous, fresh, and personal, a canvas that easily dominates the wall and stands out from all its surroundings."

Hugo Reisinger, looking the show over, agreed with the critics and paid $500, the painter's price, to make "Morning Snow" his own.

The great event of the spring of 1910, however, was sparked by the National Academy of Design. Early in March, its jury of selection was deliberating on its choices for their forthcoming semiannual show. The older members mourned the passing of an era when these had been pleasant occasions; when the plums went to those who deserved them, not to young upstarts; when theirs was

Boy on a Dock; drawing.

the delightful task of choosing between portraits of subjects who were so plainly ladies and gentlemen. Now one had to look at pictures largely of plug uglies. Some of the blame *might* be theirs, of course. After all they *had* accepted good old Billy Chase's smelly dead fish. They sighed, then firmed their jaws and made amends for past weakness. The liberal jurors of the year before were either absent or overruled, and the tories put that disrupting revolutionary, Henri, smartly in his place by rejecting two of his paintings.

Here they made a very serious mistake. Henri, prompted by Sloan, had been debating for several months the possibilities of a show to capitalize on the success of the Eight. He had, however, been largely occupied with getting his new school started, with his new wife, and with moving his belongings to a large studio in Gramercy Park. When the report of the jury's action reached him, he exploded. Those precious stuffed shirts had rejected his portrait of his bride!

Sloan was more than ready to lend Henri a rebellious hand. He hated the Academy. With the energy so often expended on causes rather than on canvas, he enlisted Arthur B. Davies' sympathy and money and set out to hire a hall. He finally located one, a three-story building at Twenty-Nine West Thirty-fifth Street that could be rented for $1,000 a month. Walt Kuhn, an independent young artist with boundless energy and enthusiasm, joined forces, and in less than three weeks the "Independent Artists Exhibition" was ready to open.

The organizational skill that accomplished this remarkable feat was a credit to Henri and bespoke the months of time and thought he and Sloan had given to the problem in the past. Scores of artists were invited to contribute, the rate of $10 per entry scaling down to a bargain figure of $30 for four. Paintings, drawings, and sculptures arrived by the hundreds. There was no jury. Each artist made his own choices. There were no rejections.

The old brownstone building on West Thirty-fifth Street was refurbished as cheaply as possible by willing volunteers. Bellows, whose "Floating Ice" at the Spring Academy Show had just been characterized by the *Globe* as "a sterling performance not excelled in the Exhibition," now found himself with house paint brush in hand, giving a new coat of paint to the woodwork. Glenn Coleman and Scott Stafford papered the walls with cheesecloth. Electricians clambered all over the place doing rewiring and installing a hundred tungsten lights.

The hanging committee, of which George was a member, kept the works of each artist together and then hung them in the alphabetical order of the painters' names. There remained the problem of spacing more than six hundred exhibits and the fair allocation of the lights. Everyone was short on sleep, but the common excitement and the stimulation of a joint effort for a worthy cause was sufficient compensation. No one was prepared for what followed on the opening date—April Fool's Day.

The public was admitted at eight o'clock in the evening, and George squired Emma. Like most of the other artists, he came very early, impatient to see what kind of a reception their show would receive. Eugene Speicher was there with his fiancée, Elsie Wilson, whom Emma liked at once. The Henris were pleased that the hanging committee had broken their alphabetical rule just once by giving the place of honor to the portrait of Marjorie Henri that had been spurned by the Academy. The Sloans came, the Glackens, sharp-eyed Davies and moustachioed Lawson, deaf Maurice Prendergast and his brother Charles, the Shinns, and bad-man George Luks. Some of the participants had fortified their spirits before they came—who knew but that the opening might be a failure? One of these made the mistake of saying coyly to Emma: "You're going to marry G. B. and you can make or break him." With utter Gibson Girl hauteur she replied that she had no intention of marrying anyone!

The public arrived, slowly at first, then in droves. It became difficult to move from floor to floor, then from room to room, so great was the crush. Rumors spread of dangerous overcrowding, and that police had been called to control the mob. Every one inside the building was electrified. No art exhibition in America had ever created such a sensation.

Next morning the artists' eager fingers, picking up their newspapers to hunt for the inner critical section, were amazed at the front page headlines: "Panic Averted in Art Show Crowd/Spectators in Jam at New Exhibition/Police Preserve Order."

They read on: "Traffic regulations of the police brand at an art show in New York, decidedly new, had to be applied to the crowd that went to the reception of the Independent Artists' Exhibition . . . Fully 2000 visitors passed through the door and at 9:30, when the police were called, about 500 persons were outside the building waiting for a chance to get in. There was no disorder at any time, but there was much nervousness. The arrival of the police averted a panic."

The old guard among the critics had their say: "The charm and mystery of good painting is sadly neglected"; "brutal draftsmanship"; "color that is coarse and opaque"; "a vague feeling of ugliness."

These comments were in the minority. Most reviewers were thoroughly pleased with the inclusion of so many artists they had never had a chance to see before. They hotly debated the radical use of artificial light. One critic expressed the hope that this show might lead to the establishment of a big, free, and cooperative exhibition gallery where every man should be able to find an open door to an open road. Henry Tyrrell of the *World* summed the show up in the words a courtier addressed to Louis XVI the day the Bastille fell: "It is not a revolt, sire, it is a revolution."

Bellows gave Joe Taylor his own impression of the exhibition and of some of the artists in a very long letter. Here are some typical excerpts:

"Such a salon has long been in the wind but this time it just seemed to happen. The groans which arise after every Academy exhibition resulted in a definite undertaking this time. There are two types of pictures that fail to 'get across' at the Academy, those which are too bad and those which are too good . . .

"There are many kinds of things we can class as too good. . . . There is a large class of things done which are taboo for reasons quite outside the sphere of art, one very principal reason being morality and morality of a very dinky distinctiveness. It is immoral to paint prizefighters with blood on them no matter how beautiful their bodies in action, but perfectly moral to paint pictures of pirates gracefully frozen in gently ferocious attitudes if you make them nice stage pirates. It is immoral to blurt out a witty idea in half an hour expressing one's self with a paint brush, but quite moral to labor six months and say nothing but 'see how well I can model nipple pink.'

"Then there is some strange disease in people's mind which makes them imagine themselves arbiters of beauty and creates a constant demand that pictures be 'beautiful.' As if Shakespeare had always gone around writing sonnets. The work of art which is a criticism of manners and morality, which presents the cruelty of life, is a horror to these smug individuals; and believe me the

Academy and the Woman's Foreign Missionary Society is full of them. And so, the Exhibition of the Independents.

". . . After what I have said you would expect wild fire, shocks, scandals, putrescence etc. etc. Not at all. There isn't even anything startlingly new. I think the big impression is that of manliness, frankness and love of the game. That is always new.

"There is tremendous variety of points of view but most of the things drive hardest after the fundamental,—the individuality of an idea, the particular quality of a subject which makes it tragic, dramatic, causes us to halt and wonder; what in painting we call character.

"The soft tender color of our great master dreamer Arthur Davies . . . the tremendous nature which [Rockwell] Kent can do . . .

"John Sloan paints a clown making up. It is a picture to dream over. It's funny how when you look at this picture you think of all the human sensations a clown must have in his life. You catch yourself wondering whether he has a wife and kids and how much money he makes. Sloan is wonderful this way. . . .

"Ernest Lawson is so different and so bully to boot. He has taken the scientific and rather cold blooded color of Monet in his paintings of the vibration of light and added a quality and dreaminess of color which has in addition to character the charm of a jewel . . .

"Prendergast whose pictures [are] so often laughed at are to me the most refined of decorations and here I contradict myself. But surely one of this fellow's works gives a wonderful sense of quiet and repose and would add dignity to any place where repose was the order . . .

"Henri in addition to his masterly portraits has an ocean which has the wonder of the sea in it; the Terror and what is the sea if it isn't terrible?

"This is the way I have become used to looking at pictures."

Before the Independent Show closed, one of the papers noted that the drawings had sold much better than the oils. George could testify to this as his returns on eight entries amounted to $500, realized through the sale of three drawings to one Joseph B. Thomas of New York City.

The National Arts Club in Gramercy Park made him a life member, with the condition that he present to them an original work of art of his own to be appraised by its own Art Committee at $1,000. He obliged with "Summer City," which he had priced at $800 the year before. It was a fair assumption that his growing reputation had increased its value during the last eleven months.

Everything seemed to be going his way now. On May 14 the press broke the story of his appointment as morning life-class instructor at the Art Students' League. Such an assignment clinched his status as an independent, professional artist. The salary of $1,000 a year gave him an assured income for twelve months. He was grateful for this, especially now that he hovered on the brink of matrimony.

Arrangement—Emma in a Room; *lithograph, 1921.*

THE HOLY ESTATE

» 1910 - 1911 «

» V «   *"I decided I'd marry you or bust. Well, I haven't bust yet."* George Bellows

Exactly when it was that Emma made up her mind to marry George will probably never be known. By February 14, 1910, George scented victory but still had no positive assurance. He gave his annual valentine an introductory bit of doggerel, so inane that a single quatrain will suffice as a digest of the whole:

> "For I confess to you, my dear,
>   That now my brain's a-tingle
> To me it is a fearful thing
>   To write my love a jingle."

At the same time he drafted a letter which may or may not have been sent. It was the most romantic letter of his life. To mid-twentieth century ears it reads almost as though he were drunk when he wrote it; but abstemious George was intent on expressing his ideas in the alien medium of words. Just as Henri, the teacher, always encouraged genius to find its proper channel, guiding Clifton Webb into the theater and Vachel Lindsay toward poetry, so Joe Taylor of Ohio State had early singled out Bellows' graphic strength and fostered it at the expense of his English composition. There were sonnets in his system, but not Michelangelo's genius for putting them in verbal form.

George. began: "I want you to take this letter to some quiet place where you'll be alone in front of the log fire where you can think of me tenderly.

"And now the year has returned again to Valentine—and again I write you my love. I feel strangely moved. My song is awkward and I use blundering words. Can I tell you that your heart is in me and that your portrait is in all my work? What can a man say to a woman who absorbs his whole life? . . .

"From the first I have studied to make you love me that we might join together maybe that little company of great hearts whose lives become poems . . ."

He went on to review in detail his five-year courtship, beginning with their first meeting at the school and his first introduction to her parents on Christmas, 1905. He touched deftly on their one great misunderstanding. Yet he maintained his masculine dignity to the last: "And now may the Gods of good Fortune grant me the boon of owning between us a log fire in perpetuity where I can whisper you a Valentine."

Although the compass needle of Emma's emotions had long since focussed increasingly on George, she still vacillated. At twenty-five she realized that an independent career was not for her. None of her numerous talents, the piano, golf, and tennis, was good enough to promote her from amateur to professional standing. She had certain social pretensions which George would refuse to emulate even if he could. Her father's dwindling success in business had made her practical side aware that she wanted security of a kind that George's profession was highly unlikely to give her. Yet life, however gay she made it sound in her letters, had increasingly less savor without him.

Shortly after receiving his Valentine's Day effusion she permitted herself to end a letter with: "I give you my most charming smile and anything else you want."

Electrified, George immediately notified Columbus that he needed a house. He had laid the ground for this extraordinary request during the Christmas holidays. When the appeal came, his mother, sister, and brother-in-law gave his father no peace until the old gentleman, in a wholly uncharacteristic gesture, loaned $10,000 to his son.

As usual, George knew exactly what he wanted and Emma, who probably had not yet consented to anything more than an "under-

standing" between them, was willing to help him get it. Two adjacent houses, almost identical, were up for sale on East Nineteenth
Street, only a few steps from Henri's new studio in Gramercy
Park. George leaned toward one because it had a large and romantic tree in the backyard, but sensible Emma favored the other
because it had a coal chute directly from the street into the coal
bin. Emma's choice was decisive. William Glackens would have
turned this vaulted chamber into a wine cellar; but there was no
tradition of such gastronomic refinement in either the Bellows or
the Story family, and the bin remained dedicated to coal for more
than forty years.

By April their "understanding" was on a sure footing. Emma
wrote: "You see I can't let you stay in peace for two minutes. You
have distracted my mind very much . . ." Intimacy was implied in
the formality of her ending: "Thanking you for past favors and
hoping for your future patronage . . . very respectfully yours . . ."
She dated the letter "1909," corrected this and noted: "I was only
a year late this time. Please smile."

Exhibitions, a house of his own, and love proved disruptive to
George's painting program. In May his new patron, Joseph
Thomas, who lived almost across the street from his new property,
arranged for Bellows to spend some days watching polo at the
Gould estate in Lakewood, New Jersey. There the speed and clash
of ponies and mallets enthralled him. The bright colors of the
players' uniforms, the tangy smell of fresh turf chopped by flying
hooves, and even the elegance of the spectators caught his imagination. He wrote Professor Taylor some of his impressions:

"I've been making studies of the wealthy game of polo as played
by the ultra rich. And let me say that these ultra rich have nerve
tucked under their vest pocket. It's an Alladin's lamp sort of game.
You wish to be a hundred yards to your left, you kick your heels—
and there you are. Sometimes there's a conflict of wishing and
Alladin No. 1 or 2 goes over the genii's head onto his tender
clavicles and he doesn't get up.

"The players are nice looking, moral looking. The horses are
beautiful. I believe they brush their teeth and bathe them in
goat's milk. It is a great subject to draw, fortunately respectable

... I also had a victoria and coachman of my own which I utilized as if born to the purple."

Back in New York he turned one of these sketches into an oil, "Polo at Lakewood," and reported it triumphantly to Emma: "I've just completed my best picture so far—so sayeth Robert Henri—a Polo Game. Peach of a subject." In May he tried his hand at another canvas, "Spring Idlers," which never satisfied him.

Emma's capitulation was now complete. On the twenty-fourth of the month she wrote: "Your letter arrived about an hour ago. I ripped it open and devoured the contents and then smiled. It was so consistently gloomy I had to ...

"I have just been reading in *Life* that a London dispatch says 'women are gradually losing their beauty because of their athletic amusements and their masculine habit of thinking.' What do you know about that? Further insult is added by saying we are no longer soft, lovely, dependable creatures but hard as nails, angular and argumentative. Please think this over carefully and tell me what your ideas are on the subject.

"It is a glorious morning and if you were here I'd take you gambolling in the green fields. Oh! dear why aren't you here, but never mind I'll see you Thursday. Telephone whether you are coming to dine or not.

"I love you."

She had agreed to marry him but was in no hurry to set a date. The tenants moved out of 146 East Nineteenth Street, and almost before the horses had pulled the van away George was in and around and over stairs and plumbing and window sash, a folding rule in his big hand and all kinds of ideas in his balding head. Emma looked in from time to time with contributions of her own. There was no question but that the basement and ground floor must be made into an apartment, for they would need the rent. Still, reasoned Emma, one would need a maid, part time at least, in so large a place, and for all George's egalitarian theories, servants should *not* share the same facilities. He humored her in everything. After living in a communal barn of a room for so many years he cared nothing for the fuss of gracious living, but the studio on the third floor was his domain, and on it he lavished the better part of his time as carpenter and general utility man.

To give the studio sufficient height he raised the whole roof eight feet and was highly amused when Emma reported later that the change had involved a mere eight inches. He put in a broad balcony across the length of the south side and built racks and cupboards in it for the storage of paintings and tools. He loved making shelves and cabinets and hinged devices of one sort or another, and his saw and hammer often sounded late into the night, while loads of shavings, permeated with the smell of wood-work rather than oil paint, were carted away in sporadic profusion.

The house raised three plain brick stories above the street, adorned with a fine Federal period doorway and broad shutters. Inside, the narrow hall was made even narrower by the steep stair-case, but each of the two rooms on the first two floors was ample and high, and provided with fine Greek moldings and a fireplace for those logs that had become something of a symbol to the new tenants. Easel painting was abandoned all summer long, although George did not neglect to keep abreast of the reviews and articles that concerned him. Thus he noted with satisfaction the Brooklyn *Standard Union*'s appraisal of the appointment to the teaching staff of the Art Students' League of "George Bellows, independent artist, factor in the first salon held by [the Independents] and a firm believer in individuality and broad, free, unrestrained art. A cable was sent to Robert Henri, who was in Holland, acquainting him with the appointment, as the artist is a fervent and ardent disciple of Mr. Henri . . . There is a devotion to the Independents' work in the League and it was in response to this sentiment that the artist was appointed.

"To say that the news spread like wildfire in all art circles is of trifling interest compared to the comment, discussion, and amazement it caused in the Independents' camp as well as the conservative."

All this made fine reading, but Bellows was amazed to discover what he was supposed to be doing: "He is now engaged in a series of prize fighting pictures which he will exhibit in the fall." Still, who could have imagined the most heralded painter of his generation stooped over saw horses or laying floors?

Up the Hudson steamed two bulky battleships, which anchored off the northern end of Manhattan near George's favorite vantage point. He painted them thus, neglecting his carpentry for a day or two, fascinated with the contrast of their man-made scale against the giant ramparts of the Palisades. Then he returned to his house-building.

Emma wrote in August: "I have just awakened and my thoughts are in a state of chaos more or less. I haven't two connected ideas about anything except you . . ."

Shortly after this, Ethel Clarke stayed with her for a few days and prodded her into an admission that "something might happen eventually."

"Why so mysterious?" asked Miss Clarke.

"Because you can't be engaged without a ring, and we can't afford one. And anyway, I don't *want* one. George says it's 'bourgeois.'"

Shortly afterward Emma and Ethel were sharing a room at a friend's house, and Emma became more explicit. She was combing her long hair with short, nervous strokes, her face very pink, when she turned and said as casually as she could: "My friend George and I think maybe we'll be married next month. Perhaps we'll choose the twenty-third of September."

Not to be outdone in blandness, Ethel replied easily: "Going to have a clergyman or a justice of the peace?"

The wedding date came on apace. It was Emma who did all the planning. They both agreed that a marriage concerned only the participants and they wanted no fuss or furbelows or families. But the Storys were eager to be there, and Ethel Clarke insisted that Emma must have an attendant. This meant that George ought to have a best man, and at the last minute he rounded up a brother Beta, a journalist named Cob O'Brien. The question of place came up. George had long since discarded his hereditary Methodism, but Christian Science included no marriage service, and Emma, for all her devotion to George, balked at the humdrum office of a city magistrate. They had seen something of Arthur Ketchum, the rector of a small Episcopal church in the Bronx, and they finally decided to ask him to perform the ceremony. The wedding party was to form at 146 East Nineteenth Street, marshal its forces, and descend on the church in a body.

Emma's last letter to George from her father's house, dated the twenty-first, reflects her talent for organization and her well-founded mistrust of George in matters of detail:

"Dearest

". . . I think I will come in on the nine o'clock train Friday morning [the twenty-third] as I will have to go up to Tiffany's and get a ring. Mother will come on the 10:15 and meet us at the house so you had better telephone Arthur Ketchum that we will be up there about half past twelve or a little after. It is quite a distance and I don't think we will make it at twelve. Be sure and ask him what station we get off at on the subway. I remember everything but that. Also you had better telephone to the Long Island Station and make sure (maybe you have done this) the train schedule has not changed. They usually do switch around this time of year.

"I think stopping off at Sag Harbor is a fine idea [they had not asked George's parents to the service] and thought of it myself but forgot to mention it. Everything is moving along serenely here and a be-autiful silver dish has arrived from the Otis Edwards. I am quite overwhelmed. I'll come over to the house Friday morning about ten o'clock. Be sure and be there . . ."

The day of the wedding, Emma arrived on schedule at 146 East Nineteenth Street to find George still hard at work on the house and in a fine state of disarray. She herself had chosen a plain, severely tailored black suit, and a small, hard, black felt hat, a practical costume suitable for a social worker or for an artist's bride. George dug up some money, and she went off to Tiffany's to buy her wedding ring. There she encountered one of her former classmates from the Chase School who raised a startled eyebrow to see her in such extravagant surroundings. "Just shopping," Emma said casually, happily implying that she did this every day.

Back at 146 the rest of the wedding party began to assemble. Now separated from his carpenter's tools, George was becoming aware of the day's larger responsibilities. While the mother of the bride and the maid of honor, Ethel Clarke, went to work on the paint spots liberally spattered all over his suit and hunted around for some shoes to replace his dirty tennis sneakers, he paced up and down, intermittently telephoning the clergyman: "Hold your horses, Doc. We're coming." "Doc" Ketchum's reply was invariably soothing: "I've nothing else to do all day."

Emma returned from her shopping in good time, but Cob O'Brien, the best man, was an hour late. When he did arrive he added a touch of sartorial splendor with his checked vest and spats. There was a further delay when he discovered that the bride had no bouquet. Off they started for the subway, when Emma, who knew her man, turned to George: "Where are we going? Do you know the address?" "Oh my God, No!" shouted George and rushed back to the house to call "Doc" for directions.

By subway, then by trolley, they journeyed for an hour and a half to St. George's Church in Williamsbridge where Arthur Ketchum, a one-time actor, performed the brief service that made George Bellows and Emma Story man and wife.

Once on the trolley again, the small party decided that the pace was too slow, and at the subway station the best man and maid of honor dipped into their cash reserves, miraculously found a taxi among the hansom cabs; and principals and entourage drove in crowded splendor to the National Arts Club in Gramercy Park where George had ordered ice cream, cake, and coffee, to the great amusement of the worldly best man.

Despite all the delays, George had picked his train well. They had finally rejected the idea of breaking the journey at Sag Harbor and went straight through to Montauk Point while it was still barely daylight. He had arranged, with rare forethought, to be met at the station. Emma never forgot the drive into the darkness surrounded by sand dunes and autumnal red grasses. They arrived at their boarding house "under a sky spilling over with stars."

Montauk was wild, stark, and still relatively isolated. A day or two after their arrival they went out for a walk, arm in arm, since they were alone. George looked fondly at Emma's tapering pale left hand. He stopped still, dropped her arm and demanded: "Where's the ring? What do you think people will say about us here without it? Don't you ever take it off again!"

To him the ring was much more than a badge of morality, although it was that, too. It symbolized the climax of the most sustained campaign he had ever waged since he won his place as shortstop on the Brownie team. Emma, bowing her lovely white neck in surrender, went back to retrieve the ring from the bureau where she had left it and wore it forever after.

One incident almost marred the honeymoon. Another young couple at the boarding house had suggested that they share a carriage and drive out to the lighthouse. The Bellows' accepted. Everything about the excursion was splendid—the view, the shapes and colors, the surf—but when the other pair departed early the next morning, their part of the bill had not been paid. George was furious at having been gulled, and Emma teased him about it mercilessly.

He was doubly angry, for their honeymoon budget, skimpy to begin with, could no longer pay their way back to New York. Enough money remained, however, in the groom's pocket to get them to Sag Harbor where Anna Bellows melted in happy sentiment when she saw her son march up the steps of Captain Davis' mansion, his bride on his arm. For his eighty-year-old father, the event marked a milestone. His only son had married well (in every respect except money), and he was making a mark for himself in his chosen field. The old man gave them his blessing and enough of his purse to see them home.

They were tired when they reached the handsome doorway of 146. They had crossed and recrossed it together many times before, but George bent down, reached out one long arm, and carried her across the threshold in the best romantic tradition. Laughing softly so as not to disturb Doctor Fox who had rented their downstairs apartment they tiptoed up the narrow staircase to their own.

Not long before they were married George had said earnestly: "I love you, but I'm not the type to pick up your handkerchief every time you drop it." "That's all right with me," she had retorted, "I'm a strong gal." On that basis they settled down after their fashion to the holy estate of matrimony.

The honeymoon continued at 146. George's indigent friends and acquaintances renewed their old habits of claiming his hospitality, although now they not only expected a spare cot in his studio but a meal as well. This kept Emma perpetually on the alert to piece out a stew or cut bread into thinner slices. Fortunately for her, George's interest in food was confined to its quantity and plainness. The French cuisine appealed to him not at all. Roast beef, chicken, and stewed tomatoes were his staples, and when Emma protested that stewed tomatoes did not go with anything else he ignored her. Cake or pie were the only desserts that he wanted, and he managed to look glum whenever anything else was offered him.

These restrictions on the family menu had the advantage of making housekeeping simple for Emma. If she wanted a change of fare—and they had the money—she could always persuade her husband to take her to Petitpas or Maxim's where they were sure to run into the Henris, the Sloans, or the Glackens. They often teamed up with the congenial Speichers, whose wedding had almost coincided with their own.

George and Emma both loved music, and Ben Ali Haggin's mother adored them both, especially George. Early that September she had offered him a season seat in the MacDowell Club's box at the Metropolitan Opera House. George indicated that he would need two for the coming year. Mrs. Haggin, unperturbed, gave him two, and for the first year of their married life they heard, in regal state, the great voices of their day—Amato, Caruso, and Emmy Destinn. After the final curtain they usually walked home, while George startled passersby and householders with reprises of the chief arias, promising: "I'll be as good as Amato one of these days."

The grandeur of a box seat was not without its penalties for Emma. At the awesome premiere of Puccini's "Girl of the Golden West," for example, George spotted Ethel Clarke in the topmost balcony and spent a good deal of time between the acts waving to her gaily, to the amusement of the house and the mortification of his wife.

He rewarded Mrs. Haggin with the gift of a sketch he had made on his honeymoon, "Montauk Light and Point." She, in turn, invited them to spend a week at her palatial summer "cottage" at Onteora in the Catskills, where George painted every day without much success. In the evening there was always a sumptuous dinner, immaculately served, followed by music, and George on more than one occasion rendered his hostess' favorite song, "Oh, dry those tears and calm those fears. All will be sunshine tomorrow." He disapproved of the "bourgeoisie" as a class in principle, but he could not help liking a good many of its members.

Shortly after their return from Onteora they attended an uproarious party at Kathleen McHenry's studio. In the din George and Emma missed the name of a short youngster with a lantern jaw, just back from France and full of the virtues of Impressionism. "None of this pure color stuff," roared George, Henri's ardent disciple. "You can't bring out real color without black, and plenty of it." "Black just muddies up the whole thing," retorted the newcomer. "The only time to use it is to accent an outline . . ." They were off, the adrenalin spouting freely, and when they parted company George was in something of a huff. All the way home on the subway he growled, grumbled, and refought the argument, but as he ushered Emma into 146 a name flashed into his mind. He tore upstairs to the telephone on the landing outside the studio, got his late antagonist's ear and yelled, "Is your name Kroll? Leon Kroll? Say, I've heard of you. Stay right where you are. I'm coming back!" Deserting his bride, he spent most of the night arguing furiously—and happily—with the man who from that evening on was one of his closest friends.

The Bellows', in turn, entertained in their big studio. Usually their guests were fellow artists, but just as he had no fixed subject matter in his pictures, George had no one type of friend, so that parties in his home usually comprised an assorted jumble from all imaginable walks of life, including such personalities as socialite Gertrude Vanderbilt Whitney and anarchist Emma Goldman.

Short and stocky and forthright, Miss Goldman was the provocative champion of philosophic anarchy. The press and the general public hated her cordially, for she made it a habit to embrace every advanced cause that promised complete freedom to the individual. Theoretically she did not believe in violence, but her lover ineptly attempted to murder Henry Clay Frick, and it was known that she had corresponded, however innocently, with the assassin of President McKinley.

During the fall of 1910, Miss Goldman was concerning herself with problems of censorship, a wonderful question to debate at any and all times, and George loved an argument.

"If a policeman interferes with a man walking naked on Fifth Avenue," he asked her in his new studio one afternoon, "would that be censorship?"

"Are you going to reduce this to the absurd?" she countered, somewhat annoyed. "But my answer is that it would be censorship. Let him go naked if he wants to."

George was delighted: "I sometimes feel like doing it in the hot weather." Then they got down to the more serious business of the dynamiting of the Los Angeles *Times,* a recent incident that had raised a furor against liberals of any kind.

To the morning life class at the Art Students' League Bellows brought his own brand of Henri's doctrine and presented it with his customary force. "What should interest an art student," he said, "is exploration, not adaptation. I have no desire to destroy the past. I am deeply moved by the great works of former times but I refuse to be limited by them." He urged his classes to regard convention as a shallow thing and to override it at will in search of a hidden truth.

During the transfer of his effects from the Lincoln Arcade Building to 146 East Nineteenth Street, the artist's innate sense of order had taken him in hand long enough to set up a pair of remarkable record books. The first he entitled "List of the Works Painted and Drawn by George Bellows from 1905," and he added the following note: "This catalogue includes only works preserved for interest or merit. I think it includes everything of any value." In it he listed his pictures in order of their execution, noting the size of each and the month of the year in which it was painted, the price (which he rarely filled in), the exhibitions in which it appeared, the sale, if any. He often included a quick small sketch of the composition or a description of the subject in a very few words. Under entry Number 23, "The Cross-Eyed Boy," he wrote: "Owner Miss Emma Story," and later he proudly amended it to read "now Mrs. Bellows."

The other document comprised a clothbound, leather-cornered day-book on which he printed "Sales and Proffesional [sic] Income Geo Bellows." On the inside of the cover under the heading "Public Collections, Paintings," he began a column with "Pennsylvania Acad. Phila. 'North River.' " On the flyleaf he titled another column "Prize Awards," and began it with "1908 Second Hallgarten Prize, N.A.D. 'North River.' " Then, at the top of page one, inscribed under a bold "1908," he started the record of the dollars and cents he had earned from his art. He began with an error, for his two entries under that year were the Hallgarten prize and the sale of "North River" to the Pennsylvania Academy. The prize he had won in 1908, but the sale belonged to 1909. By his reckoning he had made $450 in 1908, $600 in 1909, and $1,500 in 1910, not a bad showing for a promising yet still insecure young artist.

The entries in the painting book showed very little accomplished in 1910. If an artist is to live by his profession, he must paint. By November he had settled down to business again, fitfully as always. He went over his sketches made in Lakewood the preceding April and turned up one that recaptured his imagination. The camera of his mind focussed on the drama of the polo players rushing past a group of elegant spectators. These seemed almost to form a barrier along the edge of the field, containing the action swirling beyond it. He called it "Crowd at Polo." Then he tried a sentimental piece which he called "Candlelight," which he later destroyed. The dichotomy of his normal forcefulness and the new tenderness he had found in marriage had not yet merged into a single rhythm. Then, in December, he struck out in a familiar vein with "Blue Snow, the Battery," which one critic would shortly denounce as "assault and battery."

As Christmas drew near, George and Emma sat together in the studio and argued happily over which picture to send where for the coming shows. The reviews that fall had been promising; especially when Dr. Bode of Berlin had complained in the German exhibition that he had hoped to see more of the "throbbing life of New York harbor." He was refuted by the Englishman C. Lewis Hind, who thought that a national art ought to be something more than just an illustration of scenes. "It should be an interpretation of the spirit of the place, an evocation of the time . . . Something of Homer's force I find in the work of George Bellows, in his 'Bridge' arching the indigo water, rough, frank, original, true . . ."

Very much in the simple, powerful vein of Homer's "Santiago Harbor" was Bellows' first painting of 1911, "Shore House," a great, dark lonely scene developed from one of the sketches he had made at Montauk during his honeymoon.

The stock of paintings at 146 was numerous, but many of the best were out on display. George had to choose the right ones for the Academy's winter exhibition and for Columbus where his demands on lighting were being met, but especially for his first one-man show to be mounted in the Madison Gallery in January.

To the followers of contemporary art half a century later the importance of a one-man show appears an anachronism. In the nineteen-sixties no young man or woman would dream of applying for a teaching or "artist-in-residence" position at the age of twenty-eight without citing at least a dozen such exhibitions in their record. In 1910 only an artist with years of group show competition and the consequent accolade or condemnation of the critics behind him would find a gallery willing to risk weeks of its space on a single man's production. Still, the Academy show came first.

But the omens this Christmas were auspicious, for the critics approved his works at the Winter Academy. The *Sun*, for example, took a gentle crack at the Old Guard before settling down to drop a spotty shower of sunlight on George: "The post of honor is occupied by President John W. Alexander's 'Summer Day.' It depicts two slender maidens at an open window through which the soft light filters. A pussy cat is at their feet . . . Precisely the kind of picture that the President of an academy should paint . . . George Bellows is one of the most gifted of our younger men. A pupil of Robert Henri, Mr. Bellows has swum out further into the turbid seas of realism than his master, has developed a more forthright manner. Consider his 'Polo Game.' Its rhythmic violence, its crash and go, betray not only a close study of Degas but the movement of horses in life. It is a breezy, brilliant picture, full of air, crisp, telling strokes and resounding vitality . . . "

The *Post*, commenting on the same picture, was all praise: "George Bellows displays a new side to his versatile gift. [The "Polo Game"] is not merely the rattle and rush of the subject . . . a conscious elongation of the figures of the onlookers, a stilting up of the ponies' legs beyond natural proportions show that Mr. Bellows is not merely retinal, but is seeking an expression as well for the elegance as for the animation of his theme."

All this was splendid background for the real test that waited at the Madison Gallery, 306 Madison Avenue, early in the new year. His twenty-four canvases there would represent a synopsis of his first six years in New York. He included as good a sampling as he could find of all his varied interests—portraits and street scenes, views along the Hudson and in New Jersey, prize fights, polo, Coney Island. Some had already been tested out on the public, such as "River Rats," "Stag at Sharkey's," and "The Stone Fence"; others had never left his studio before. He was twenty-eight years old; he had reason to be proud, striding around the empty gallery, hands in his pockets, before the opening. That a certain Briton, Miss Carlisle, was exhibiting a group of her pastels and miniatures which included some of Her Majesty, the new Queen Mary, and the royal children, troubled him not at all. This was *his* show.

The opening was well attended, but it was the reviews, not the congratulations of his friends, that would tell the real story, and George and Emma waited impatiently for every paper. So powerful was the impact of the show that the critics were shocked into caution.

One of them called his brushwork "as slashing as that of a sabre" and cited "Crowd at a Polo Game" as "ineffectual bravura," but liked his newly painted "Shore House," noting its affiliation with Homer. Another found his "strongarm method to hold a knockout punch in every one," and called his art "irresponsible." Still this critic ceded it such palms as that Henri or Chase might have fathered "Little Girl in White." The *Sun* repeated its erudite likening of "Polo Players" to Degas, although it regretted that Bellows could not equal the French artist in "the consummate art of concealing art," whatever that dainty phrase may mean. It did admit that the walls "reverberated" with his individuality and speculated whether he would pursue his own or follow the Academy's idea of "Beauty."

Joseph Chamberlain was enraptured. He heartily congratulated a painter whom he found "gentle, idyllic, romantic when he feels that way. When he feels the other way he gives us realism, but realism alive, representative, full of significance and therefore of spirit. Mr. Bellows is to be congratulated on this show. It is the real thing."

Before they were married, Emma, loyal to her sister Lillian's standards, said: "George, I don't want to have any children, the whole process is so troublesome—but you do. So I suppose we could adopt one or two?"

"No," replied George emphatically. "If I'm going to raise 'em, they're going to be my own."

Soon after the opening of the show at the Madison Gallery it was apparent, to Emma's physical distress, that a little Bellows was on his way. Morning sickness, viewed by a loyal Christian Scientist, was "Error," but an error that must be borne if it could not be ignored, and Emma bore it perforce. The child would certainly be a boy because George always got what he wanted. Between themselves they called the forthcoming member of their family "John."

Bellows had won his battle of the lighting in Columbus, and the Art Association had asked him to arrange an Independent Show there. He would be well represented along with all of the Eight. The pictures had been sent and Henri had been persuaded to make the journey from New York to speak at the opening. But when the paintings arrived, they suddenly stirred up a merry little tempest in the capital city of Ohio. The New York press, getting wind of the story, lost no time in ridiculing the rustic morality of Columbus. The metropolitan version, true in the essentials, ran as follows:

The librarian of the Carnegie Library had looked forward to unpacking the pictures in the delicious anticipation of being surprised. He was not prepared to be scandalized. He called in the art supervisor of the public schools who was simply aghast. With commendable heroism the two assumed personal responsibility for the morals of the city and decreed that Arthur B. Davies' nudes, four etchings by John Sloan, and George Bellows' "A Knockout" would *not be shown*. Henri, hearing of this, promptly wired that he would not come unless Davies' pictures were reinstated. Faced with this manifesto, the self-appointed committee hastily decided to hang all the offending pictures in a separate room from which the general public would be excluded, thereby setting up a "Chamber of Obscenity" akin to the one in the Naples Museum. This action mollified Henri, and the guards of the locked room were growing rich on bribes.

The Columbus Press denied this version with dignity. It did admit that the Bellows prize fight picture had been withdrawn since certain ladies on the art committee pointed out that pugilism was forbidden in Columbus, that to display any picture of the subject was illegal too, and that they could not assume the responsibility.

In the end only the big Bellows drawing was barred from public view.

Henri reached Columbus where he rewarded several hundred persons with a talk that was unfortunately more than two hours' long. A reporter noted that he rambled, often began an idea only to find himself stuck on the word "that," after which he would meditate a bit and confess that he had lost the thread of his argument. But he "held his audience with occasional glints of humor and the frank good nature with which he took his hearers completely into his confidence."

To the assembled lovers of art, Henri, the famous painter, rebel, and radical, appeared to be "tall with strong but irregular features, a short, bitten-off moustache and eyes which seem to squint all the time. His hair is sparse and black, he wears his clothes in obedience to his theory that they should serve only to express the motion of the figure back of them."

Disapproval of "A Knockout" by his home town disturbed Bellows not the least, and he maintained the pace of production in his studio that he had established before Christmas. His first picture of 1911 had been the "Shore House," shown at the Madison Gallery. He followed this study in remoteness with "Docks in Winter," exploring the horse's mane brushed by a snow-flecked gale. Then he abandoned the darks of his oil palette in favor of pastels, and in the warm tones of summer polished up his "Mardi Gras at Coney" and a polo sketch. In the same medium he tried his hand at a football theme. Thus he moved from landscape pure and simple to the human figure in tension and relaxation; from cool tones with a broad, wet brush to bright tones with a finer, brittle crayon—one change of pace spelling another in a rhythm that matched his own dynamic mood.

This alternation he continued through the early spring with two big canvases. "Snow-Capped River" was inspired by another visit to the wintry Hudson. In "New York" he presented a remembered synthesis of a mid-summer traffic jam, the Madison Square area packed with heavy delivery carts, patient Percherons, and crowds of pedestrians, the stolid buildings closing in on the sweltering scene. He virtually plucked this canvas off the easel to include it in the Spring Academy Show.

Inspiration began to wane, and his next essay, "White Hudson," displeased him. He painted Emma reclining on a divan which he exhibited a few times before he destroyed it. He made a few minor sketches during visits to the Storys in New Jersey. Aside from these the late spring and early summer were unproductive. He was, as always in such fruitless periods, restless and irritable. He fiddled for a while with portraits of his mother and his father-in-law hoping that a change of subject might rechannel his flagging energy. It did nothing of the kind.

The season, however, brought with it fresh problems and rewards.

A year before, the Independents had made so strong an impression that a successor show was much in demand. Rockwell Kent wangled rent-free exhibition space on Thirty-third Street for a month—a good beginning—and set about lining up artists to join him. The Eight were essential ingredients to the venture's success, since they still had the headlines. Robert Henri was their unofficial leader. Unfortunately, Kent and other young hot-heads planned to issue a draft manifesto proclaiming that no one showing with them might enter pictures at the Spring Academy. Henri wanted no part in such polemics. He had been leading the battle against exclusion of any kind by anybody for too long a time to back such a conditional clause. Kent, who preferred rebellion against institutions rather than against ideas, was miffed. Without Henri's support he sensed disaster to his enterprise and poured out his grievances to Arthur B. Davies.

Quiet Davies, whose appearance was as deceptively gentle and vague as the spellbound nymphs he painted, was developing a taste for revolution and also the ability to lead one. He gave Kent a pledge of full endorsement, promised to persuade Prendergast and Luks to join with him from the Eight, and put up the money for the catalogue.

Thus, informally and unnoticed, the leadership of the Independents passed from the dynamic but generous hands of Henri to the subtler and more fanatical fingers of Davies. Henri had taken his own stand but had no objection to a respected colleague taking another. Preparations for the show went forward rapidly, and although only three of the original Eight were included, the names of such individual experimenters as Alfred Maurer, Marsden Hartley, and John Marin appeared in the catalogue. Some of the past and present Henri students showed, others declined, among them George Bellows.

Glackens, Shinn, and Sloan also abstained, for it made no sense to any of them to practice the very doctrine they opposed in theory. The sharp-eyed reporters were quick to note the names of the absentees, found out the story, and played it up much more prominently than the exhibition itself.

"It is sad," observed the *Sun*, "to think of dissension arising so soon among the artists who like to be known as 'independent.' " It regretted that Henri would not be seen, and added: "Neither will George Bellows, whom the Academy persists in recognizing these days. Mr. Bellows, has two canvases at the Academy, and even the fact that one of them is hung in the 'morgue' did not drive him to the Independents this year. And another of the Independents of last season who has withdrawn from the new grouping is John Sloan.

"Sloan will be missed from the 'Kent Tent' as the new independent organization has been dubbed . . ."

Some of the paintings that might have gone to the Kent Tent were now in a traveling group exhibition in Detroit, whose *Free Press,* under the caption "Ultra Modern American Art is Shown at Museum," opined: "George Bellows is tremendously interesting even to the point of exciting controversy . . . To some he represents genius; to some he seems a poseur without gifts. At least he claims attention." The *Journal* was all on his side, stating flatly that he shared with Whistler perception beyond that of the average artist; and that the friends of his paintings will be "those who appreciate color, harmony, composition and colossal technique . . ." A third commentator mocked: "The 'Polo Crowd' can only escape being crushed to death by the divine intervention of Providence," and "the water in 'Up the Hudson' does seem to run up hill."

Hugo Reisinger took strong exception to this last statement, as he demonstrated by deeds, not words. In April he bought "Up the

Hudson" and presented it to the Metropolitan Museum. It is true that he paid only $300 for it—his price, not George's of $500, but the painter could hardly refuse any offer when he considered the picture's destination.

Very few artists under thirty have been able to point to one of their works in so eminent a collection. The deal indicates that George had a very shrewd idea of the long-range value of a reputation, and also that Hugo Reisinger had not built up his handsome fortune with hands entirely dedicated to worthy causes. The most rewarding aspect of the whole transaction was the willingness of the Metropolitan's trustees thus signally to assert their approval of George Bellows, Artist.

Three hundred dollars was welcome cash to an expectant father, and the month was further gladdened by a check for $900 more from the Columbus Art Association, George's price for "Polo Game."

These solid testimonals to his talent gave encouragement when it was needed, for the Manhattan press was busily condemning Bellows' interpretation of his adopted city. The *Times* could only say that his "New York" moved the "beauty-loving observer to bleak despair, so devoid is it of the element of charm." Another reviewer was willing to call the picture " 'amazing'; we only wish it were composed of finer art." On top of these abuses came the news that the Carnegie jury in Pittsburgh, hitherto so receptive, had turned down both his entries to its annual show.

Further west, Chicago made amends for eastern insult. The *Examiner* waxed lyrical: " 'New York' rings with sincerity . . . No wonder Bellows is tagged with the Gotham personality . . . This artist's work is worth going to see: it is a lesson in individuality in art."

So mixed a bag of criticisms perfectly matched Bellows' temperament at the time. The upper floors of 146 East Nineteenth Street began to warm up uncomfortably by May, and George and Emma spent more and more time in the relative coolness of Upper Montclair away from the clash of iron-wheeled drays and the ever-increasing honks of automobiles, all tolerable enough in winter when the front windows were closed, but nerve-racking in the open season. Emma's increasing girth annoyed her, especially when it precluded her usual sports. George was uneasy, missing his tennis games and long walks with Emma, worried about her, about the coming baby, about himself because he could not seem to paint any more. His good-natured father-in-law was driving him crazy. Although he was the regular shortstop for the strictly amateur Upper Montclair ball club, games and practice sessions provided only momentary solace for his restlessness.

The break came in mid-July. Robert Henri, having decided to forego another summer in Europe, was fidgety too. The primitive isolation of Monhegan Island, that solitary sentinel off the coast of Maine, beckoned to him again in harsh contrast to the sophistication of Paris or Madrid or Amsterdam. He craved competent, congenial junior companionship, a group sympathetic to his point of view and respectful of his personality. This clannishness, this sense of interdependence within a group that never wavered in its allegiance to its head, was typical of Henri's method of living. Student Randall Davey accepted his teacher's invitation without hesitation; veteran George Bellows grasped at it as Salvation's straw. He could not bear to leave Emma, but he had to escape from the accumulating tensions in Upper Montclair. Nobody knew this better than Emma, who heard him out and then virtually told him to go. It was the hardest and wisest sacrifice of her life.

Just before Bellows left for Monhegan, Emma's home town reported on the first post-season baseball game of the summer with the Commonwealth Field Club: "All of Upper Montclair turned out for it." The contest was tense throughout with the score tied in the ninth inning and George, on first base for a change, had a lively time making eleven put-outs. In the tenth inning, a member of his team "had to put up an umbrella to protect himself from a shower of peanuts rained on him by his admirers" as Upper Montclair forged a three-run victory.

The glow of this success remained to help lift some of George's gloom two days later as he parted from Emma at the Upper Montclair station. With their baby due in another six weeks, she had lost her Gibson Girl figure. Her innate stoicism spared George the torment of her tears. After his train pulled out she trudged back the familiar mile to her parents' home alone, while he joined the Henris and Randall Davey at Grand Central Station, all poised for Boothbay Harbor, Monhegan, and the open force of the Atlantic

Ocean. Hot, dull, crowded New Jersey was soon behind him, physically at least. Bellows shed the emotional regret of leave-taking with each jounce and crash and rattle of the wheels on the leaping track beneath carrying him closer to a new adventure.

For the next four weeks George and Emma wrote each other almost every day, penning a unique record of his enthusiasm for his new environment, her contained but uncomfortable loneliness in Upper Montclair, and their sometimes frantic misery over their separation. His letters are also penetrating documents for the study of the emotional tides that govern an artist's life.

They reflect in an odd way the difference in their natures that constituted both a mutual attraction and a frustrating barrier neither of them could overcome. Thus when George, the humblest of men in the face of art, described a sketch as "a beaut," or relayed a word of praise from Henri, he was deliberately putting himself out of character for Emma's sake, trying his best to convince her of the nobility of his calling. It was not enough that she loved him as a man, she had to learn to love art as well, not with the lip-service she readily gave it, but with the same understanding passion that ruled his own life. He never succeeded in this mission, but he never gave up trying.

His first report was mischievously addressed to "Miss Emma Story":

"Dearest, And all the other cuss words I call you or have ever invented to express just that thing. By this time of night I have usually been severely kissed many times, and it's not late now.

"I hope you will forgive me for not having written to you for nearly a year, but circumstances have been such that it has seemed almost unnecessary. And as you have been in touch with nearly everything that has been going on I have brutally let the business slide.

"Over if you want more

"I didn't have any trouble in getting away, but neither Henri's trunk or mine came on the train for no good reason, so we are both wearing many of Dave's things. Dave you must know has no small nature although he is extremely short in the legs. His arms and feet are full to the brim and his garments, except trousers, will do . . .

"This is the most wonderful country ever modelled by the hand of the master architect (read this line to Pop; then send clipping to Sag Harbor.) You have received the pictures I sent [postal cards from Boothbay]; They are feeble. We are staying at a regular summer hotel and there are more summer people here than natives . . .

"Well, if the trunks come we're hard at it tomorrow, and believe me you'll see some pictures. We've got the best tools in the world, the best place and the best company that any artist ever had to create masterpieces.

"We're in with the chickens and up with the sand fleas.

"There are no mosquitos, snakes or mice.

"It is pretty cold to swim but I'll try and keep clean. The face hairs are thriving like Elephant's Ears and I love you . . .

"My dearest love to John . . ."

To this Emma responded:

"Dear Old Squill

"Are you mad or do you want to create a scandal in this town by addressing a letter to 'one in my condition' as 'Miss?' . . . You all must be playing perfect havoc in that hotel and I tremble more than ever when I think of you with that moustache surrounded by fair dames and damsels . . .

"Ma and Pa depart for unknown parts Friday night on the Albany boat to be gone until Tuesday. We [her brother Ed, his wife and their new baby] are left to hold down the house and I hope it will be cooler. The last two days have been vile . . . Aunt Eliza blew in yesterday and settled the fate of your progeny. Prepare for the worst. It's a boy. Oh! G. B. I miss you and love you most terribly. . . . I just live for the postman's footsteps . . ."

Three days later George wrote again: "It is a cold morning and my hands are almost stiff from chill as I am writing. It was pretty hot here yesterday. Must be pretty bad where you are if it's hot here. Yesterday the wind came from New Jersey and several mosquitos arrived on the wings of the wind.

"The boxes with the canvases and palettes have not yet arrived from Rabinowitz, and Henri and Dave haven't been able to work. I have my sketch box outfit and I've painted seven little beauts all of which will make beautiful big canvases if I succeed in enlarging the idea in size. The Island is only a mile wide and two miles long, but it looks as large as the Rocky Mountains. It's three times as high as Montauk and all black and grey rock. Beautiful pine forests and wonderful varieties of all kinds . . .

"The meals are not interesting except for pie and cake which are bully . . .

"I wish I could be here in the late fall. We'll come back some time and spend Sept. and Oct. and ½ Nov, get a snow storm and the fall color . . ."

Emma, too, allowed a gap between her first and second letters:

"By candlelight. Mother and Father having gone and Ed being upstairs with his family I am left alone to gaze at your forgotten can of Prince Albert and derive from its familiar outside what comfort I can . . ."

She reported being deluged with letters and with gifts for the baby. She told of her daily doings, of people seen: "This letter seems full of dry facts," she concluded, correctly. "Well my dear I hope you miss me more and more each day because it would be a tragic thing if you should become used to life without me. I give you a thousand kisses, sweetheart, so goodnight."

No letter reached Monhegan on August 12, George's twenty-ninth birthday, and he was feeling very forlorn when one arrived the following day:

"I have just unexpectedly received your sweetest letter and at the psychological moment. I came in tonight nearly fainting with fatigue, late for dinner, and not thinking I could eat. Gee, but I wanted a letter from you . . ."

The baby's arrival was much on his mind:

"Do you think, Dear, that I will be home in ample time to do everything you want if I come on Sept. 2? Is it possible to calculate the approaching harvest with any certainty? I guess not . . .

"I feel a great pride in working so hard, in getting strong and stronger, in being browned by the sun and hardened by work. And it all has such a wonderful meaning. It seems that everything I do is to make you proud of me and very, very happy which, when you are, gives me the finest sensation in life."

He still took orders from Henri:

"We [he and Davey] are now going down with 'The Boss' to look over the last pictures with a lantern. I have just been requested to report.

"Sweetheart Sweetheart G."

The next evening he again had his pen in hand:

". . . I tramped all over the ocean rocks today and my outfit is easily portable, and the basket ball shoes clutch the cliffs like a fly's feet . . .

"Shall I send you the key [to 146] or will you just wait until I get back?

"I hope you're not too lonesome dearest. I'm drowned in work and go to bed by nine o'clock . . . If you were with me we could tramp the wild places all day and night and be alone together again; and sit by the sea in the night wind; and watch the moon lay a silver carpet over the ocean. We could slip over the velvet covered rocks down at the Sea's brink and watch the waves reach for us, and you could laugh at me for being timid and afraid of those crystal green hands which are so clean and cold . . .

"We two and the great sea and the mighty rocks greater than the sea, and we two greater than the rocks and sea. Four eternities . . ."

A day later his letter was brief:

"I'm tired as possible tonight. I painted 3 big canvases today. One is a bird. I now have 20 pictures for a week's work. How's that? And I don't feel like painting out any of them either. . . .

"I learned a great deal this trip. I'm falling dead in my tracks. The bed is three feet away. Good Night.

"A thousand kisses Geo."

His next letter exulted: "Well dear sweetheart I painted a sure enough masterpiece today which walks up to the 'Shore House' and says 'Hello, Kid, I'm with you.' It's 'An Island in the Sea' [Manana]. Mrs. H happened in the Barn when I brought in the prize and called it 'the picture of the year.' Bob [Henri] is with his wife on the subject."

Within twenty-four hours, his spirits began to flag. He put the following in a pink envelope:

"I painted two more canvases today. It was the most wonderful day we have had, yet it changed so rapidly I did not get a great picture. I really don't know how good they are, but they are fair, I guess. They make 23 pictures. . . .

"Tonight when I came in I felt like I needed a change, but I guess the morning will bring renewed enthusiasm. There was some surf today and I tried it, but it's very difficult as you know. However we'll hit at it again."

Emma's letters continued in their usual vein. Her niece was to be christened, and she had loaned her a garment intended for their own infant. "Father and Mother came home tonight from a very dissipated four days. They sailed up the Hudson and down the Hudson and blew around in an Automobile and are now in bed resting from their mad revels . . . Your description of that moon and the rocks, pine trees, etc. almost made me weep. I wanted to be there so . . . Well in the interests of humanity I must go to bed though I am not at all sleepy . . ." But practical matters were always on her mind. She was busy sewing garments for the baby. She sent on the insurance policy with the query: "Do you think $6000.00 is too much? I leave it to your fine judgement." She thought September 2 would be time enough but he must be back by then, for Upper Montclair was scheduled to play the Commonwealths again on that date and he must take part in "that ge-rand occasion." She had thought of something for him to do on his return "very needful and ornamental as well and I think you will enjoy doing it. This is for the dining room. I am not going to tell you what it is now because I do not want to distract your thoughts from higher things . . ." She also dutifully caught the bait of the colored envelope and guessed he had begged it from the waitress.

George, after his mild fit of depression, resumed his normal zest:

"I think we should insure for $10,000. I know very little about insurance; but I don't believe you make any money having a fire.

"I painted one *big* fellow today in the Barn, a memory of yesterday's sunset. The most beautiful color and the boldest sky characterize this effort and it's a beaut . . ."

Emma relaxed with such repeated expressions of undying devotion as these now arriving daily from Monhegan:

"Dearest G. B.

"All your letters have come, and each is nicer than the last. Today came one telling me of 'An Island in the Sea'—such a wonderful and poetic name that I long to see the picture that is such a corker . . . All those great things you do make me so happy and

proud. Just think how John will feel when he sees them. Oh—
(that means a large hug). I take long walks with you every night
before I go to sleep . . . How does the moustache look now? You
haven't mentioned it of late. Can't you get Mr. Henri to sketch a
picture of you as I should like to know just how you look . . .
Every time I hear music I think of you . . ."

And later:

"Having just read your letter, that came in this afternoon's
mail, for the hundredth time I feel I can't go to sleep unless I tell
you I love you once more." She reported the gift of an "Alfgan,"
made by Laura Monett for "John," and explained its use. Other
presents were coming in. "Mother and Father tripped off merrily
this morning for the Seashore to be gone over the week end. They
had not a definite idea where they would land but thought it
might be somewhere near Asbury as there is a C. S. church there."

On Monhegan, the days of intense excitement and work took
inevitable and sudden toll of George. He plunged into so de-
spondent a mood that Emma did not keep the letter that reported
it. Then he rallied back toward normalcy. On the back of the
envelope of his next communication he scribbled: "Read this first
if they come together."

This text reflected the uncertainty of his state of mind:

"Having become rather dull with the brush as you may judge
from my last letter I joined the ball game today. . . . Well, I had a
barrel of fun until after hitting a three bagger I turned third on
the slippery grass and twisted my old bum knee again. So I'm
afraid there's no more baseball in me this year. . . .

"Henri is much too busy to draw moustaches for you so I sheep-
ishly enclose a slight representation of my own."

Next day he was a soaring optimist, full of dreams and great
good humor:

"Knee much better today. Some more fine work. 5 more panels.
Everything going fine. Paint rags arrived from Rabi. I have 24
panels painted, only 6 more blank ones and have written for more.
The moon has left us but the stars do it just as well. Great wonderful clouds in the starlight tonight. My head is full of millions of
great pictures which I will never have time to paint.

"I climbed all over this rocky mountain today, feeling a wild
spirit of adventure, but with thoughtful care of myself. When I

remembered my wife and child I got none too close to the edge of the precipice.

"I climbed into the Lair of the sea eagle where human foot had never trod, and what do you think happened? I lay on the ledge for a while in some soft long grass watching the clouds above and the mighty sea below, when suddenly the thought got into my head: 'suppose that—' and just as suddenly I arose and climbed out again."

Emma, apprised of her husband's bout with despair, knew exactly how to respond. Her reaction was immediate and warm, full of small, homey touches:

"Football," for the "Delineator," 1912.

"Your last letter written on that gloomy Friday almost made me weep. When I read it I just wanted to put my arms around you and tell you a thousand foolish things . . ." She reminisced romantically and apologized for writing in pencil. "Dad was tickled to death with your letter and thinks you're a great wit . . ."

When she heard about his knee, however, she was all Christian Science:

". . . You just exercise that knee well and don't let me hear a word about your not being able to play any more ball. You have to perform on September 2nd so you might as well begin to know your joints are all right now."

Then she told him what she wanted for the dining room: "a two-fold screen. Framework to be of wood painted white and inside to be of some sort of stuff like unbleached muslin with birds of gay plumage flitting over it. Very gay birds . . ."

George maintained his new exhilaration: "This island is endless in its wonderful variety. We painted today in what is called Cathedral Forest, and it is a majestic place. Gothic spires everywhere. Tomorrow a storm is predicted. The surf has started tonight and [I] will probably be down on the rocks tomorrow morning.

"I have one beauty of the surf now. The canvas I call 'Lunatic's Delight' is really a dandy . . ."

He wound up his note with plans for his return ten days later and his usual sentences of devotion. To these he added a postscript: "Important. Send me at once three pair socks. Sure can't get any here."

Inspiration had failed him again:

"I've been walking around all day in a dream doing nothing. A cold grey day. Deadly.

"I slept well last night, but have no energy or interest. Tomorrow will be better. There's a fine sky tonight and we've just seen the 'Northern Lights' make a bright green slit in the north sky.

"I carried two big canvases over to the cliffs, saw nothing, did nothing but sit down and grow awful homesick for you . . ."

Emma went through a brief period of sharp physical discomfort which she ignored except to say:

"This will be a short epistle as I feel very restless and do not think I can sit still long enough to write you much. Father will get the socks for you tomorrow and send them P.D.Q. . . . . Your island must be a most beautiful place and I am dying to see it.

"Dearest, I can't write any more . . ."

Mr. Story, however, was alarmed. According to his way of thinking no prospective father would have gone off into the wilds when his first born was so nearly at hand. He liked his son-in-law well enough, but was honestly puzzled about painters and their ways. He was annoyed with his daughter's fortitude in the face of her first delivery, and he certainly did not relish the thought of being the lone male to cope with the climax when it came. Artfully, he took his pen in hand and wrote George that he was worried about Emma.

A wire came promptly from Monhegan signaling immediate return. Emma met this firmly by telegraphing: "Nothing happened. Do not think of coming home. Will write tonight."

Emma had the right touch. George was a little ashamed at having panicked and made no immediate reference to the incident when next he wrote. He talked about a lobster party at the McEveretts' studio. He reported on "12 pictures and 30 panels now in three weeks, not mentioning what I scraped out. Yesterday I worked all day on a surf picture and made a mess. Then turned around and in an hour painted a crack. When I came into the Atelier this A.M. Henri had been in and printed a card with 'PRIZE' and tacked it on the frame. So there's one more success . . ."

He called her "brave and bully" to let him go and then thought himself "damn brave not to get awfully homesick before." When finally he mentioned her father's letter, he spoke of the complications of packing all his pictures and ended, "Be Brave Dear old Pal. I love you madly . . ."

Departure time brought mixed emotions and a shorter letter:

"Dear Mrs. Bellows

"It's very late tonight. We've been down at Henri's studio looking at sketches and I'm tired out fine . . . We were in the woods today. Henri has done some wallops of the woods. Dave did a good one today. I don't know whether mine are much or not. They are pretty good.

"If I can get two more real birds I'll be very content to stay.

"My moustache now looks great like this!

"I've thought of something else to build, a two-story Fire Proof top to the house to store all the things that John is getting.

"Received another letter from your Dad. He must not expect me to strain myself too much in this wit business . . ."

By September 1 he was packed and fretting to be off. Thirty small panels and a dozen canvases painted in barely a month, paints, palette, and his new socks represented most of his luggage. Davey, the Henris, a handful of lingering summer visitors and a goodly number of fishermen went down to the bulky wharf and waved him good-bye. With all of them he had shared some part of his own amazing vitality.

George arrived in Upper Montclair in plenty of time, too much in fact for his volatile nature and anxiety of mind. The hospitable Story house was small and hot. Emma's "condition" provided a magnet for half the female population of the town, and her husband found himself increasingly pressed into the company of his father-in-law, with whom he had only one real bond: the inadequacy of their sex confronted by imminent maternity. When the great day came and Emma uttered her first grudging groan, the two took to their heels and disappeared in united misery and apprehension until their time of trial was over.

Mrs. Story and her daughter, as dedicated Christian Scientists, scorned the medical profession, but they had heard that a doctor was a legal requirement at such a time as this. An elderly, good-natured neighbor who had retired from his practice as a homeopathic physician now offered them his presence and his pills. Since nothing in his pharmacopeia suited the situation, he very sensibly forebore any interference with nature, while Emma's patience and healthy constitution saw her through her ordeal. On his return, George found her tired but proud, even though the name "John" was obviously no longer appropriate. They decided to honor Grandmother Bellows in Columbus, and called their first child "Anne."

Billy Sunday; *lithograph, 1923.*

REVERBERATIONS
FROM AN ARMORY

» 1911 - 1914 «

» **VI** «   *"I expect to change my methods entirely when I*
           learn what I can in a new direction."
                                            George Bellows

Early in the fall of 1911, the Bellows family removed from Upper
Montclair to 146 East Nineteenth Street. The advent of Anne had
marked a milestone in the lives of her parents, but her perpetual
care and feeding posed an infinite number of milestones into the
future which neither of them felt equipped to manage. Mrs. Story
knew what to do about babies, and her daughter did not. From the
first, Emma disliked the whole process. Diapers, she thought, ought
not to be necessary, but she could invent no substitute. Bathing
the child appalled her until she discovered a pronouncement of
Mary Baker Eddy's which stated that daily ablutions of an infant
were unneccessary to its health, whereafter she postponed the
ordeal as often as she could. Emma handled the baby gingerly,
astonished and rather afraid of her, almost giggling in her attempt
to cover her sense of inadequacy. As for George, he was so awe-
struck that he hardly dared to touch the child.

Anne was installed in the front room of 146, while her mother
adjusted as best she could to maternity, and her father rocked away
furiously in his studio as he tried to pick up the thread of his work
where he had left it in August. He could still see so clearly the surf
creaming over Monhegan's granite ledges and hear the wind combing the stiff thin grass on the headlands. All around him were his
panels and canvases, as bold and powerful and grey as the island

itself. The contrast of white foam and black rocks and of luminous mist and light breaking through dark clouds to shimmer on the swell were effects that showed his new interest in atmosphere. He was familiar with the work of the French Impressionists and their approach to this phenomenon, but he was searching for his own solution in an entirely independent way.

From this stock of new material George worked on four large canvases, characteristically choosing separate motives for each: "Evening Swell," "The Sea," "The Rich Woods," and "Three Rollers." His growing concern for color appeared not only in the paintings themselves but in the record book where he noted "The Sea" as an "Analogy in Blue Green," and "The Rich Woods" as "Pyramid in Yellow Green." But by November this spurt of activity waned. He tried his hand at a portrait of a Scotchman which he ultimately destroyed and then turned his hand to the decorative screen that Emma so earnestly desired for their dining room.

The Gramercy Park area was tenanted largely by serious artists and by wealthy Bohemians who dabbled in painting and other intellectual pursuits and especially delighted in scooping up large sections of the community for parties. Among the Bohemians, almost directly across the street from 146, was a huge bear of a man, Robert Chanler, who talked in an almost unintelligible growl, painted splendid decorative screens, and performed erratic feats of Herculean strength. It was said of him that once, having ordered his wife out of their Paris hotel, he heaved her unpacked trunk right out of the window. When he fell under the spell of the notorious Lina Cavalieri, Chanler's brother, already in a mental institution, promptly cabled: "Who's looney now?"

Chanler's parties attracted the top-crust intellectuals of Manhattan as well as the sweepings of its gutters and lasted noisily until dawn. George enjoyed the conviviality when he was present and, after leaving, still enjoyed vicariously the hubbub from across the way. Emma disliked it intensely. On one occasion when George was away on jury duty, she decided she could endure no more of the racket from a Chanler party and called the police to stop it. When a good-natured bluecoat responded, he found himself in no time at all a welcome guest with a bartender's apron around his waist and his cap on Bob Chanler's head. Under the circumstances the law settled for discretion, and Emma experienced one of her rare defeats.

With Chanler's screens in mind, George set to work on a strong, light, two-panelled frame, and decorated it with one of Emma's favorite characters, "The Jaberwauck," as he entered it in his book. It was done in plenty of time to survey their Christmas with benevolent "eyes of flame." But by then, too, George had resumed his normal pace at the easel.

Everett Shinn, ex-Philadelphian and member of the Eight, found himself centering his interests on the attractions of Broadway. Spectacular light, rich color, and the fugitive character of each theatrical performance lent themselves admirably to his talent with pastels. Shinn, however, was not the type to stand forever on the sidelines transcribing what he saw. In the winter of 1911–1912, he built a tiny stage in his Waverly Place backyard. With careful direction this platform could be used by real actors, preferably two, but possibly four at a time. The casts consisted of Shinn himself, his wife Flossie, the Glackens, and a variety of other artist familiars, including Ben Ali Haggin. The sole orchestral instrument was a vintage upright piano played by Emma Bellows. A maximum audience of fifty-five could just squeeze itself into the open-air "pit" at one time.

Shinn also wrote the plays, broad parodies on the melodramas that had enthralled the "opera-goers" of the nineteenth century. "Ethel Clayton, or Wronged from the Start" and "Hazel Weston, or More Sinned Against than Usual" had their partisans, but "Lucy Moore, or the Prune Hater's Daughter" was the odds-on favorite. All were replete with innocent heroines driven out into the snow, glowering villains, noble heroes. Both the *Times* and the *Tribune* honored the "Waverly Place Players" by sending reviewers to the opening performances. Shinn was as amazed as he was delighted when bits of his script were taken up by vaudeville troupes. Eventually, some achieved international stature and, in translation, were performed in the provincial towns of Europe.

In this impromptu theater Emma's little talent found an outlet that she greatly enjoyed, and George sometimes took part in the performances, his buffoonery drawing an appreciative response. On other occasions he stayed at home and, as nursemaid, made the acquaintance of his small daughter. Anne was far too young to remember her father's behavior, but visitors to 146 have recorded it. He was shy in her presence, awed by her small size and apparent fragility. Gradually he overcame his timidity in his own violent way, tickling her, tossing her energetically in air, and fairly hypnotizing her with his *basso profundo*. When both of her parents were out for an evening there was usually one of George's indigent friends bedding down for the night in the studio to cope with the ten o'clock feeding, the problems of infant gas, and the stabs of a roving diaper pin. If no nonpaying guest was available they would call on Ethel Clarke or some other friend to keep watch over Anne's quite healthy and normal slumbers. Long before she could talk the little girl learned quiet reserve and amiability, characteristics that stood her in admirable stead as the Bellows household continued on its impulsive and tumultuous way. George and Emma fought from dawn until dusk; afterward some peace might descend on the Bellows household.

George was painting again. He began in December with "Snow Dumpers," a dynamic composition of canted tugs and pawing horses keeping an uneasy balance under the sweep of the Brooklyn Bridge. January saw a brief change of pace in "Winter Road"; by February he was reworking the dock-side theme with "Men of the Docks," one of his starkest and most monumental interpretations of life in the metropolis. He was so pleased with it that he plucked it off the easel, whipped it into a frame, and entered it in the Spring Academy show where the critics immediately singled it out: "A significant study of individualism in art"; "free from affectation"; "a significant picture of the year." They admired its solid simplicity, its directness, its "tense, crisp air."

James Huneker, however, inclined to disagree with the majority opinion. In a searching study of the ills of the National Academy of Design, he concluded that in comparison with similar exhibitions sponsored by Philadelphia, Pittsburgh, and the Corcoran Gallery in Washington, the Academy revealed itself as neither "national" or even "local," but essentially "parochial." He considered the exhibits mediocre and castigated the artists for not presenting their best. In this category he put "Men of the Docks." It was, he thought, "a good Bellows . . . Yet—Bellows seems to be pulling the same old trick. He is a realist, not a poet; nevertheless he can sound certain Walt Whitman chords if he cares to. For one thing he is to be praised—he never sings the songs of the oppressed.

"No pitying socialistic note spoils his virile art . . . Labor is not precisely sacred, nor is it precisely a curse. It just happens, for mankind must eat, and in the sweat of its brow. Bellows shows the working man as he is."

Robert McIntyre, ex-Henri pupil, now a critic and a dealer in the firm of his uncle, William Macbeth, added his perceptive opinion: "Should anyone look for a literary parallel to Bellows he would, I think, stop at Kipling as the one who most nearly approaches it. Both deal with the great realities of life, its humor and its pathos, and both treat these in a big, general way. Kipling, however, is a preacher, a moralist, who not only reveals to us conditions as they already exist, but who shows us what, in his eyes, they ought to be. Bellows is a democrat, content to take things as they are, not grieving that they are not otherwise. Thus he paints fancy free, following no conventions save those laid down by himself, keenly sensitive to all that suggests life, supremely happy in his work."

One year later Philadelphia belied Mr. Huneker by awarding "Men of the Docks" its Sesnan Medal. Long before that, Bellows himself would seem to have denied Mr. Huneker's observations on his Socialism by becoming a regular, unpaid contributor to Socialism's foremost publication, *The Masses.* Its art department was run by John Sloan, a member of the party. Yet for all his own sincere verbal protestations in favor of labor's cause, George could not conceive of committing his art to a social message until the atrocities of World War I forced him, along with the whole population of the United States, into a grim appraisal of human society.

Henri had long been an enthusiastic Socialist; Bellows promptly followed in his footsteps. Bellows' youthful confrontation with the squalor of New York's slums had made the prosperous, middle-class life he had known in Columbus seem stale, privileged, and "bourgeois," and he rebelled against it in theory. Living as he did in a consciously "intellectual" group, Socialist aims were obviously admirable. His natural generosity prompted him to sympathize with underprivileged humanity, but his inbred sense of financial responsibility, like that of the Communist Diego Rivera, kept his prices up as high as he could push them whether he was selling to a magnate or the Alumni Association of Ohio State University. However passionately he might argue the virtues of equality, poverty, and brotherhood, it never occurred to him to moralize on these ideals in his paintings, his real medium for expression. He stood before his easel, his brush and his pigments becoming as one with his subject, disciplined only by his skill in handling his materials.

In the early winter of 1912, three artists were disconsolately viewing the unvisited showrooms of the Madison Gallery where their latest works were on display. With neither viewers nor buyers to distract them, Walt Kuhn, Jerome Myers, and Elmer MacRae had plenty of time to discuss their disappointment and what to do about it. It was Kuhn who recalled the amazing success of the first Independent Show and proposed that they organize another. The recurrent idea of a general exhibition had become something of a will-o'-the-wisp to fame and fortune that seemed to lose its followers in the leaderless quagmire of artistic individuality. The three unhappy exhibitors adjourned to the cosier privacy of Myers' studio, behind the New York Public Library, and debated what might be done.

A successful exhibition would require the sponsorship of some organization, certainly as broad in its membership as Henri's Independents had been, and just as surely not exclusionist, as the "Kent Tent" had proved the year before. Surrounded by Myers' pictures of clustered immigrants and "the great unwashed," the idea of the Association of American Painters and Sculptors began to take shape. A year later its first exhibition would shake American Art to its foundations and deeply affect the destinies of all Western art for at least half of a century.

The eager trio looked about them for a suitable *dramatis personae* and decided that a proper president would be J. Alden Weir, a wise man in the politics of American art in 1912. Weir represented the type of independent impressionist about whom the National Academy had flung its hopeful, if flagging, arms. His acceptance as head of the new society guaranteed that the exhibition would make a genuine effort to find room for all artists, and that it would not be an explosion within nor a bomb without the moribund walls of the Academy.

A sculptor was needed for vice-president, and Gutson Borglum seemed the ideal man. He was relatively young, yet already endowed with a reputation for ability and a sense of scale that would, before long, find him carving colossi from the faces of whole mountains. He accepted the invitation.

In no time at all seven of the original Eight (Shinn abstaining) agreed to participate. The project appealed enormously to Bellows, and he joined without question. Thus, a year before its debut, the exhibition was assured of a dignified slate of officers and the whole-hearted backing of diverse, eager, and able American artists, conservatives and liberals alike, dedicated to the advancement of American art.

Then a serious crack opened across this image of sincere, united effort. When the newspapers heard that Weir had accepted the presidency of the American Painters and Sculptors he was badgered unmercifully to explain how he could remain an important figure in Academy circles and at the same time head up a rival organization. Weir, exasperated by the reporters' consistent refusal to believe that there was no conflict of interests, resigned the presidency.

Who would take his place? It was Myers who settled the problem by suggesting Arthur B. Davies, a retiring individualist who had never directly organized anything in his life. Many of the group hardly knew him at all, but they needed a president, and he was urged to accept. He said he would on two conditions: (1) that contemporary European art be included and (2) that its nineteenth-century background be represented too. These qualifications entirely changed the original purpose of the exhibition, but nobody bothered about them at the time. After all, the planning by the Eight for the still-born Independent Show of 1909 had actually embraced the possibility of inviting certain English painters to contribute. The important thing was to persuade Davies to accept the nomination. Once he did, the members returned, relieved, to their studios and went on painting.

To these external alarms George Bellows seems to have paid little, if any, attention. He, too, was in his studio, but instead of painting he was drawing his head off. He first turned to summer themes while the February snow filtered along his window sills and the scrape of shovels rasped along his sidewalks to counteract the rumblings from the Third Avenue "El." One of these black-and-whites, "Luncheon in the Park," served later as the basis for his splendid oil "A Day in June"; the other, "Splinter Beach," appeared a year later in *The Masses.* Then, in what he described as a vein of "slapstick humor," he depicted his initiation into the Beta fraternity more than a decade before. This drawing he sent to Joe Taylor in Columbus with the request that he offer it to the *Makio* for reproduction if the yearbook wanted it, presenting it to the university. He could afford this generous gesture, for just as he made it, a request came from *Collier's* to illustrate a sentimental little story, "The Roar of the Room," for their forthcoming May issue at $150 for three drawings.

In 1912 all periodicals depended on hand-drawn cuts to embellish their fiction. Some were already experimenting with news photographs for their documentary articles. A few others were cautiously exploring the possibility of illustrations in color. Sloan and Glackens, whose oils sold poorly, if at all, supported themselves in large part by their illustrating. If Bellows could establish a name for himself in this field, he could improve his income in an entirely agreeable way, as Winslow Homer and others had done many years before.

The *Collier's* commission proved a success, and before the year was out he had accepted five other offers for illustrations. To the *Delineator* went three drawings of football subjects, and three more of the same subject were printed in *Everybody's. Harper's* ordered five to accompany "The Darkened Path," a story of adventure in Africa, while the *American Magazine,* with admirable logic, considered him the ideal artist to design four scenes from a tale of the prize ring entitled "The Last Ounce."

The same journal had previously been pleased with his scenes for a rather silly canine story, run under the title of "Uncle Bung," although these drawings had caused George more trouble than all the rest. The script was concerned with the newest fashionable breed of dog, the bull terrier. George's experience with dogs was limited to his childhood when his own pets had been big and shaggy. The new bull terrier was still a rarity on the New York streets, and the artist was obliged to get his information about it from photographs clipped from any handy source. From this practice he developed the habit of collecting photographs of other animals in the hope they might some day come in handy. Animals were rapidly vanishing from the New York scene. There an artist could hire a human model with no trouble and at little expense while even the horse was beginning to lose its parity with automobiles and trucks, and the "latest" dog could be seen on a leash only at rare intervals. The inevitable goat of the shanty Irish was disappearing from the New York panorama with more rapidity than the Indians on their reservations in the West.

Through these illustrations, the Bellows family was richer by $1,000 in 1912.

The tenets of Socialism and Anarchy continued to occupy Bellows' thoughts and conversation. He had joined Henri in the support of the Ferrer School, named for a young philosophical anarchist who three years earlier had been martyred for his cause. The institution's aims were to give "modern" methods a chance to develop the individual, stressing excellence at the expense of mediocrity. The importance of the arts was not neglected, and in March, 1912, the school borrowed a number of Henri's paintings for an exhibition. It also engaged a minor poet, Bayard Boyesen, recently relieved of his duties at Columbia University because of his political views, to lecture on the new style in painting and the precepts of philosophical anarchy. Boyesen spoke of the great work being done by Henri pupils under thirty-five "like Kent and Bellows." He then read an extraordinary "honor roll" of all the "great philosophical anarchists of former eras," a list that might have startled many of those included, such as "Pheidias," the protégé of Pericles; "Michelangelo," the darling of the Medicis and the Renaissance popes; aristocratic "Lord Byron"; and "James Russell Lowell."

April provided the newspapers with two dramatic headlines: the unsinkable White Star liner *Titanic* on her maiden voyage struck an iceberg and carried fifteen hundred souls to the icy bottom of the Atlantic Ocean, and the Lawrence (Massachusetts) Mill Strike came to an end after two months of highly publicized stupidity and violence. The spectacle of a giant and invulnerable ship rearing in majestic agony and slipping out of sight must have appealed to the romance so indelibly a part of Bellows character. More important to Bellows' intellect was the victory in Lawrence of the International Workers of the World.

The I.W.W., popularly known as "The Wobblies," represented to the misinformed American populace the specter of lawlessness, undisciplined violence, and the worst excesses of rampant Anarchy. As recently as December, ordinary citizens had considered the movement discredited when the MacNamara Brothers had confessed their responsibility for the bombing of the Los Angeles *Times*. Now the I.W.W. emerged so triumphantly as the workers' champion that Ray Stannard Baker, writing in the *American Magazine,* observed that the dispute had shifted labor's usual slogans from the conciliatory note of "A fair day's wage for a fair day's work" to the revolutionary slogan: "Abolition of the Wage System."

The master mind behind the Lawrence Mill Strike was "Big Bill" Haywood. The press saw him as a man of brute force; and his career justified this reputation. He was a professional Anarchist, an apostle of righteous violence from his jutting jaw to his oversized feet, an impatient dynamo whom Ramsey MacDonald, England's first Labor Prime Minister, described as "a bundle of primitive instincts—a torch amongst a crowd of uncritical, credulous workingmen."

With the triumph at Lawrence in his pocket, "Big Bill" paid a call on his old friend Robert Henri in Gramercy Park. The newspapers, alerted, noted that Henri and Haywood had certain characteristics in common. One wanted to force life into the conventions of contemporary art, and the other wanted to force more people through industrial strictures into life. Both had a radical habit of mind. One commentator wondered if, in all the earnest discussion, poor, soft-hearted "Big Bill" was allowed time to enjoy the Henri pictures around him.

Bellows, as donor of one of his less important paintings in support of the strikers' cause, was surely included in the session. Both he and Henri certainly subscribed to the reasons for the strike. Both would have had reservations about some of the means that secured the victory. They agreed with the philosophical ideals of equality urged by the Anarchists, but neither artist could endorse the blind outrages or assassinations so often associated with Haywood.

.   .   .

Despite the pleasure of discussing the nuances of Anarchist codes, Bellows had more professional problems on his mind. The Association of American Painters and Sculptors (now under A. B. Davies' direction) was planning a huge demonstration of the importance of art—a single effort. The real problem was some kind of continuity in the process of bringing American art to the public. In New York, the MacDowell Club was trying this out on a small scale. But New York, big as it was, was not the United States of America. Just as every artist should have a place to show, so every American should have the opportunity of seeing the artist's products.

When Cornell University invited Bellows to contribute to a collective exhibition, his ideas began to crystallize. Dotted all over the United States were colleges and universities where, hopefully, the most promising minds of the country were being trained. Here, as he wrote Joe Taylor, was an opportunity "to introduce some real genuine interest and instruction in the Fine Arts."

"Literature," he continued, "receives much attention in the Universities. In some institutions Music, and in some Architecture [are recognized] while the arts of Design, Drawing, Painting and Sculpture [are forgotten] outside of here and there a foolish class in academic drawing or more foolish lectures on painting by some nice old dub who happened to visit the Louvre . . . In other words the great institutions of learning devote most of their energies to very practical affairs and produce lots of Lawyers, Engineers, Doctors, etc., but the spirit of the Arts which is the Father and Mother of Civilization is ignored." He followed these larger observations with practical details—simple showrooms, minimum expense, the willingness of artists to cooperate in continual loan exhibitions.

The Bellows outline of the status of the arts in American institutions of higher learning in 1912 was accurate for his period. Except at Harvard, where Charles Eliot Norton had won respect for his teaching, very few other institutions offered any art at all or, if they did, the quality of instruction merited Bellows' anathema. Two decades later, American education became aware of the values of general education in the arts. At the time, George's voice was that of a John the Baptist roaring through an academic desert studded with the bones of defunct neo-Classicism.

Suddenly summer was at hand. The Bellows family had no specific plans but did have a great many arguments about them. George could not wait to return to Monhegan, while Emma had no intention of going there. She could not admit to her dread of the water, so recently confirmed by the *Titanic* disaster. Instead she pleaded that Anne was too young to be moved into such unfamiliar and primitive surroundings. When news came from Columbus that Ben Monett, George's brother-in-law, was dangerously ill, Bellows capitulated; they spent much of the summer amid the heat and the mosquitoes of Upper Montclair with the Storys.

Bellows began the summer season with a portrait of Dr. Walter Quincy Scott, for whose image the Ohio State Alumni were willing to pay $300. Meanwhile, Emma busied herself with arrangements for a circus to be staged for the benefit of an Upper Montclair charity. The majority of the entertainers were highly paid professionals, while the management was strictly amateur. As a result, the sponsors lost a good deal of money, but the performances brought back vividly to George the sights and smells of all the Big Tops he had seen as a boy. These inspired two powerful canvases: "Outside the Big Tent" presents a narrow glitter of light from the sideshows cutting between the barker and the crowd in the foreground with the elephantine mass of the tent humping up against a black sky; "The Circus" offers an interior view, a bareback rider on a white mount circling within a luminous pool fringed by the silhouettes of the acrobats and the audience. Both pictures echoed Henri's fondness for contrasts of light and dark tones. Color was purely incidental.

Then bad news came from Columbus. Ben Monett died. George hurried out to comfort his widowed sister Laura and his parents. The price of his ticket to Columbus was, as he put it, "$40.00 nine dollars," a big chunk out of the family budget, and Emma perforce remained behind. A day or two later he wrote her his reactions:

"I haven't had a letter from you yet. You don't love me any more. This is Sunday night and I had to go to church *once*. We had a very happy dinner tonight. The Family seems to be rather relieved that Poor Ben is out of trouble and the reaction is towards a lot of happy thoughts. It is not the gloom I feared and expected.

"Father is too weak to travel, but spruces up now and then. He has a wonderful old head. Howard [Monett, his nephew] seems to be quite a business man, making all kinds of deals and investments. I think he will be quite a shiner.

"Everybody seems to own autos here, and the city looks green and clean. I haven't been here in the summer for years, and winter visits made me think the town a very bald place . . .

"Everybody wants to see you. You seem to have the reputation of being a great beauty and a swell dresser . . . I am so gloomy with wishing for you that they all think I have changed for the better being more grown up and dignified. I go around as if in a dream with large, sad and silent eyes. How different it would be if we had $40.00 nine dollars . . ."

Practical Emma had heard tales of his family's well-stocked attic and made some suggestions to which he replied:

"Just as I said our attic is full of clocks. I have a choice of four or five. One is a rather tall mahogany affair and runs by weights with a mirror in front. Maybe I will bring two. Some are black walnut, some mahogany. I will also try to bring the big lustre pitcher. I think the little one is broken."

His next item shed a sharp light on their economy:

"Brother Ben left me a thousand dollars in a legacy which settles our financial troubles for half a year or so."

He played tennis with Joe Taylor who gave him one of his watercolors. He also kept a sharp eye out for business. Bob Patterson, one-time captain of the Brownies, gave a luncheon in his honor and included among the guests a number of prospective patrons. Bellows also arranged for a big show that fall, and spent a day "with sister and Howard going down to the Carnegie Library and looking over the Gallery. It's a fine room and we will do it up right with the thousand bones I can count on. [You] must come here in November . . ."

Clouds of mosquitoes rose to welcome George back to Upper Montclair in August, and although he and his family took refuge in New York, the thermometer maintained a steady, gentle climb, eyeing the Bellows' tolerance. This cracked when Mrs. Haggin invited them again to share her peaks and glens and rushing streams in Onteora. Anne was returned to the Storys in New

Jersey while her parents hurried off to the Catskills. There, surrounded by hospitable luxury, George loafed and sang and
painted ten small landscape panels.

About this time the New York *Herald Sunday Magazine* ran a
long article on Bellows, partly biographical, sometimes inaccurate,
but wholly enthusiastic. It quoted the artist's opinions on the
principles of painting and on his objectives:

" 'I can't see anything in the worship of beauty which some
people seek to develop. Beauty is easy to paint; just as easy as
something grotesque. What really counts is interest.'

" 'Many painters specialize these days. It's all wrong. If a man
can paint at all he can paint anything that he knows or feels.'

" 'I admire the man who tries to do a big thing with the imple-
ments at his hand. Even if he fails to please, he has done something
worthwhile.'

" 'Learning to draw or paint is comparatively an easy matter.
But to say anything—you must have ideas. You can paint perfectly
and still be as uninteresting as a college professor giving a dry
lecture.'

" 'According to my view, drawing and painting is a language.
You can be great or small, glad or sad, in its use according to what
you have to say.' "

These observations have a particular significance since they
were made when Arthur B. Davies was quietly shifting the original image of the first exhibition of the Association of American
Painters and Sculptors into his own. Probably he himself did not
know how large a door he had unlocked when first he persuaded
his colleagues to include modern Europeans and their nineteenth-
century background. With Davies' financial backing, however,
Walt Kuhn was presently in Europe utterly entranced with what
he saw. So great and so broad were Kuhn's enthusiasms that Davies
joined him and, together with Walter Pach who happened to be in
Paris at the time, the trio hastily assembled a huge number of
marbles, bronzes, oils, and drawings to be shipped to New York
the following winter.

Word of their activities began to seep out along the eastern
seaboard and penetrated inland at least as far as Hartford, Connecticut, where the Director of the Gallery, Mr. Gay, gave his
opinion on the new French "isms" of Mr. Davies. Mr. Gay, for a

Connecticut Yankee in 1912, had a remarkably liberal disposition toward post-Impressionism. He conceded that Van Gogh, Gauguin, Cézanne, Hans von Marées, Picasso, and Matisse might be iconoclasts, but that "these men are simply the more zealous crusaders in the movement of art to rid itself of the laggards who have sold out to the sickly, imitative photographist." At the same time Gay stated his belief that Rembrandt's "Night Watch" was a better picture than anything Van Gogh had produced.

The interviewer, James Britton, added a postscript of his own: "New York has its own Post-Impressionist of importance in the young recruit from the West, George Bellows. Bellows has done some revolutionary portraiture and some startling representations of prize-fights, wrestling matches and circuses." Britton considered him, along with Philip Hale of Boston and Brandegee and Duveneck "as individual as any of the foreign 'futurists' and very much more able, technically, than most of them."

If Davies ever saw this article he must have smiled quietly under his moustache. Bellows certainly read the report, for he cut it out and tucked it away in his clipping folder. It was, for him, good publicity, but he was busy that October with his first portrait of his daughter Anne, "My Baby." In this picture he tempered the normal vigor of his palette to a delicacy worthy of Mary Cassatt and disciplined his brush to almost dainty strokes, achieving a tenderness of interpretation that makes one wonder how an early viewer could have said: "It looks as if it had been painted with a broom."

The first big Bellows show in Columbus opened in mid-November and he, Emma, and Anne settled in with his parents on South Monroe Avenue for a prolonged stay. The Pen and Pencil Club promptly turned over its club rooms for him to use as a studio. His home town looked over its prodigy and liked what it saw. The *Journal* wrote:

"Word pictures of artists are usually drawn to represent men with long, flowing hair, a large Windsor tie, and a coat daubed with paint . . . Mr. Bellows does not wear his hair long nor does he wear a Windsor tie or a coat spotted with paint." George must have been amused to have it implied that he had any option about his hair, while Emma took full credit for the coat. As for diminutive Anne, not yet fully mobile, she had only to take the measure of her Bellows grandparents, one aged seventy-four, and the other with the whiskers aged eighty-three, and make an easy peace. Her grandfather was a frail old man, slow and often inaccurate in his responses, partly because of his deafness, but increasingly so because of senility. Grandmother Anna showed her years very little. She was as large and hearty and folksy as ever. She heaved her giant body heavily from kitchen to dining room to parlor at its accustomed pace, her tongue busily dropping the earthy phrases she had learned in Sag Harbor, that her daughter-in-law from Upper Montclair found hard to accept. Emma, however, "coped" as only Emma could, partly because she adored George and partly because she was fond of her mother-in-law.

George loved every minute of their prolonged stay at his old home. The stir he was making in local circles came as manna after the relative anonymity of New York. One morning he spent so long with the students at the newly formed Columbus Art School talking about the wonders of the Maratta system of colors that both he and the class forgot the lunch hour. He had the miraculous quality of so infecting others with his own enthusiasm that he reinfected himself, to the mutual delight of everyone.

In his improvised studio, George painted cheerful portraits of almost everyone who was willing to sit. Perhaps the most welcome of them all was Professor Joe Taylor. These sessions with his former teacher were replete with discussions on art and literature and politics and everything else under the sun. He felt closer to Taylor than to anyone else in Columbus with the possible exception of his mother. When the sittings were over, George made a Christmas present of the portrait to Joe.

Two leading ladies of Columbus society, Mrs. Albert Miller and Mrs. Harold Arnold, were young, beautiful, and thoroughly agreeable subjects. For the first he used a cool palette of whites and blues, drawing freely on his studies of Sargent's swift, mellifluous strokes to cut the outlines across the grey ground of the painting. Mrs. Arnold's portrait struck a more Whistlerian note in the warm browns and yellows of her dress and in the full-lighted modeling of her head. Quite clearly, the artist from Columbus was out to show the capital city of Ohio what a man could learn in New York.

Christmas came and went. There were receptions and parties in honor of the artist and his wife. His exhibition, wrapped in eulogies, had left the Carnegie Library for the less prejudiced critics of Toledo and Detroit. His father was clearly failing, and the doctor was frank in saying that he might linger for months or that he might go at any time. There had never been closeness between father and son, yet there had always been a deep affection, and George was reluctant to leave his mother at such a time. Still he had a responsibility for the forthcoming exhibition of the Association of American Painters and Sculptors. He had, as a member of both its "Executive" and "Reception and Publicity" Committees, to be on the spot to see it through.

When the Bellows family returned to New York it found the art world in a state of pandemonium. Presiding over this confusion with an energetic hand was Arthur B. Davies, his full lips tucked more firmly than usual under his broad moustache, his eyes shining more brightly behind his steel-rimmed spectacles. He had leased the Armory of the "Fighting Irish" Regiment at Lexington Avenue and Twenty-Fifth Street from mid-February to mid-March. Meanwhile, he directed the activities of his devoted aides from a nearby rented office. No detail was too small and no personality too formidable for this inspired man to deal with as he saw fit. Vice-President Gutzon Borglum, accusing Davies of breaking the letter and principle of almost every tenet of the group's constitution, resigned in a fury less than ten days before the opening. Davies calmly selected a less famous, but more pliable, successor.

Before this unfortunate incident, the president had shrewdly called a special meeting of his executive committee. Following the custom of many other organizations, he asked blanket approval of all his actions. He knew that the opening of the exhibition was certain to evoke a storm of criticism from sensitive temperaments offended by the placing of their works, by the lighting, by any number of petty chips already poised on restless shoulders. He also suspected, rightly, that when the full extent of the European participation was realized, there would be reproaches from many of the founding members. The meeting, therefore, was asked to resolve "that the policy expressed by Mr. Davies in the selection of paintings and sculpture be approved by the members [and] that the Improved plan of arrangements submitted on that date, as well as Mr. Davies' policy regarding the distribution of the works be approved." The timing was perfect. A vote of "no confidence" at this point would have meant the ruin of the show. The resolution was passed.

Some details could be carried through in orderly fashion. The pine tree symbol of the American Revolution was adopted (inappropriately, as it transpired) and used for posters, the cover of the catalogue, and for badges. Bountiful Mrs. Whitney contributed $1,000 for ropes of laurel, potted palms, and firs to relieve the drabness of the Armory's interior. A catalogue was miraculously produced in ten days. It was unalphabetized, sometimes inaccurate, and incomplete, but for these shortcomings its compositors could hardly be blamed. There was no consolidated list of entries, and new paintings appeared daily, even after the opening.

The space within the Armory was made available to the association only five days before it opened. In that short time, eighteen compartments had to be constructed and covered with fireproofed burlap. This took three days, leaving only two days for the orderly mounting of thirteen hundred paintings and sculptures. Whatever justifiable charges of dictatorship may be laid at the door of Arthur B. Davies, it was his meticulous planning that made the resultant miracle a reality. Along with a handful of other dedicated, frantic artists, George Bellows worked like a galley slave day and night. He liked having a hammer and nails in his hands, and his alert blue eyes scanned every canvas that passed through his carpenter's hands.

Publicity had presented no problem. Borglum's abrupt resignation kept the pot boiling, and Walt Kuhn proved to have the ability to whet curiosity without actually giving out any positive information. Guy Pène DuBois, a former student of Henri and a rabid anti-Academician, could be counted on to promote the venture through *Arts and Decoration.*

Henri himself had joined the first organizing forces of the Association. He had been responsible for the Eight and for the first Independent Exhibition. He enjoyed associating with any group that wished to promote American painting, provided it was not exclusive. Yet when the Association asked him to make its European selections he declined because the choices would not be exclusively his. From that point on he had withdrawn more and more from active participation in the movement, doubtless piqued by Davies' rising star. But he kept his ear to the ground, and just before the opening he paid a visit to the Armory.

Through the chaos of packing boxes, pedestals, unhung canvases, unplaced shrubbery and bustling artists Henri made his way to the French area. There was little there to surprise this veteran of Paris and Madrid except the large and blatant proportion of the European representation. The Association had been formed to promote independent American artists. When Davies accepted the presidency he had stipulated only that the exhibition must "include" European art. Since a third of the show, embracing within itself one whole compartment exclusively dedicated to forty Redons, was given over to works from abroad, it was evident that Davies had either changed his original ideas or had dissembled from the start. Clearly, the Armory had become a salesroom for the products of Germany and France.

With this conviction churning in his mind, Henri turned a corner and encountered Davies himself standing with Walter Pach in a veritable pool of Fauvist pictures. The situation was embarrassing for all. Something had to be said. It was far too late for Henri to charge President Davies with deceit, for there had been abundant opportunity for any member of the Association to keep himself informed. As casually as he could, Henri suggested that the pictures were hung a trifle low. Davies ignored him. Henri then observed to Pach, reproachfully, that he hoped as many Americans would sell their pictures as the French, and went on his way vowing that the Americans would never work for the French again.

If George Bellows shared his teacher's opinions, he said nothing about it. All around him was a fascinating new world of ideas, of expression, and above all of color. His visits to Stieglitz's tiny gallery in the past had been a wholly inadequate preparation for all the European developments in the last decade. He fairly haunted the Armory while the show was on.

The preview for the press was charged with tense inquiry, the journalists eager to see what the exhibits were, and the artists on tiptoe to gauge what reception their work would receive.

The immediate reaction was, in fact, splendidly mixed. The triumphant *avant-garde* of the mid-twentieth century has been so

busy heaping derision on critics who found the Europeans outrageous, that they have largely overlooked the more open-minded
reviews of which there were a goodly number. It is true that "an
explosion in a shingle factory" makes more dramatic reading than
"Cézanne's sober studies . . . can hardly shock," or than "Van
Gogh, too, is not subversive." It was the public, as well as some
journalists, who treated the exhibition as something of a side
show, and thus inadvertently opened the floodgates to foreign
modernity.

Bellows fared well in the reviews. One that ran for two
columns bracketed him with Myers and Prendergast, noted
that he would "avail himself of the gospel of freedom without being swamped by it" and went on to cite his "Polo Game" for
special praise. Of the thirty artists covered by the article this was
the only painting specifically singled out for comment.

The following night, with the reviews ringing conflicting strains
in their ears, the members of the Association turned out to receive
their invited guests at the formal opening. Even though all the
important public officials who had been sent invitations, from
President Wilson down, had declined, four thousand curious
people wearing their free badges milled about the eighteen compartments and bought the catalogues peddled by excited art students. They studied the sculptures and the paintings, commented
according to their individual tastes, and went away—and stayed
away.

During the next two weeks panic grew among the Associates.
Where was the general public? Admission was only twenty-five
cents, but nobody seemed to want to pay it. What had gone
wrong? Every real or fancied art critic was shouting his opinions in
the papers, the posters were all over town, but the floor of the vast
hall was largely empty day after day except for some of the partici-
pating artists among whom George Bellows was always included.

The American part of the exhibition claimed very little of his
attention, for he was familiar with the paintings and with the men
who had made them. It was the European sections with their new
ideas which drew him. So preoccupied was he with these new discoveries that his record book shows no paintings at all for the
months of February and March and not so much as a single draw-

ing. The impact of the Armory Show upon him was immediate and profound.

For the rest of his life he constantly mulled over the lessons he had learned at the Armory. He would never tolerate derogation of the serious experimenters, and he consistently championed Duchamps' "Nude Descending a Staircase" even after he had come to doubt Duchamps' artistic integrity. Here his views coincided with those of many of his contemporaries among the painters and the critics. Yet he differed from most of them in one respect: no matter how much he might experiment with the new gospels, he never let them engulf him. During the next decade many of his associates, including Arthur B. Davies, attempted the same feat and were hypnotized in half-comprehending imitation. George's own perception never faltered. It was only sharpened by the experience.

Two weeks before March 15, the announced closing date, the inexplicable miracle occurred. The men and women in the streets began to pour in by the hundreds, then by the thousands. Some treated the exhibition with the hauteur of the *cognoscenti,* some as a curiosity, most as an amusement park. Magazines were now adding their comments to those of the daily papers, a fact which might partly explain the change in public interest. *Life,* for example, had a full page of cartoons with such captions as: "If the paint sticks out so thick you can hang your umbrella on it, 'It stands out in virile contrast to the older masters and is an artistic triumph' "; or, with less originality: "If it is a picture called 'Afterglow' and if it looks like an explosion in a tomato cannery it is 'Above the heads of the people' "; or one durable old gag: "If it is a picture that you like and others like, why, of course, it is no good at all."

A physician, pontificating in the *Saturday Evening Post,* gave his professional opinion: "One could easily recognize the germ of value which has been forced into performing capricious pranks by instigators with ocular aberrations and hallucinatory obsessions." A letter to the *Tribune* explained Duchamps' controversial "Nude" as "the diagram of a shudder." *Arts and Decoration* carried a laudatory note from Guy Pène DuBois, and also included the observations of John Quinn, a prominent collector, who stated flatly: "Life is growth; stagnation, the failure to grow, is the great tragedy of art." Mr. Gregg, of the *Sun,* wrote a long article for *Harper's* extolling with real perception the work of the French Post-Impressionists and the European sculptors. And ultimately Royal Cortissoz, the arbiter of conservative taste in New York, neatly summed up the opposing points of view: "It is a fine and stirring exhibition [which] includes some of the most stupidly ugly pictures in the world and not a few pieces of sculpture to match them. But while these will undoubtedly make a 'sensation' of the affair, it is plain that the latter was organized with no sensational purpose, and it is not freakish violence that gives the collection as a whole its tone. That is determined by nothing more or less than a healthy independence in most of the types represented."

Under the *Sun's* sympathetic headline, "Cubists Migrate: Thousands Mourn," the Armory Show came to an end on March 15. Long after the closing hour, when the last of the visitors had finally been persuaded to leave, the members of the Association celebrated with dances and champagne. Thirty-six hours later the exhibits were on their way to Chicago, the partitions to the dump, and the Fighting Irish Regiment was forming up as usual for the Saint Patrick's Day parade. Almost coincidentally with these obsequies, George Bellows found himself engaged in a very different activity.

As an Associate Member of the Academy, Bellows was asked to serve on the jury of selection for that institution's Spring Show. Three hundred spaces were available and there were twelve hundred entries. The Academy's jury of thirty contrasted strongly with the normal art jury of six or seven. Its members were drawn largely from the conservative group that George saw only on rare occasions, and against the radical impact of the Armory Show their offerings were timid and sedate. Yet this extraordinary contrast of points of view furnished him with the dichotomy that made him a great artist. His offering, "Little Girl in White," went safely through the hypercritical maw.

On March 23, a telegram came from Columbus. "Senility" had carried George Bellows, Sr., off to the wonders of that Methodist heaven he visualized so well, and his son hurried West for the funeral. Anna Bellows was tearful but composed. The estate was

in excellent order as one would have expected. The will left
$3,500 to the First Methodist Church, much smaller amounts to
other charities, and the remainder, totaling $52,000, to Anna
Smith Bellows. Newspapers noted that the old man had given a
considerable part of his holdings to his wife and children some
months before; of this transaction there is no other record.

Years later, George wrote the following two paragraphs:

"My father, with but a few months of school in his youth, became an architect's apprentice at eighteen, moved to Ohio by
canal boat in 1850, and made a modest living thereafter as contractor, architect and builder. By charging much less than his
worth, and by investing in 'Worthy' causes, his fortune remained
reasonably easy to calculate.

"He was a wonderfully fine man, and yet having been born in
1827, and being fifty-five when I appeared, his point of view, his
character even, belonged to so remote a past that I look upon
many of his ideas to this day with amazement and sorrow. Certain
things he could not discuss. On religion, the church, and respect
for the Law he was beyond reproach."

The half century of extraordinary physical and emotional
change that lay between father and son had been a frustrating
barrier. Yet much of George's character had been modeled on his
parent's—his thrift, his stubbornness, his passion for fine materials,
his enthusiasm, and his devotion to the idea of full measure of
performance.

Immediately after the funeral, Bellows returned to New York
where new problems awaited him. Like most of his fellow artists,
he was anxious to know how the Armory Show had succeeded
financially, but "Little Girl in White" at the Academy was raising
a small controversy of her own that was of more immediate concern. She had been hung prominently in the Academy's "Vanderbilt Room," the choicest area available. One morose critic, who
pointed out that the Academy's opening had coincided with the
Armory's demise, had nasty things to say. After chirping merrily
about the necessity of St. Patrick purging his Armory of snakes and
vermin that, under the guise of art, had made merry for a month
on his premises, the scribe mellowed a little, noted that Bellows
showed indiscriminately with both the Independents and the

Academy, and finally melted in praise of "Little Girl in White."

Then "Little Girl in White" was awarded the First Hallgarten Prize of $300, and the press went vigorously and virtuously to its typewriters. The Academy's jury of selection was also its jury of awards. This year three members of the jury were recipients of awards. "Favoritism," "Nepotism," "Horse-trading"—even the Philadelphia *Press* took up the cry, and the *Inquirer* demanded that: "The Academy Council, for the sake of dignity and reputation, should look into this matter."

Calmer heads had their say. In a letter to *American Art News*, Charles Vezin pointed out that the majority of the Academy's jurors were die-hard academicians, and that the vote of any single individual among twenty-nine others would, if so cast, be a negligible factor. "How this works out is shown in the case of George Bellows, a member of the jury, the brilliant young 'progressive,' a former critic of this very thing. He was a member of the jury, the majority of its thirty members believed him entitled to the prize, and willy nilly he got it."

The suggestion of collusion galled George, but he kept his temper and his peace and the $300.

The affair of the "Little Girl in White" was sour in his mouth as he came to grips with his final responsibilities for the Armory Show. This had attracted forty thousand visitors and had sold two hundred items. Yet the exhibition had run deeply in the red, so deeply in fact that when Davies called a meeting late in April the treasurer's report was greeted with a horrified silence. DuBois was the first to break it. He rose to his feet, said "I resign," and walked out. Henri, Bellows, Mahonri Young, and others followed suit. Jerome Myers remembered that: "It was rather a marvelous demonstration of the fact that artists are not especially businesslike in the acceptance of an unsatisfactory situation. Dignity rode high as one by one the members left in silence."

For many of the members this was the end. Davies and Walt Kuhn somehow found the money to pay off the Association's debts before the year was out, but the impact of the show remained with Bellows for the rest of his life.

George, like his father, was not a man to plunge suddenly into waters he did not know, but rather felt his way into unfamiliar currents with an inquisitive toe. Sloan, now art editor for *The Masses,* importuned him to contribute, and for the next four years, until the magazine's demise, George regularly sent drawings to *The Masses.*

Bellows thoroughly enjoyed the association of the people involved. He admired their Socialist ideas, although from time to time he would grow impatient with what he considered their piddling campaigns, such as one against the newly formed Boy Scouts, and he often threatened to join Emma Goldman and her Anarchists.

All through April he drew—and the meetings at *The Masses'* office were pleasant ones. Usually, when an issue was "put to bed," about twenty people assembled. The Editor, Max Eastman, read poetry while the various departments quarreled cheerfully about their contributions. Dolly Sloan, her diminutive form in a chair that left her tiny feet a good six inches off the floor, kept an adoring eye on her harrassed husband. Art Young and John Reed usually rushed in late. During the whole rather casual business of forming an issue the conversation rambled from politics to art to letters. The names of Brieux, Gauguin, and Picasso were common currency, while beer and macaroons spurred them on in their objective to "do big things" and to "give the people what they ought to have whether they like it or not."

Bellows drew for *The Masses* for a month. Then Ohio State University waited again on his doorstep in the person of Dr. Mendenthale ready to sit for his portrait; the Carnegie International Exhibition awarded him its Third Class Medal for his "Circus"; and the National Academy of Design elected him a national Academician.

Not quite thirty-one, this eloquent Socialist and vigorous participant in three Independent exhibitions became a full partner in the most conservative and exclusive art organization in America.

In Bellows' mind, his election was second in importance to the portrait of Dr. Mendenthale. He wrote a rather anxious letter about this picture to Joe Taylor stating that the subject had arrived on a Friday and already had departed:

"He certainly is a fine old boy.

"He likes the portrait very much . . .

"Emma says it's a fine likeness. It's very hard for me to tell. It's alive anyways. I think it's as much of a likeness as the others at least . . .

"Robert Henri and Guy DuBois think it's a beaut . . ."

Not every one was of the same opinion, for a little later the artist asked Taylor for his own, adding that: "the Doc likes it very much although he writes that his wife failed to 'get it.' He tells me it is hung very badly in the Library. If you'll get it into a good light you'll find it has fine color and strong drawing. I don't think myself it's a marvel of a likeness . . ."

Among the drawings he submitted to *The Masses* was one of the slums, entitled in proper Socialist fashion, "Why Don't They All Go to the Country for Vacation." He now turned this into his most monumental painting of life in the tenements. Tall buildings crowd in on a swarming street, a horse car pushes its way among carts, sportive urchins, and scolding mothers. Higher up, figures lean out of windows and over fire escapes, and festoons of laundry dangle in the hot still air. "The Cliff Dwellers" provided the picture with a better title than that of the original drawing.

Other aspects of the city claimed his attention as spring gave way to early summer. "A Day in June" and "Approach to the Bridge, Night" show a dramatic change of moods. One canvas is bright and warm and still, the other seems dark and turbulent, a great sweep of lighted pavement swinging up to the distant bridge and a thunderhead elbowing its way across the moon. Later, he commented that the bulk of the painting of this second picture had taken no time at all, but that he had spent two days on the horses in the lower left-hand corner.

In one of his letters to Joe Taylor he wrote: "We are going to Monhegan this summer, I think." Evidently Emma required a considerable amount of persuasion, but George had no intention of repeating the discomfort and frustration of the summer before. He had given in then; it was her turn now.

In July, Henri, who was spending his first summer in Ireland, received the following epistle:

"Dear Irishman:

"The food is very good at Monhegan this year, and my room-mate neither snores, sneezes or wheezes. They have wonderful lobsters and fruit (at the other hotel) but the Lady manager is very nice so we stay at the Albee House for dinner.

"Of course you knew we had gone to Monhegan.

"Financial condition never better.

"N. Rabinovitz [a dealer in paints and canvases] slumbers on in the Ghetto while the artist colony on Monhegan curses him to the High God. I waited nearly three weeks for white and borrowed three tubes a day from different victims.

"Cap't Stevens—you remember him—has offered us the freedom of the city, had us to dinner [in his lighthouse], gave me a high-ball, four cigars, a fresh mackerel and asked me for a sketch. I haven't touched a razor since arrival and I expect to return to New York looking as good as M. Leon Dabo . . .

"Anne is the most popular person on the island, holding continual reception when she goes out and swimming in the cold sea every day at the beach near the public dump."

Bellows saw Monhegan with different eyes that summer, and the one hundred and seventeen paintings that he eventually listed from this stay invite a rather startling comparison with those of two years before. Once in a while he reverted to the plastic simplicity of "An Island in the Sea," and more rarely to the crowd at the dock greeting the mail boat or a cluster of fishermen cleaning their catch. But the majority of his output showed a larger approach, great strokes from an inch-wide brush as in "Rock Bound" or the broad streaks from the palette knife in "Cream Surf." At times he seemed almost to model in paint the contours of the ocean and of the rocks repelling it. The forms sometimes became so broad as almost to shed their immediate identities and stand as symbols of assault and immobility. Into the endless surge of the Atlantic he put the maximum of Marsden Hartley's weight and added more as he studied the combers plunging against headlands, raking the coves and crevices with hungry hands, breathing a waiting interlude over the beaches.

Leon Kroll also spent that summer on Monhegan. Perhaps it was from him that George learned Winslow Homer's dictum on how to paint the sea: "Do it with one wave, not more than two."

Certainly it was Kroll, long fascinated with the pure colors of Impressionism, who encouraged Bellows in his experiments with his palette. There were some dark paintings; the natural rocks invited this. But in general Bellows forgot Henri's caution: "Never change the tone of a color or from one color to another until you have to," and his brush dripped with undiluted hues. The hot palette of the Post-Impressionists, Gauguin and Van Gogh, the tropical chromisms of the Fauves, never shone more brilliantly than in "Autumn Flame." Although he was now making much more meticulous color notes in his book, he did not include the proportions used, so that this painting, described as "purple-red, yellow-green and blue," emerges as a study in red-orange. Such a choice of colors he preferred that summer, although in his new-found freedom he often substituted straight yellow for yellow-green. What he had learned from the Armory Show was inescapable, while the paintings remained pure Bellows. Nobody else could have done them.

His enthusiasm knew no bounds. When a fisherman from the island of Mattinicus argued that *his* island was much smaller and much more attractive than Monhegan, there was nothing to do but go aboard his boat and see it. Inevitably, Emma and Leon Kroll went along. With them were the George Washington Smiths, an aristocratic couple from New York who apparently could not enjoy life without George Bellows. The trip was rough, and in their small, smelly boat Emma earned her passport to a heroism. Arriving at the tiny farming islet of Mattinicus, they were shown what sights there were in no time at all, and Bellows put these into the back of his mind for a further visit: no picture postcards, but an isolated environment that Winslow Homer would have admired, a tiny slip of land dumped far off the coast where human beings continued to face the precarious challenge of existence with dignity.

The fisherman was all hospitality. George and Emma were given his room on the ground floor, and the fisherman's wife was ordered to set up sleeping quarters in the attic. The elegant Smiths were delegated to a windy out-house. There remained the ubiquitous bachelor Kroll, who was finally bedded down in the attic too, although a hastily erected screen was entirely ineffective between himself and his host and hostess.

Next morning, the whole entourage was dancing its way back over a sparkling sea to grim Monhegan.

September came, and the summer visitors disappeared like exotic plants wilting with the first frost. The Bellows family stayed on all through October. It was a glorious month, the scattered hardwoods standing brilliantly against the solemn firs of Cathedral Woods. Bellows could not tear himself away from this radiant pageant. When the leaves blew off with the first fall gale, the sea churned up new brilliancies of blue and green in the thin, clear air of Indian Summer. He turned out forty-two pictures in thirty days, some large canvases among them; but at length even his incredible energy flagged. Inspiration cannot last forever, and of the last eleven of these paintings, he destroyed three.

Outside their house, the wind skittered the fallen leaves as George and Emma, ineptly assisted by Anne, reviewed his summer's harvest. The packing cases were duly labeled "146 East Nineteenth Street," and passed, one after the other, over Monhegan's massive dock. The cadence of the winter sea grew stronger day and night. On the last day of October the Bellows family returned to New York.

Exhaustion took its toll. Three months later Bellows described his state of mind in a letter to Joe Taylor dated January 25, 1914:

". . . having been busy for the last three months doing nothing at all . . .

"Since returning from Monhegan November first I have painted just one thing so far, a dismal failure to be put away with those hopeless hopes that some day I may straighten out.

"Pipe after pipe, and cigarette after cigar I sit and rock in profound discontent; and the effort of standing on my feet and fighting a canvas is too much. I look like a healthy pig. Tobacco is a curse, also a blessing. I wish I could enjoy just enough of it to be good for me.

"I am so tired of depending on my past summer for present interest that I hesitate to state for the thousandth time that I painted a great many pictures and arrived at a pure kind of color which I never hit before. And which seems cleaner and purer than most of the contemporary effort in that direction . . .

"I did have a great summer, and with the memory of working almost every day with some success and with the present depression I am longing to go right back now."

Technical problems raised by his new and independent inquiries into the methods of Europe's younger men as opposed to Henri's dogma of traditional techniques were very much on his mind. Both avenues were demanding, and he could not abjure either.

"Having got what I can out of the modernist movement for fresh, spontaneous pure color I am now turning my attention to the 'Secrets of the Old Masters' (to be read with some humor), hoping that what I have done will not lose its freshness with the passage of time. I have come to the realization that permanence demands more care, and while I am certain that my pictures are as 'stable' as any *modern* technic, I also realize that there are grave dangers in too much spontaneity and haste.

"I am glad that most of my good pictures have been on new, nearly white canvas, and that I used permanent colors and good mediums. But the Old Masters got different results and I want to know how they did it . . . I expect to change my methods entirely when I learn what I can in a new direction, that direction being the isolation of drawing and coloring into two distinct processes and over a perfectly prepared canvas of pure white. This is the process of Rubens, Titian, Velásquez, Hals and the rest and the proof of the pudding etc.

"This seems to be an extremely original attitude nowadays. All this is very hopeful, of course, and I am not beyond hope."

The Armory Show had fired him for the first time with the magic of color. All summer long he had fairly shaken with excitement as greens and blues and vermillions raced with each other over his panels in an intoxicating sequence and with so much success. But why? Henri had taught him a well-balanced but limited palette. Hardesty Maratta, whose prepared pigments George considered the best in the world, advocated a color "triangle" or "triad," three complementary hues in different degrees of light and dark and intensity. But Bellows had been experimenting with a vague concept of "color unlimited." Why had the results been so satisfactory?

He found part of his answer in a recent book by Denman Ross, Lecturer at Harvard. As Monet was "The Eye" of nature, so Ross was "The Eye" of pigment. He was also a perfectionist, a connoisseur, a romantic philosopher, and a verbal analyst-extraordinary in the uses of paint. Like Bellows, he was an idealist in everything that did not touch him very closely—then both became hardheaded realists.

It may have been the brief but highly provocative conclusion to Ross' "On Drawing and Painting" that set George to study the whole text intensively, for Ross aimed point blank at a democratic *nostrum* and demolished it:

"Consider, for example, the ideals of Equality, Fraternity and Liberty . . . Shall we be led by these ideals or shall we be led by the contrary ideals of Superiority, of Exclusive Demotions and Self-Sacrifice? Shall we seek liberty of action, or shall we give up all thought of liberty for the sake of some interest, some ideal by which we are possessed and controlled . . . some excellence and perfection we want to achieve, which is so important that Liberty seems to be nothing in comparison, Fraternity an incessant and irritating interruption and interference, and Equality quite contemptible in view of the Superiority for which we are prepared to suffer everything?"

"The reader . . . if he does not share my interest, if he does not share my ideas and my ideals . . . must shut my book at once and never open it again."

George read it from preface to conclusion many times.

Ross' treatise was full of material that appealed directly to Bellows. Thus: "I love to see the human body in vigorous action. Attending wrestling bouts when I can, I am constantly watching for the best moment, a moment of consistency, unity, order and beauty . . . I have no interests in 'holds' nor do I care who wins . . . I am not going to give up my idea of wrestling because the pose is one which is impossible to hold for any length of time. I am not going to be limited to subjects of still life." Bellows might have written those lines himself.

On other points, however, George disagreed violently with the text. Ross stated bluntly that the Post-Impressionist's aim was to exhibit himself: "The Post-Impressionists believe in nothing but themselves, and there are writers just like that who tell us that they want to write 'not Literature but Life.' It was in view of this declaration that somebody said: 'Life is worth living, of course, but it is no longer worth reading.' Nor are the pictures of the Post-Impressionists, Futurists and others of the same brutality worth looking at." To an artist like Bellows, who championed Duchamps' "Nude Descending a Staircase," these were fighting words.

When Ross stated that we should never have any art until the public learns to discriminate between good work and bad, his reader could heartily agree. Even when the author castigated the trade unions for not stressing the quality of the work they were producing, George, an ardent supporter of the labor movement in any form, was obliged to concur. And the two were as one in supporting the credo: "The only hope for art . . . lies in the establishment of standards of excellence."

The meat of Ross' book, however, lay not in such generalizations, but in the very specific study it made of nearly sixty different set palettes. Some of these were austerely limited to only two colors, others to three or four. One that particularly interested Bellows, who later used it in several of his pictures, was a very varied combination that Ross noted as being particularly reminiscent of Rubens.

George rocked much of the winter away in his studio, tobacco smoke wreathing his big balding head in blue and gray, with "On Drawing and Painting" resting on his knees as he battled with its contents.

For three months the problems of color churned away in his mind, while he limited his own performance to three black-and-white drawings. The lustrous possibilities of the lithographic crayon appealed to him, an indication that for all his new-found intentness on the spectrum he had by no means shed his concern for design in depth. "Disappoints of the Ash Can (Real Tragedy)" poked fun at the hoboes he remembered from Columbus; and a half century later Max Eastman, reminiscing on *The Masses,* recalled: "We were coarse enough at least to play a role in creating what has been called the 'Ash-can School of art.' Indeed George Bellows' revolting lithograph . . . of two bums picking scraps out of a refuse can was the *ne plus ultra* of that school." "The National Game" he executed in two versions, the first in the ink-and-wash medium that had been his mainstay during his college career. Of "Prayer Meeting," a satirical recollection of a visit to the tiny Methodist church on Monhegan, he wrote Professor Taylor: "That's what I wanted to do to Billy Sunday, and didn't get a look. This I will always regret. I have not yet been handed my church papers. I suppose I should ask for them."

February saw Bellows back at his easel. In "Love of Winter," a scene of skaters in Central Park, he tried out a palette of red-purple, red-orange, yellow and blue, so gay a combination that it reminds one of Glackens; yet the end result as usual put the emphasis on the forms themselves rather than on their surfaces.

The Montross Gallery mounted a show of two dozen of George's paintings. He sent some nineteen of the panels painted the summer before, but salted in a few larger canvases, including "Love of Winter." None of these sold, but his five-year-old version of "The Palisades" found an immediate buyer at $600, a good start for 1914. He shipped his "Polo Crowd" and "Snow Dumpers" to the Pennsylvania Academy but neither of them found a buyer. Then came the Spring Academy, and he was electrified by the results.

Two years earlier, in 1912, Bellows had begun a large portrait of Dr. William Oxley Thompson, the distinguished president of Ohio State University. He had no commission for this work, but the subject appealed to him—a big, bluff figure in academic robes —and he no doubt hoped that it might appeal to the University's Alumni Association or some generous patron of the institution. After a while his interest languished and he put the painting aside. Some months later he returned to it, and the results were so satisfying to him that he rushed off a letter to Joe Taylor, describing how he worked:

"I am full of enthusiasm this night. After having Thompson's portrait photographed and sending [off] copies . . . and not particularly good ones at that, I looked at the Portrait two days ago and decided it was very punk.

"I have raised hell with it in the meantime and am sitting back now admiring myself, for she came through at last. I really think I've got a beauty, and I never worked so hard on a portrait in my life. It was a long series of experimentings to get everything to do its work with the rest. There is not a square inch that hasn't bothered me to death.

"I went at it yesterday and painted the whole thing over fresh, getting everything into the new wet skin of painting and without disturbing the head or the hand or the vest which I have always liked but which I painted on some since you saw the picture. I can now feel good about this work which has been challenging my ingenuity since I started it. There isn't a stunt I didn't try . . . Every little part is now what I started out to get and the color of the whole is the richest thing yet . . ."

If his enthusiasm was shared by any one connected with Ohio State, it was not sufficient to attract a purchaser. The canvas rested with other unsold pieces in a stack under the balcony of the studio, was critically reviewed at intervals, and then was returned to storage. In the spring of 1914, Bellows decided to let the public see it for the first time. He wrote Taylor:

"I am sending the Thompson portrait to an exhibition this month where I can see it in a gallery. Sometimes it looks like what I want; sometimes it looks dull and dark, which of course it is and always will be. The blacks have been painted over too much. But in a good light it has great dignity and is really 'awfully' sober."

The Academy jury not only liked the painting, but hung it in the "Place of Honor" and awarded it the Maynard Prize as the best portrait in the show. For a time George expected the accolade from the press to sell the picture to Ohio State, but nothing came of it and he had to content himself with the prize money of $100. At about the same time the Carnegie International in Pittsburgh awarded his "Cliff Dwellers" its Third Prize and the more satisfactory sum of $500.

Willard Straight, man of affairs, decided that it was time his portrait was painted. His relative by marriage, Gertrude Vanderbilt Whitney, suggested Bellows, and sittings began promptly. The two men struck it off beautifully from the start, for they had

Self-Portrait; watercolor. No date.

sports, books, music and the theater as common enthusiasms. Unfortunately, however, the sessions were punctuated by incessant telephone calls. Emma or the maid would answer on the landing, and Willard Straight would apologize, rise, take over the receiver, and settle some urgent affair of state. Recapturing the pose and the mood was difficult, and the finished painting reflects more of the successful businessman than of the sportsman and connoisseur. The sitter had no objection to this, and promptly handed over a check for $1,500.

Early in June Bellows worked on another portrait that satisfied neither himself nor his model. Then his mind was swinging into focus on Monhegan again, and he began "Fisherman's Family" in which he represented himself with Anne on his shoulder and Emma by his side, standing above an imaginary harbor. At the same time he blocked out a big canvas, developing his drawing "River Front" into a monumental scale. The lure of the island, however, was stronger than his compulsion to finish either picture. The exaltation of the summer before made him impatient to try out his new discoveries in the field of color. By the middle of June they were on their way to test them.

Monhegan was foggy that summer. They rented a cottage on the solitary street parallel to the harbor where they were comfortable enough, and there was excellent company, for the Randall Daveys had decided to come along. A number of older artists had adolescent daughters ready and willing to pose for portraits when the weather made it impossible to work outside.

George started in at once with a fair-sized panel he called "Family Group," choosing a setting behind his cottage with the harbor and Manana in the background. For this and for the first two portraits of the summer he used Denman Ross' "Rubens Palette." In July, he reverted to a very simple triad of blue, yellow, and red to produce what is perhaps his finest portrait of his wife, "Emma at the Piano." She sits, half-turned away from the instrument, her right arm extended and her hand resting on the keys. Her handsome, even features appear in three-quarter view, her magnificent eyes illuminating the broadly modeled face. The arm and hesitating hand and the ivory fronts of the piano keys form a powerful horizontal across the lower part of the canvas. Henri's simplicity and strength and dramatic contrasts of light and shade are all here, yet Bellows' master never achieved so striking a blend of intimacy and universal charm.

In its externals, Monhegan presented the same opportunities it had the year before. Rocks, trees, and surf had not changed. The baseball diamond still suffered the scrapes and tramplings of amateurs' sneakers. Evening after evening the ceilings of the inn or of the Bellows' cottage rang with song. The Fisherman's Band elected George to membership, a unique honor for an off-Islander.

There was the inevitable costume party for which he acted as master of ceremonies, outrageously dressed as a cross between a pirate and a confidence man, his costume topped off by a jet black wig and a high hat. But Monhegan did not seem the same.

Bellows had changed. He cursed the fog that kept him inside until his restlessness drove him out to grope and slip and stumble among the thick gray veils shutting out everything he wanted to paint. But the Island's magic that had twice fired his giant energies failed him now. The "continent" he had discovered in 1911 had shrunk to the dimensions of "An Island in the Sea."

As he struggled to understand and to adjust, the "Century of Peace" came to an end, and Europe went to war.

The Enemy Arrive; *lithograph, 1918.*

THE WAR YEARS

» *1914 - 1918* «

» VII «   *"If you think, you see democracy looming large for
the whole world."* George Bellows

The Bellows family had hardly settled in their Monhegan cottage
when, early in July, 1914, the heir to the Austro-Hungarian
throne was murdered in Sarajevo. The daily mail boat brought the
news along with the newspapers. Blowing up royalty was always
worth big headlines, and conversation around the dinner table at
the Inn that evening surely centered around assassinations: that of
the Archduke's aunt, the Empress of Austria; of the King of Italy;
and, only a year before, of the King of Greece. No one on Monhegan had much sense of the horrendous pile of diplomatic tinder
accumulated in Europe's backyard.

Unlike Colonel House, reporting to President Wilson one
month before the murder that "it needs only a spark to set the
whole thing off," Monhegan and the rest of the United States
gossiped about the event and thought little of the consequences.

On August 1 the European nations began to issue declarations
of war across their neighbors' doorsteps like passes to a free-for-all.
Monhegan knew that Europe was always fighting about something; indeed, the smoke from the last Balkan War had hardly
settled. Every intelligent person knew that war, especially on a
large scale, was immoral, useless, and ridiculous. Eyebrows were
lifted disapprovingly over Germany's dismissal of the guarantee of
Belgian neutrality as "a scrap of paper," but when 335 European

divisions began to shoot to kill, most of the residents of Monhegan went on with their fishing or their painting as though nothing really serious had occurred.

The war went on, too, gradually becoming a small disturbing fact that Bellows, as well as America as a whole, could keep tucked away in the back of his head for a while, even though Paris nearly fell and was saved only by a miracle of German misjudgment. Good weather found the artist working in the open, trying out variations on Ross' color combinations, or bringing back to his palette the black he had temporarily discarded. In the studio he continued these experiments. "Julie," for example, he executed entirely in red and a much neutralized yellow and black, while "Geraldine Lee" is almost a synthesis of the spectrum. He produced thirteen portraits that summer, and his good opinion of them is indicated by the prices he asked: $1,000, $1,500, $2,000.

Unlike the summer before, George felt no impulse to linger. It was already plain that another "John" Bellows was due in the spring and that something would have to be done to enlarge their living accommodations at 146 East Nineteenth Street. The studio was sacred to painting, and the three rooms on the floor below it were already barely adequate for a family of three. The rent from the ground floor apartment was still welcome, although George's account book showed a steadily improving income from sales, commissions, and class and lecture fees. He and Emma decided to turn the basement into a kitchen and dining room, and George spent the whole fall on these alterations. A kitchen demands shelves, cupboards, and cabinets, exactly the sort of carpentry that appealed to him. His booming voice, caroling operatic arias or hymn tunes, as his fancy dictated, rose over the scrape of saw and plane, and the thud of his hammer was heard up through the stairwell, past the apartment, to the second story and into the empty studio. Emma, who took her second pregnancy in stride, listened to him contentedly as she stitched a wardrobe for herself, another for Anne, and a third for the coming child.

William E. Story, defeated in the battle of fine linens and laces, moved with his wife into the new first-floor apartment. Their rent was assimilated by baby sitting as George and Emma's battles continued above and below stairs. The Storys provided a continuous refuge for Anne from the incessant conflict that composed her parents' lives.

Although he did no drawing or painting until January, Bellows could not entirely desert his art. In the last two weeks of November, for example, he served on four juries in three different cities, giving his best judgment in an atmosphere of haste, general confusion, and the tensions of vested interests, all of which he hated. "Time is needed to estimate any work of art. Space is needed to show any work of art. Congenial company is essential in the hanging of pictures together. Freedom is necessary for the development of all art. Freedom to create and freedom to show," he wrote the editor of the *Globe,* which had published a letter praising the existing method of selection.

One of the juries that prompted this explosion was a small one, appointed a year and a half before to select the paintings for the forthcoming Panama-Pacific Exposition in San Francisco. Besides Bellows, the other two members of this group were J. Alden Weir, the American Impressionist, and John Alexander. Both were staunch members of the Academy with whom Bellows got along tolerably well. The experience seems to have been a relatively pleasant one, except for the necessity of haste and for the violent opposition of Robert Henri, who categorically refused to submit his work to the selection of any jury. How his stellar pupil and two other academic friends succeeded in getting around this ultimatum is unknown. Very probably they simply asked him to put in what he chose, for a show of American paintings of this scope without a contribution from Henri was unthinkable. Even so, the episode rankled in Henri's mind and was not helped soon after when George's "River Front" was awarded the exposition's Gold Medal for the best picture in the exhibition, while Henri's entry drew only an "Honorable Mention."

Over New Year's, 1915, George dropped his carpenter's tools long enough to pick up those of his vocation. His first essay was minor in that it was devoted to giving the finishing touches to "River Front," the painting that would so soon bring a mighty accolade from the other side of the continent of North America.

Into this painting he compacted and reviewed a number of ideas that had stood him well in the past. A familiar swarm of small boys basks, dives, or wanders around the foreground. The long pier links them with the further line where the funnel of a tug seems almost to collide with the sails of a two-master headed downstream. Bellows organized in rectangles and triangles a picture full of Cubist mannerisms, yet gave it a certain restricted depth enriched with the intimate wriggles and struggles with shirts and trousers taking place in the foreground. The painting has the richness of "Forty-Two Kids," and an emphasis on limited space that was also his own.

He contributed to two big traveling shows, one that began in Los Angeles, California, and wound up in Worcester, Massachusetts; another that toured the Middle West; and a third that went as far west as Denver and, through Canada, touched the eastern seaboard at Baltimore. The mere bookkeeping of where and when dozens of paintings happened to be, provided a full-time job for Emma. Laudatory reviews poured in from coast to coast. Yet fresh as the praises rang, the job of the artist would always be to keep on painting.

The *Metropolitan Magazine* sent him to Philadelphia with John Reed to report on Billy Sunday, then "preaching" in Philadelphia. The revivalist had energy, lungs, and showmanship. He had also a knowledge of the Old and New Testaments, perhaps as good as that of a Methodist from Columbus, Ohio. Billy Sunday capitalized on the Revivalism of the nineteenth century and the tensions growing in America over World War I. His sermons were phrased in such picturesque vulgarity that the most illiterate could understand him and the most precious intellectuals came to cheer. Billy Sunday swept across the nation, filling its biggest urban halls or circus tents. He cajoled, threatened, and pleaded for penitence to overflow-audiences night after night. Confessions, conversions, screams, tears, and shouts of exaltation, mixed with his hoarse-voiced exhortations and good old-fashioned Methodist hymns, were standard accompaniments to his triumphal stands.

To George, this whole gaudy show was a sham. The faith of his father might no longer be his, but he held it in deep respect. Billy Sunday was pulling down one of the vital props of his past, and Bellows hated him for it. He and Reed took in several meetings, sitting under banners that trumpeted "Christ for Philadelphia—

Philadelphia for Christ." They endured the garish lights. They heard thousands of throats responding to the choir master's urging: "Stand Up, Stand Up for Jesus." They heard Billy's account of the battle of David and Goliath: "He socked him on the coco between the lamps, and he went down for the count, after which the kid chopped off the big stiff's block and the whole bunch skiddooed." They heard him out on pastimes: "Sow a card party and you'll reap gamblers," and "Sow dances and you'll reap prostitutes."

Bellows compressed the whole hysterical performance into a drawing he called "The Sawdust Trail." The platform cuts sharply between the indistinct rows of the worshippers responding to the choir master on the one side, and the foreground pageant of Sunday leaning over to grasp the hand of a convert, female adorers being removed in a happy state of exposure and, over all, "Ma" Sunday giving an air of matronly respectability to the whole shoddy show.

Bellows told *Touchstone Magazine* exactly what he thought about Billy Sunday and his revivals: "I like to paint Billy Sunday, not because I like him, but because I want to show the world what I think about him. Do you know, I think Billy Sunday is the worst thing that ever happened to America? He is death to imagination, to spirituality, to art. Billy Sunday is Prussianism personified. His whole purpose is against freedom; he wants religious autocracy, he is such a reactionary that he makes me an anarchist. You can see why I like to paint him and his devastating 'Sawdust Trail.' I want people to understand him."

He cordially detested Billy Sunday, yet there was an undeniable force about the evangelist that he unconsciously admired. In a later lithograph, complete with cynical reporters, overacting derelicts, and enchanted auditors, he showed his villain vigorously straddling two desks and throwing out an arm with something of the power that Michelangelo gave to God in "Creation of Sun and Moon." Bellows thought highly of vitality, and Billy Sunday at least had that.

In March he settled down to painting again. First he reworked two of his 1913 Monhegan sketches and sold them promptly at $200 apiece. Then he turned to portraits and produced "Paul Manship." This young sculptor's star hung high, and art circles in

New York exclaimed over his graceful, cleanly modeled styliza-
tions on Classical and Renaissance themes. Manship, after years at
the American Academy in Rome, was full of the latest news
from the European ateliers, and these sittings at 146 were exciting
ones for both men concerned.

The baby's arrival was imminent in April. Emma awaited her
ordeal with her customary calm. "George wants a boy, so of course
that's what it will be," she stated. "George always gets what he
wants."

Ethel Clarke came to dinner on April 22. When the meal was
over, Emma said in her casual way, "I've just called the nurse,
George, so you'd better call the doctor." His regular doctor was
out of town, but there was a new medical shingle hanging out
across the way, and Bellows had no trouble persuading its owner
to lend a hand in this crisis. Then, nervous, the prospective father
paid Miss Clarke the unusual compliment of walking home with
her. "I'll call you in the morning," he said when he left, "but I
know it is a boy."

The next morning he telephoned. "Is everything all right?"
Miss Clarke asked. "And, oh, what is it." There was a pause. "Yep,
everything's O.K." Another pause. "Same kind," and he hung
up.

The baby's birth was in itself characteristic of the informality
and improvisations of the Bellows household. George had let the
unknown doctor into the house, then closed the front door behind
him and escorted Miss Clarke to her rooms. The newly-graduated
physician found the patient's bedroom by himself. The baby, on
the point of arrival, was unfortunately upside down, and the doctor had no idea what to do about it. The veteran nurse told him
what steps to take and almost at once the new Bellows baby was
safely in the world. Emma, completely in control of herself, asked
what the sex of the baby was. "A girl, and I hope you don't mind."
"Not at all," replied Emma almost gaily, having scored over
George. "Will you please introduce me to my daughter." At this
point the harrassed doctor exploded, "I don't know her name, nor
your name, nor your husband's name. *My* name is Dr. Smith!
Howdy do." And they shook hands.

George settled the problem of his second daughter's name in

characteristic fashion. The Speichers were their most intimate friends. He turned "Eugene" into "Jean" and rushed to the telephone to secure the consent of the delighted artist.

With the advent of Jean, Emma replaced her part-time help with a full-time maid. From then on a constant succession of servants kept 146 in order. The turnover was frequent, for Emma could perfectly well keep her house in order by herself when she had to, and she was a strict mistress. She would tolerate neither inefficiency nor trifling peculations. Once she found a new maid taking home a large chocolate cake baked in Emma's kitchen. "You may leave the cake with me," said Emma without rancour, "and you may take yourself and your belongings home. And don't come back."

The domestic changes occurred so often that George had trouble with servants' names, especially since he rarely saw them. He settled the problem by calling them all "Flora," until Emma protested. After that he called them all "Dora."

Anne Bellows, aged four, was already a thoroughly professional model who rather enjoyed the concentrated attention her father gave her when she sat for him. This she did in April, setting her small form into a big chair, an extraordinary contrast to Judge Peter Olney who came almost daily at this time to have his portrait painted. To the world at large, Judge Olney's reputation rested on his distinction as a referee in bankruptcy, but the inner circle of his acquaintance admired him also as a past president of the Harvard Club of New York. Any member who survived this honor was entitled to have his likeness hanging on the paneled walls of the club house. One Charles C. Burlingame, a Harvard man and a lawyer, persuaded the hale and hearty judge to sit for Bellows.

A portrait painter must not only produce a likeness, but also establish a rapport with his sitter that will give him the necessary insight into the character behind the features. Judge Olney was accustomed to wielding his gavel in the courtroom, in the Harvard Club, or in any other place he happened to be. He started to establish this identity from the moment he ascended the narrow stairs to the studio. His steel-blue eyes and harsh voice immediately made it clear who was running the show, and he became a self-appointed authority on poses, colors, and expressions. George bore the judge's didacticism longer than usual, for the commission was important to him. Then he met obnoxious bluntness with judicial finality, saying in effect: "Save it for the Bench, Judge. *I'm* running *this* show!"

He had tried Olney the year before, but neither was satisfied with the results, and the judge was caustic on the subject of the high color palette. Now in April and May of 1915, Bellows tried again, this time using a seated pose and stressing the massive head and features in full light, underscoring the effect of craggy self-assurance. The judge finally expressed himself as satisfied with the result, and they parted on amicable terms. George tinkered with the portrait's tones for a month and then, just as he was imitating the members of the Harvard Club in their mass exodus for the summer, he took the finished canvas to its destination. The somber setting in the Harvard Club and the discreet lighting changed the effect of color and disturbed him.

He wrote Joe Taylor: "I have just finished one of the best things I've ever painted and today delivered it to the Harvard Club. It's a blow to see a thing hung in a place not suitable for pictures . . . But it's so rich it can't be altogether killed, and it doesn't look quite so musty as the rest of the coal cellar portraits." Quite unconsciously, he had deposited a tinderbox in the Harvard Club ready to ignite at the first member's "I'll be goddamned!"

During the Olney sittings the crack liner *"Lusitania"* was torpedoed without warning off the coast of Ireland. Women, children, and American citizens were among the thousand lost. International law could obviously crumble when Germany, squirming under Britain's blockade, reverted to the Neanderthal instinct of self-preservation. In the United States, war news began to supplant the latest local murder in the tabloids. The country was shocked, disapproving, and more determined than ever to dissociate itself from the unprincipled piracy that held Europe in its grip. President Wilson announced his "too proud to fight" doctrine in spite of the small band of fire-eaters pressing for involvement.

Bellows wrote Joe Taylor in June on other matters: "Wish you could see my things for the past two years. I have been trying to discover dignity in powerful colors. I have been painting with the pure stuff and arriving at a richer statement with more reserve than before. This sounds paradoxical. But great, dignified masses can just as well or better often be made with powerful colors as with grays. Would you like to see Whistler's reserve in pure Orange and Blue? It can be done."

Then he launched into their summer plans: "We are going to Ogunquit, Maine . . . Ogunquit is not as hard to reach as Monhegan or as far." Even his mother was joining them, so why shouldn't the Taylors? He ended his letter with: "Come on, Joe, beat it East!"

Ogunquit represented a compromise in the Bellows family. George wanted Monhegan again, and Emma, who dreaded the water especially with German submarines drowning American citizens without warning, wanted none of it. If George must have Maine, let him stay ashore. Emma, with two small children of her own as hostages, won the day for Ogunquit, where they spent an uncomfortable summer.

They rented a cottage on the major road of the little Maine fishing village. Artists, musicians, and people of little talent had only recently discovered the place. But Kroll came and Henri too, and George was anxious to mend the fences damaged by the Panama-Pacific episode. Old Mrs. Bellows and the Storys came. Everybody met in the Bellows' living room of an evening, and the opportunity for song was an opening George could not resist. There were beach parties complete with driftwood fires, Jean sleeping by Emma in a wad of blankets, and Anne dancing like a seasprite by herself on the sand.

Yet the summer was a poor one for the artist. It was foggy, and his best paintings of the season were two studio nudes. One, "With a Parrot," was promptly bought by Gertrude Vanderbilt Whitney. The other, "Torso of a Girl," evoked a proper criticism from his mother, the daughter and granddaughter of whaling captains: "It's bad enough, George, to paint a girl with both of her breasts bare, but to show only one is nasty."

The Henris arrived late, giving fair warning in advance. They brought with them an incredibly beautiful girl of sixteen, Lucie Bayard. As a member of the Henri household she helped Marjorie, posed for Robert, and attracted all of Ogunquit's youth into the Henri circle. George made the mistake of asking the girl to pose for him. He produced a splendid portrait, but Henri, the Panama-

Pacific Exposition still rankling, took this invasion of his household hardly. The summer came to an uneasy end.

Throughout these vacation days, little flecks of rumor from New York began to cloud Bellows' horizon. Ensconced in its new, low-ceilinged palace on Forty-Fourth Street, the Harvard Club was attempting to maintain the best standards of Cambridge, Massachusetts, as its oldest inhabitants understood them. Dark paneling, thick carpets, and discreet light discouraged anything lively in this *sanctum sanctorum*. George had been disappointed about the way his portrait of Judge Olney appeared in these surroundings. The members of the club who saw it during the vacation season were scandalized. Where were the sober black and whites of Hopkinson and Sargent? These colors used by those Socialist painters were as vulgar as any of them had seen at the Armory Show. Still, it was summer with most of the important members away.

Labor Day came, and in its wake the Sons of Harvard returned from Nahant, the Berkshires, Newport, and Southampton to do battle with the market and the courts. Some of them were so well advised in the arts that they had a course with Charles Eliot Norton, and the kettle of discontent that had simmered all summer now broke into a shriek of protest that threatened to burst the clubhouse. Mr. Burlingame, responsible for the whole situation, wrote an embarrassed letter to the painter:

"There's an awful how-do-do about the portrait of Olney. He [the judge] has now come out in the open and said he cannot bear to have it hung on the walls of the Club . . . Of course those chaps up at the Club don't know the difference between a portrait and a Uneeda Biscuit advertisement . . ."

The storm at the Harvard Club reached an almost undignified peak, and Mr. Burlingame wrote again, urgently: "The Committee of Art and Literature, so-called, has recommended . . . that the portrait of Mr. Olney not be accepted . . . As was said by a famous lady to a strong man of old, 'The Philistines be upon thee' . . . Meanwhile I think the portrait had better go back to your studio."

During this urban whirlwind the unsatisfactory summer in Ogunquit had come to an end. George, impatient and proud as a wounded bull, refused to compromise. He wrote the secretary of the Harvard Club that he was shocked to have Mr. Burlingame offer to settle the crisis through his private means: "This would not satisfy me for the shoddy respect in which my work has been held by the Art Committee of the Harvard Club. Nor do I wish to have my work pass into the possession of anybody who holds it in slight regard. But when I am solicited as a distinguished painter to undertake the commission of a portrait, when after months of earnest consideration bringing all my energies and ability to bear on the matter, and when the result in my own judgment and in the judgment of the men most competent . . . to judge is a most unusual success then I feel and rightly that the matter has been successfully concluded . . .

"The Harvard Club owes me fifteen hundred dollars . . . I will settle for seven hundred and fifty dollars, if I am also allowed to retain the painting, and I will not deviate from these terms."

The eminent art critic Forbes Watson had been squeezed into defending the Club's position. Artists do not ordinarily risk alienating the press, but Bellows wrote him "with a certain feeling under the collar," caring nothing about the consequences. He began his lengthy letter with a complimentary paragraph, and then launched into his grievances:

"For all I know this is the first letter written by an artist on the 'Sins of the Critics.' Let this, then, be the title of the work.

"You certainly could not expect me to be pleased or flattered with what you wrote about the portrait. I like the canvas for precisely those qualities you say it does not possess.

"About the business—the moral situation in regard to the work in question, there are no two statements of the case . . . A man is commissioned to do a work to the best of his ability. This he does. It is only in the case of the artist among all other men that the client presumes to pay if he pleases. Doctors, Lawyers, Shoemakers, Plumbers, when they do their work to the best of their ability, have to be paid. The client has a standing at law, unless he can prove absolute negligence.

"The artist is afraid of the law and afraid of creating prejudice against himself. The client usually gets away with his scurvy trick . . . What picture, may I ask you, in the Club's collection is a better work? I think that you will admit they are all very ordinary things . . .

"Every one of you critics has the complacent idealism of believing you are helping 'the cause of art.' . . . With this in mind you all become school teachers, giving out marks of good, bad and indifferent.

"Helping 'the cause of art,' the bourgeois is only strengthened in his distaste. The casual reader would imagine art dead or dying . . .

"I am glad I do not feel this way, and I am glad that I stand almost alone in saying so . . .

"Now the cause of art is the war on stupidity. The critic should realize that he is not competent to teach the artist. He may be competent to teach the public.

"What the world needs is art, art, and more art; art in social and economic relations, in religion and government. We have a vast deal of science, of flying machines, singing, talking, moving, hearing, tasting, smelling, feeling machines, but great emptiness of imagination, a great barrenness of beauty.

"For all men who are sowing the seeds of imagination and beauty you should fight with unqualified enthusiasm. Let their faults and their failings go to hell. You at least cannot help them. They are usually well known to their victims and obvious to the enemy."

In the end the Harvard Club paid him nothing. He showed the portrait many times. It took no prizes. Two years later he could look benignly back on the whole episode:

"I painted a famous old man for a famous New York Club House. I put my kind of imagination into it. I wanted to make him live just as he was. It seemed to me that if the club members wanted him painted, they would want him as they knew him. And then I made a canvas with the color that belonged to life, full of it; but the art committee of the club sent the picture back. And now I am very glad of it. I like it around, because it has come to be regarded as one of the best portraits I have ever painted."

The picture is certainly full of both color and force. The fact that George depicted his sitter as the personification of Old Testament justice is perhaps the reason that the Harvard Club found it hard to live with.

In spite of his furious preoccupation with the Olney portrait, he could not have failed to note as 1915 drew to a close that the year had been a good one for him financially. The Rhode Island School of Design had paid him $1,000 for a portrait of Walter Littlefield and $959.04 for "Rain on the River," although in its time that painting had been called "ultra modern" and "freakish, affected and doomed to an early grave." Three Monhegan sketches, "Emma at the Piano" and "Paddy Flannigan" had been bought by private collectors. The Chicago Art Institute had thought $1,300 a fair price for "Love of Winter" and had awarded "Anne in a Big Chair" its Second Harris Prize of $300. Lectures, classes, and illustration commissions had yielded $650. When someone abstracted his drawing "Reducing" from the *Masses* office he collected $50 in insurance, although he never charged the paper a cent. All in all his tally for the year went into the ledger "Income from My Proffesion" as a tidy $6,530.54.

Into the New York winter scene Isadora Duncan swept with assured grace and the relentless purpose of establishing a permanent School of the Dance. It would, of course, be *her* School where her chosen girl disciples, the "Isadorables," could learn through the movement of their bodies the finest sensations of their minds. The capitals of Europe and their captains of finance had sympathized and promised, but since England and the Continent were doing their best to bayonet themselves out of existence, Isadora now sought help at home.

Her agent had discovered an enormous room for her to use as a rehearsal hall and as a setting for her inimitable self. She shut out the view of the city with long draperies of her favorite blue and livened the space with rosy scarves and brilliantly covered couches tucked away in the less lighted spaces. A piano, pianist, and Isadora completed the scene, except when the Isadorables swept gracefully in to practice their numbers and decorate the couches. Here the brilliant woman whose first two children had drowned in the Seine and whose third had recently died in infancy set out to rebuild her tempestuous career.

Over the years of trouping through the higher levels of entertainment Isadora had perfected a unique form of the dance and had also flooded her not-very-selective mind with a lobster-trap assortment of ideas. When the wealthy of the world showered her with personal assistance but failed to support her school, she became convinced that there was something inherently wrong with money and that her only hope rested in the underprivileged. She developed an unfortunate custom of treating her audiences to an enthralling performance and then breaking aesthetic distance to make a rambling speech across the footlights. Her harangue against money brought silent embarrassment to her tuxedoed backers in the front row and thunderous applause from the gallery. In one way or another, she tided herself over bad debt after bad debt and maintained her elaborate rehearsal hall as a magnet for the intelligentsia, the dedicated, and the curious.

Bellows found himself entirely in sympathy with her theories about society. He was also heart and soul in support of any movement that would promote the importance of art, and he was enormously impressed with Isadora as a person. The great actress Eleanora Duse had said of Isadora: "But she has strength! What strength!" when the actress had come to her after the drowning of her children. George had strength too, and he admired it in others.

Her studio was not far from East Nineteenth Street, and without any urging from Henri, a long-time devotee of Isadora's, George and Emma spent an evening there. Isadora received her guests in a recumbent position, gracefully offering her hand with a gesture that confused some of the newcomers. When Ben Ali Haggin's mother said graciously: "Please don't get up," Isadora retorted sweetly, "I have no intention of doing so." The dancer's personal beauty and charm, the loveliness of her every movement, the drama of the setting, and the compatibility of the gathering caught George up in a warm embrace. Artists, authors, all kinds of interesting people made it the kind of environment he loved best. Emma was not impressed and rarely came again, preferring to keep a relaxed sentry duty over her marital battlements, while George returned night after night to Isadora's place of enchantment.

Emma's confidence was not misplaced. One evening, when Ethel Clarke came to supper, George announced that he was going to look in on Isadora. Would the ladies come? They declined, and when he had gone Emma chuckled and said: "Do you suppose this will be the night she asks him to father her next child? She does, you know."

Isadora firmly believed in eugenic parenthood. With an un-shakable self-confidence she considered her own perfection of mind, body, and spirit something that should be shared only with the most suitable of the other sex. Her three children had all had different fathers without benefit of clergy or a justice of the peace. How often her invitations were rebuffed is not known. The gruff, sensitive sculptor George Gray Barnard is said to have re-fused her. George Bernard Shaw used to relate that when she sug-gested to him that her body and his brains should combine in a perfect child he replied: "But what if it had my body and your brains?" In Europe tales of this kind were not news. In America they were salacious tidbits. The press censored her conduct, and thundering denunciations were poured on her head from dozens of pulpits. She had no objection to the publicity.

Ethel Clarke was still chatting with Emma when the front door opened and closed with a bang. George, swearing lustily, tramped heavily up the stairs past the room where they were sitting and headed for his studio and his rocking chair. As he passed, Emma called out cheerily: "Did she ask you?" It was a long time before he admitted that she had.

The short days of winter rarely provided enough light for paint-ing, but new designs kept popping into his mind or old ones that wanted reworking. His restless thoughts turned to print-making, as readily done in artificial as in natural light. Years before he had tried his hand at etching, but immediately had abandoned it. Sloan had established a profitable reputation in the field, but there was something impersonal about that medium that repelled him. To cut through a layer of wax to a copper surface, the sharp point of the stylus unable to change its breadth, and to rely on acid to etch upon the plate one's inmost thoughts had no appeal for Bel-lows. For years he had found the lithographic crayon, soft but sensitive to manipulation, a responsive vehicle for his drawings. Lithography had long since been out of fashion, considered a commercial tool. But George thought of Daumier rather than Goya and realized that the crayon, thick and greasy, could produce the quality of an original drawing a hundred times if applied to the proper stone. He bought a half dozen of them and a press and began to test his hand.

His friends were shocked. "Everybody is buying etchings," they protested. "Nobody wants lithographs these days."

"Then they will," shouted George, as enthusiastic over his new medium as if he had just received a new medal. He transformed the balcony over the studio into a print shop, building cabinets to store the stones and inks and crayons of his new profession. He would sit up half the night working over old designs—"Stag at Sharkey's," "Prayer Meeting," "Hungry Dogs"—and inventing new ones. At first he cautiously executed his drawings on paper and transferred them to the stone, but the process was too slow and he rapidly discarded it to draw directly on the stone.

Collier's gave him a chance to try out his new medium by commissioning him to execute, at $100 apiece, three drawings of heavy-weight Jess Willard in training for his forthcoming bout with Frank Moran. Big Jess, the "Pottawattomie Giant," was very much in the public eye because of his conquest of Jack Johnson the year before. He was the "White Hope" who came through. Bellows paid a good many visits to the gym where Willard trained and, hunched up at the ringside, watched the champion go through his routines, interspersed with some time-honored clowning. The sparring partners were usually big men; but Willard's manager, hoping to build up some speed in his clumsy charge, hired some smaller boxers to nip around him in fast time and needle him into quicker reactions. Good-natured Jess thought this a waste of energy. One of his jokes was to raise his huge arms above his head and invite his small tormentor to punch him at will. This act caught George's fancy, and he turned it into a print for his own market under the title of "Training Quarters." It is by no means his best, but it has a peculiar interest in that two of his drawings for it have survived to show how carefully he studied the details that never became a part of the final lithograph.

Chilly spring was in the air, and with it came the perennial problem of summer plans. Sloan had already decided on Gloucester and planned to pay it a pre-season visit with Randall Davey, who happened to own a handsome new Mercedes. They invited George to join their excursion and, hopefully, to join them for the summer. The Mercedes had no windshield. Early one frigid morning, Davey rode gaily from his Fourteenth Street garage, picked up a well-bundled Sloan, and came to a stop in front of 146 East Nineteenth Street, his fist squeezing his raucous taxi horn. George emerged in a huge ulster, collar up-turned, holding in one hand an enormous piece of cake and in the other a diminutive suitcase which he had no doubt built himself and labeled in very large letters: "Anne."

In April and May he continued with his lithographs and painted only one satisfactory portrait, "Olivia Sterner." But there were diversions.

Anthony Comstock, champion of civic virtue in its every guise, disapproved the growing disregard for the laws against birth control. He had made trouble for Margaret Sanger. His present target was Emma Goldman who, with her talent for writing her own laws, was shouting the doctrine wherever she could find an audience. She was arrested in February, 1916, and her supporters registered their protest in Carnegie Hall.

The night before her trial in April, some of these stalwarts, including Henri, Bellows, and Sloan, gathered their forces for dinner at the Brevoort, and the next day cheered her through her choice of sentence between fifteen days in the workhouse or $100 fine. When she was duly released, they escorted her in triumph to receive an accolade, again in Carnegie Hall.

The Bellows family noisily debated their summer plans. George wanted no part of Gloucester, and he had found Ogunquit dull. Emma again thought Monhegan too distant and too perilous with German submarines infesting the water she disliked. They settled on Camden, further north along the Maine coast. Here were spectacular, rounded hills, a picturesque harbor, a remoteness from casual summer visitors.

They moved there early in June, and George fell into a wretched mood. His mother, his mother-in-law, his wife and two daughters, the inevitable maid who was certain to be homesick for New York—all were there leaving him in charge of an assorted harem if one discounted his father-in-law who had joined the party. Domesticity had him in its grip, and he hated every bit of it. It rained a great deal, keeping the household members indoors much of the time, each working on the other's nerves. The move had been more expensive than anticipated. The exchequer was dangerously low. He appealed to Henri for a loan of $100, which the master sent when he could scrape it together, along with the following observation: "Don't bother about the rain you are having in Camden—the weather here is rotten, not very hot, but it rains every few minutes. I've still got the 'out west' idea, but have made no plans so far."

Shortly after this Henri left to explore Mabel Dodge's new center for intellectuals in Taos, New Mexico. Sloan and Davey were lodged in Gloucester. Bellows, desperate for the familiar company he depended on, wrote Kroll, who nobly left his carefully chosen retreat for the season and moved to Camden into a shed adjacent to Bellows' house. Leon's pleasant needlings restored George's good humor, and the skies cleared. He put up a swing in the yard for Anne and went back to work.

Camden, with its miraculous fountain of water plunging into its narrow harbor, was a romantic town. There was tennis for Emma at the club around Sherman Point. The swimming was good if one could bear the frigid water. George and Leon found that they could. The house was comfortable and presently began to bulge with passing friends. The newspapers were full of news of the campaigns in Europe, and the local gossip rippled with rumors of submarines sighted off the coast. George cursed war and its futility and began to paint diligently.

The shipyard drew him like a magnet, for in it a huge wooden skeleton was pushing its great curved timbers to the sky. This furnished the theme for four major canvases: "The Teamster," "Shipyard Society," "Builders of Ships," and "The Skeleton." In them all he played the arcs of the giant ribs against the geometric precision of the scaffolding, underscoring the scale by the workmen or the small white houses in the distance. In an article written the following year he said of these pictures: "When I paint the beginning of a ship at Camden, I feel the reverence the ship builder has for his handiwork. He is creating something splendid, to master wind and wave, something as fine and powerful as Nature's own forces . . . When I paint the colossal frame of the skeleton of his ship I want to put his wonder and his power into my canvas, and I love to do it."

That summer he experimented with blacks again, and many of his paintings done in June and July are remarkable for their dramatic contrasts of light and shade. One of these, "In a Rowboat," dramatized a little incident that occurred outside the harbor. Kroll was rowing George, Emma, and Anne back from a morning at the club when a sudden squall pounced down from the great round hills with a malevolent splendor of streaming black and white clouds. The two artists were so entranced with this spectacle that they forgot the peril of their position. Then the placid waves around them became a maelstrom, dumping gallons of water into the overloaded craft which threatened to capsize. As Leon struggled to keep the bow into the wind, George whispered in his ear, "If we capsize you look after Anne and I'll take Emma." Meanwhile Emma, who still could not swim a stroke, was bailing away as fast as she could, the only calm person in the perilous situation.

From the outside came news both bad and good. In San Francisco a bomb exploded in the middle of a Preparedness Day parade. Anarchists were blamed for this outrage, and Tom Mooney was arrested. Liberals of all kinds believed that the crime was committed by others to discredit the anarchists. At this time George wanted no part of either war or preparedness therefor, and his sympathies were certainly divided between principle and circumstance.

The good news he reported to Henri: "Bum pen, Short note. Sold 'In Virginia,' $2000.00, 25% to M. Knoedler kindness of Mrs. Sterner. Return your loan with thanks."

There were picnics on the beach, with string music, song, and campfires. There were the inevitable scrub baseball games, excursions through the hills, and drives to Rockport and Rockland. Emma liked all these. George, however, was finding the mainland too tame, better than Ogunquit to be sure, but not half as exciting as an island. He remembered their earlier trip to Mattinicus, that tiny island further out than Monhegan, so remote that only by climbing the lofty hills behind Camden could it be seen from shore.

September came. His mother and the Storys with the little girls departed, while he and Emma took the mail boat from Rockland to Mattinicus.

The reef-lined harbor of the little island faces east, protected from the Atlantic by the smaller islet of Crehaven. Around the massive cube of the dock the fish houses stand on their long piles like a disorganized flock of weather-beaten herons. The tides wash against them with a powerful pulse, now high, now low. Mattinicus lacked the spectacular headlands and thick forest of Monhegan, but was more primitive, each family a self-sufficient entity with its fields, cattle and chickens, small boats, and lobster traps. George rented a small story-and-a-half house on the main (and only) street and a fish house near the pier for a studio and settled down to painting in earnest. There was a fine broad block of wood usually used for cleaning fish which made an admirable palette and there were wide doors he could fling open to watch the water lapping against the dock while cloud shadows raced over the sunlit shore and sea. The barnacle-crusted piles supporting sheds and shacks massed in vertical lines or isolated in ungainly lankiness provided him with fascinating shapes and patterns. The trim little farms, hulled down against the wind, the big ledge behind the harbor piously called "Mount Ararat," the oxen toiling away from the pier—all these were daily noted as September turned the long grasses from green to gold, and sumach splashed the rocks and firs with red and orange.

They crossed the narrow strait to Crehaven, clambered over the low, rocky hills where sheep and horses roamed at will, so much a part of the landscape that George began including them in his pictures much as he had peopled his streets and tenements with the swarming humanity of the city. The utter sequestration of these islands within the envelopment of sea and sky probed new depths into his interpretations. The finest of these, "Crehaven," with a broad line of reflected light moving in the calmness of infinity across the water, is as romantic as any of Davies' pastorales and infinitely more robust.

By October they were back in Camden, lingering through an autumn too garish to be missed. They kept fires burning in the rooms they used the most, while George sketched in colors worthy of Derain and Matisse in their most *Fauve* vein. The Sherman Point area particularly intrigued him, allowing him to splash his tapestry of tones above the cool blue of the inlet.

This he reported to Henri who had asked him to lend some pictures to an exhibition in Chicago: "I am very well fixed to accept this flattering invitation as I have available almost everything I ever did. I have just returned from Mattinicus where I had a great time and did extra fine work. I am not trying to complete everything, but rather searching for new ideas and impressions and trying to learn as much as possible . . ."

Randall Davey's season with Sloan in Gloucester had apparently turned out badly: "He didn't do any raving about a successful summer, and I hear from Kroll who heard from Snell who heard from Gloucester that there was much politics, social and moral scandal, and general atmosphere of felinity. Not for me!"

Washington wanted him to choose two Henris for a loan show at the Corcoran Gallery, but he wisely told Henri that the choice was up to him. "I am doing my best to get some of the young fellows invited—McFee, Weber, Halbert, DuBois, etc. Kent, Kroll, anybody else? I have the entire list of the old 'eight' in my hands." He speculated on the character of the jury of selection: "Are they human?"

The gold and orange turned to brown and fell away. Before the end of October, Bellows alerted Henri of his impending departure:

"We will be in N.Y. Thurs. between 12 and 3 P.M. Keep that night at least partly for us.

"Have a great surprise for my friends and an even greater special delight for Marjorie [Henri] for since May 1st the Barber [Emma] has been rubbing my head and I will have a new head of hair for my friends on that date. Will not mention that I can drive a car, although in fact I can.

"Hope your pictures will be on view Thursday afternoon. If I can shake my wife I'll be with you. My stuff should be available in the evening. With chaumping at the bit and furious impatience, Geo."

He did not forget Camden immediately on his return to New York. His portrait of "Anne with a Japanese Parasol" is entered in his accounts with the subtitle "Autumn Leaves and Purple." At the same time he painted Baby Jean with a mischievous grin, a bright blue book, and a very red apple. Then he abandoned his easel and moved up to the balcony and his lithographic stones.

The designs fairly poured from his press, at such a rate that he wrote in his book under the date of January 1, 1917: "During the past year I have made twenty-eight lithographs of approximately 50 proofs each." To this Emma later added four more titles. There is no way of determining the order in which the prints were drawn. Since "Prayer Meeting" was the first one entered, Emma stated that it was also the first one printed. She may very well have been right. But the fact that "Willard in Training" appears far down on the list, although the subject was much on his mind about the time he began lithography, makes it seem likely that he simply put down the titles as the prints happened to lie in his portfolio.

The titles represent a synthesis of all his subjects except pure landscape and portraiture. "The Old Rascal" pays his debt to Daumier, "Hungry Dogs" and "Splinter Beach" pay his debt to Henri. In "Introducing the Champion" and "Between Rounds" he recalled the prize ring which he had not touched on in painting for seven years. With "Benediction in Georgia" and "Artist Judging Works of Art" he became the social satirist. In "Mother and Children" and "The Family" he struck a note that carried the intimate tone of so many of his later prints.

"Reducing," a commentary on a current fad, prodded the eminent critic, Royal Cortissoz, into complaint. He was ordinarily good-natured toward the rebellious Bellows, but on this lithograph he took a stand:

"I wish there were more enchantment of style, of feeling, to match that which attaches to Mr. Bellows' lithographs as technical triumphs . . . The print called 'Reducing' is representative of his taste. While the husband snores in bed a fat woman reclines upon the floor and uplifts a hideous leg. He offers it as 'a study that started out in a humorous vein but developed into a drama of light and dark' . . . The subject, as a subject, might pass. It is the mere ugliness of form, an ugliness unredeemed by beauty of drawing or style, which repels . . . Life, as Mr. Bellows sees it, is singularly barren of charm. Whether he is studying the nude model or drawing the heroes of the prize ring he appears to find form an affair of brute strength, never beauty, and this view of the matter enters the very grain of his art."

Cortissoz had little in common with an artist who said, more than once: "There is no beauty without strength."

At Christmastime Bellows issued his first Christmas card. Sloan had sent his friends little etchings at this time of year. Now "The Studio," an intimate glimpse of life on the top floor of 146 made its rounds among a host of friends and admirers in New York and Columbus. The concept was purely romantic—Mrs. Story telephoning from the landing, Anne and Jean playing under the Christmas tree, these were episodes never to be associated with the artist posing his wife on the model's stand.

Yet Christmas with the Bellows' was an extraordinary event. The ceremony began at the dinner table with chicken, mashed potatoes and another vegetable, mince pie, and ice cream—then up to the studio.

George was no believer in medieval customs, but the little tree was always immaculately adorned. He always took the part of Santa Claus, without the red suit and whiskers. He sat everyone in a circle and commanded silence on the penalty that he might forget his lines. The presents were elaborately wrapped with funny inscriptions. If there was no card, he made one up as he went along. On one occasion he produced, as the *pièce de résistance,* an intricately wrapped box, interlarded with ribbons and messages, all to Emma. Revealed, the gift was a gleaming white toilet seat with the inscription: "Hoping this may end the war!" Then, for the benefit of guests, George explained the present. For a long time he and Emma knew they needed a new seat. George said that getting a new one was "woman's work." Emma said she would not buy one from a man. So George visited the plumbing shop several times, but the boss was sick and his wife (young and pretty) was in charge. Finally, he bribed a boy to make the purchase for him. At least, this was his story.

The Bellows children had already established their own small personalities in adult surroundings. Anne was quiet and accommodating. A good part of her earliest years had been spent with her grandparents in Upper Montclair where she was the center of attention. At 146 she was so much spindrift at the edge of a turbulent sea, and she found it expedient to observe life without comment. She found it easier to eat what was set before her—milk excepted—than to complain, and she developed a mysterious technique of her own in disposing of what she did not like. Given a child's tea set for four, she brought it out every afternoon and formally poured for three absent guests. When Leon Kroll, who knew about this ceremony, once asked her pleasantly whom she was entertaining, Anne looked up seriously and replied: "God and Rembrandt and Emma Goldman," the three names most frequently heard in the Bellows household.

Jean, on the other hand, modeled herself on her father from the start. Like him, she had a highly selective appetite, and when something she disliked appeared, she roared, threw her dinner on the floor, and clawed the air until she finally got what she wanted. Emma was amused by this tempestuous infant, especially when George took over the discipline. Then the house would rock for a while, and he would scratch his balding head and exclaim, "Where in hell does that child get her vitality? And her temper?"

Exhibitions were his first problems for 1917. Milch wanted a one-man show. Bellows made it mildly retrospective, but three-quarters of the canvases were of Camden and Mattinicus. A circulating exhibition went to Emporia, Topeka, Manhattan City, and Lawrence, Kansas; Nashville, Tennessee; and Kansas City, Missouri. His portrait "Geraldine Lee, I" toured Texas under the auspices of the American Federation of Arts. During the year his work appeared in Chicago at The Art Institute, The Arts Club, the Carson, Pirie and Scott Gallery, and at J. W. Young's; and in New York at Macbeth's, the National Arts Club, the Independent Exhibition, and the National Academy.

The year got off to a good start with prizes: the Pennsylvania Academy's Temple award for his "Day in June," and the National Academy's Isador medal for "Doris in the Parlor." Later in the season, "Day in June" joined Detroit's permanent collection for $1,000.

All winter and spring he continued with lithography, painting very little. Exercise came in the form of squash racquets, and then he took up a new, less strenuous game. Thanks to his parents-in-law, Randall Davey owned not only a pool table but a room to put it in. From this he supplemented his income by forming a club, the membership including the Henris, Sloans, and George and

Emma Bellows. The group foregathered frequently, the click of the balls particularly appealing to Henri, while the ladies chatted away on feminine topics as though they were at a studio session.

At one such meeting Emma came in with bright eyes and glowing cheeks, settled down quickly, and burst out happily: *"We sold a picture!"* Dolly Sloan never forgot that moment. Jealous of her husband's reputation and sensitive to his lack of sales, she never lost an opportunity to persuade John that George was a dangerous and unworthy crony. Bruised by experience and uncomfortably aware that his paintings rarely sold, John found this advice hard to ignore. Emma, who had intended no malice, cared nothing for the resultant coolness for she thoroughly disapproved of Dolly. If George noticed any change of relationship he gave no sign, continuing his enthusiasm for and promotion of the older artist and his work.

The United States was hovering on the brink of war. Only President Wilson's reluctance to involve the nation kept patriotic ferment in check. Bellows, like everyone else, felt the excitement plucking at his sleeve while his head and, he liked to think, his heart were determined to resist it. Everybody was hiring halls and making speeches, and often the artists would join the audience. George and Emma went to one of these in Carnegie Hall with the Sloans and Henris. One of the speakers was Helen Keller, whose enunciation was so poor that she required an interpreter. Dolly Sloan thought this was fine and applauded steadily and loudly. Marjorie Henri disagreed and hissed so venomously and moistly that her husband literally dragged her from the box and took her outside. Later, when George was asked what he thought of the speech, he said between the "thunder" [Dolly] and the "rain" [Marjorie] he did not hear much of it.

His work at the time reflected almost nothing of his political indecision. One lithograph, probably inspired by the San Francisco bombing, was a lampoon entitled "Prepare, America!" in which a pretty girl pins a button on the chest of a weak-chinned, foolish young man. Another, "Electrocution," graphically indicted capital punishment. He reworked two canvases begun the summer before, but continued his fascination with print-making. Sometimes he repeated earlier designs—"Dance in a Mad House" and "The Sawdust Trail" were done that spring. On other occasions he treated familiar themes, such as "The Life Class" and "The Street," in an entirely original way.

During the winter and spring of 1917, George Bellows had a decision to make that wrenched his thinking to the core. Only when Wilson defeated Hughes in the 1916 election, by so narrow a margin as to make every man recount his stakes, did Bellows grapple with the idea that what makes the immediate future is based on the men who can implement it. Wilson was no Debs, but Wilson was in the saddle, and had now won a new supporter. Wilson, the dedicated pacifist, inspired another of George's cartoons for "The Masses," a Christ in prison stripes, indicted for "language tending to discourage men from enlisting in the United States Army."

The drawing was published in one of the last issues of "The Masses," July, 1917. By that time Bellows, like the President of the United States, had had a complete change of mind.

In April, when Wilson finally asked for a Declaration of War, Bellows was writing an article for *Touchstone* that expressed his new resolution.

"I am a patriot for beauty," he stated firmly. "I would enlist in any army to make the world more beautiful. I would go to war for an ideal far more easily than I could go for a country. Democracy is an idea to me, it is the Big Idea.

"I am going to California for the summer and paint my head off—and then I'll do my stunt for democracy—if it comes out that way . . . I can see the point of view of the Pacifist . . . But where the Patriot gets it over the Pacifist in my mind is that he does not have a chance to be a coward . . .

"I hate the thought of fighting—but I am all for democracy . . . I have been called a Revolutionist—if I am, I don't know it. First of all I am a painter, and a painter gets hold of life—gets hold of something real, of many real things. That makes him think, and if he thinks out loud he is called a revolutionist.

"I am deeply interested in real life. I want to see it, and I want to paint it, and God knows I don't want to destroy it. But there you are. If you think, you see democracy looming large for the whole world. If you think, you know democracy has got to win—not in this nation or that, but freedom for the whole world."

This statement cut him off from the philosophy of his old associates, but it did not sever his old relationships among the

artists. Bellows urged the importance of *The Masses* when its dis-
solution was imminent even though his and Max Eastman's ideas
now ran in separate channels. If Wilson thought an active participation in the war imperative, George wanted to take part. He was
never an onlooker if he could help it, especially if the stakes were
high.

Thomas, his near neighbor, was responsible for their summer in
California by arranging for him to paint the portrait of the small
son of a wealthy mine owner in San Mateo. George was delighted
to have an excuse to see the West Coast. His family, of course,
would go with him.

Emma's enthusiasm was considerably less. A change of scene?
Yes. A transcontinental trip with Jean still in diapers? No. Finally
she capitulated, and set about accomplishing a domestic miracle
with recalcitrant Jean, while George went on ahead to find suitable accommodations. He had heard of Carmel, a summer colony
of artists and writers picturesquely poised on the coast midway
between the two great cities of California. At the end of May he
was there, and promptly fell in love with the place. He wrote
Henri:

"This is an artist's colony, wonderfully ugly. Looks like a Methodist camp meeting grounds (in spots). We have the 'Queen's
Castle,' the most pretentious dwelling here with lots of rooms and
a fine garden of flowers and trees looking on the sea and almost on
the beach."

The fine white sand squeaked under his feet as he hurried
along it, sometimes plunging head first into the chilly surf. Overhead the stubby pelicans, plodding their earnest echelons, led his
search for subjects south to ragged Point Lobos with its fantastic
old cypresses or north to the level ledge where the Pebble Beach
golf course cut between a rocky scarp and the towering pines and
eucalyptus that clamber up Carmel's steep slope.

"I am always very amused," he wrote in *Touchstone,* "with
people who talk about lack of subjects for painting. The great
difficulty is that you cannot stop to sort them out enough. Wherever you go they are waiting for you . . . It seems to me that an
artist must be a spectator of life; a reverential, enthusiastic, emotional spectator, and then the dramas of human nature will surge
through his mind . . . There are only three things demanded of a

painter: to see things, to feel them, and to dope them out for the public."

To an artist so recently excited over color, Carmel looked like Fra Angelico's vision of paradise on a much grander scale. Point Lobos and all the acres around it ran riot with yellow, orange, blue, and tangles of green. The sea had a warmer, deeper tone than he had ever seen before. The morning fogs created extraordinary effects of light when the sun nibbled their filaments away until only the finest ghost of a haze remained. Then pale emanations from the dips and valleys bathed the hillsides with an ethereal glow. George's pictures that summer and frequently thereafter experimented with this phenomenon, acquiring a new luminosity.

The size of California offered him an excuse to buy a Buick which he called "Georgette." This purchase reflected the rapid change that was taking place on highways all over America. A few years before, any car had been a rich man's symbol; now only the expensive ones were "Bourgeois" in George's parlance, while Henry Ford's Model T was becoming an essential element in the working man's economy. Buick had just been produced as a middle-income car, an ideal compromise for a man whose Socialism barred a Packard or a Rolls Royce, but whose sympathy with Denman Ross' doctrine of superiority made ownership of a Model T an impossibility.

Having mastered the intricacies of spark and crank, and the art of repairing punctures, Bellows proceeded to explore the countryside. But he treated landscape that summer more as an adjunct to figures. "The Fisherman," casting from the rocks on Point Lobos, was far more important to him than the setting. It was not so much the bright sweep of beach that lured him as "The Sand Team" with its heavy frame, patient horses, and laboring men. Only in "The Golf Course" does the sun-drenched mass of fields and hills dwarf the players moving across the foreground.

Again, his *Touchstone* article explained his ideas: "I have been said to have come out of the painting world slowly, handicapped with my respect for old masters. I have been accused of painting without reverence for art before I had mastered my technique. It seems to me that the only way is to get from the past what you can; think, see, live and work . . . And every artist must do it his own way.

"Watch all good art, and accept none as standard for yourself. Think with all the world and work alone."

Emma finally made her departure from New York with the children. George's mother, "Gram," joined them at Columbus looking as jolly and as huge as ever. At every stop Emma would descend to the platform to feel the cool air and stretch her cramped legs. Sometimes she stayed out so long that Anne would panic, fearful lest the train pull out without her mother, and she would find herself alone with her big-nosed giantess of a grandmother and rambunctious Jean. The heat of the Great Plains gave way to the splendor of the Rockies; then the heat of California closed in. They reached Salinas to find George posing proudly beside his Buick before he rushed forward to meet them.

Emma never cared for California. She was perhaps a little like the legendary two old ladies from Boston who went to the West Coast by way of Dedham and reported that they did not like it because it was too far from the sea. She thought the setting too opulent, the people too casual. She mistrusted the occasional sounds of Spanish around her.

George was fairly bursting with delight. He promptly painted Anne in a black velvet dress, a picture that reveals a new sensitivity to textures and an intimate penetration into the world of childhood. He painted Jean again, and two local characters. One of these, called "Padre," shows that he could interpret old age as sympathetically as youth. Then in July, he piled clothes and equipment into the Buick, chugged up the steep main street of Carmel, and made his way northward through the Salinas Valley to San Mateo and master Paul Clark, whose portrait was his reason for coming to California.

He reported regularly to Emma.

"The kid is a nice little fellow and in high key. I think I'll get something out of him . . . Mr. Clark is away in Arizona. He owns the mines where all the trouble has recently been with the I.W.W. He has a nasty job on his hands, I hear."

Bellows was staying with a Mr. Tobin, a friend of his early patron Joe Thomas: "We get up early and play two sets of tennis before breakfast. My pants are pressed every morning and I wore the Jap valet's dinner coat last evening when [my host] had the polo team to dinner."

Later:

"The first two days I painted a life-size full length of master Paul which everybody here is crazy about and which is acclaimed a great masterpiece . . . Mrs. Clark hasn't any criticism to make except a detail of the chair! (Very remarkable.)

"Mr. Tobin is a finer and finer man. He is a bank president and entertained Bourke Cockran when he was here for the Mooney business to the horrible disgust and hatred of many of his banking associates. He is a man of great culture and has a great library which he uses."

Mrs. Clark now wanted master Paul painted standing, full length. Another guest of Mr. Tobin asked to have his portrait done. A San Francisco gallery begged for a show of his work. His departure was delayed several times.

"I finished the big portrait this afternoon and have had nothing to do since 3 o'clock and nobody is home. So I am reading Balzac and going to bed. [The second version of master Paul] is quite unique in my work . . . It is very fine in color, a fine laughing head and very, very successful hands; a setting of curtains and rear light like "Geraldine," [and with] hydrangeas and elephants ears, a toy rabbit and a toy duck, while the boy holds a pencil and big book, looking over his shoulder at something that tickles him; color a green and gold." In all this lengthy description he does not mention that his model wore a Little Lord Fauntleroy suit.

The first, seated portrait has the simplicity and directness of his treatment of street urchins. In the second, the firm hand of Mrs. Clark is everywhere apparent, and only the merry expression of the face, the vitality of eyes and mouth, and the impish twist of the nose save the child from being a monument to parental adoration.

When Bellows returned to Carmel he found his Aunt Fanny Daggett who had so relentlessly tried to make him into a proper little gentleman so many years before. Life with the recently deceased Mr. Daggett had apparently mellowed her, although she was as determined as ever, almost pathetic in her strength. George promptly led her to the model stand and produced a penetrating study which he called "The Widow."

His throat grew rough and inflamed. Nothing seemed to help it.

Swimming, tennis, and hiking over the hills were remedies that he had used for every ailment, but they failed to check the choking swelling. Emma assured him it was nonsense, something to put his mind to, but eventually he sought out a doctor who promptly ordered him to a San Francisco hospital to have his tonsils removed, a safe and simple operation (in the age of innocence before polio) made safer by the snaring technique. It would be a nuisance, but he elected to go.

There were complications, fortunately not medical. He wanted to spend some time with Henri in Santa Fe. The Art Students' League had engaged him to teach for a year beginning October 1. A week in the hospital would forfeit one engagement or the other. His mother wanted to visit a while with her sister Fanny in San Diego. The Queen's Castle doubtless reeked with tobacco and profanity for days while George overrode protests and pleas. Then one morning, he bundled his mother and Aunt Fanny into the Buick, saw them tenderly aboard the train at Salinas, and headed north to the Mount Zion hospital where he was put to bed for three days before the operation.

Physical immobility gave his mind time to invent a dozen ways of plaguing doctors, nurses, and interns and he sprayed letters all over the map like Old Faithful Geyser on an accelerated schedule. The first of these, a long plaintive bit of doggerel composed "in the manner of Robert Louis Stevenson writing 'Paradise Lost,' " began:

> "Here I lie and take my ease
> And write my letters on my knees.
> Remember me to Anne and Jean,
> Anne the slim, and Jean the bean;
> Anne who laughs and Jean who squeaks,
> Jean who squats and Anne who sits
> Anne who dances while Jean has fits;
> Anne who eats and Jean who stuffs,
> Anne in collars and Jean in cuffs.
> Anne the lithe and lank and lean
> And oldest sister of Jean the Bean."

Next day he wrote directly to Anne:
"Dear Anna Banana Bolifloat,
"I hope you are taking good care of Mommie and wiping Jean's

eyes, mouth, chin, stomach and other parts whenever necessary, and keeping her and Mommie quiet and not let either of them cry because they miss me so much, and thinking about your daddy very often, and keeping my studio clean and entertaining all the visitors and writing lots of letters to me."

Then he informed Emma: "I am having as good a time reading, writing, dreaming as could be expected, and am prevented from too much smoking which is doubtless good occasionally . . . I have sent [Mrs. Clark] a tentative price and a rather exhaustive letter on the subject as I am at a loss really about what to do or say in this regard [$2,000.00]." He had missed intimate professional camaraderie at Carmel and kept in constant touch with Henri who suggested a way out of his contract with the League. Why not plead inability to travel and get someone to stand in for him for a month? Bellows wrote Sloan at once, keeping Davey's name in mind in case Sloan could not accept.

He tried every means to cajole Emma into coming to see him, but she wanted no part of illness or hospitals or doctors. His last attempt was practical, for he dreaded the thought of a long, lonely drive: "I might feel a little weak on Saturday and would feel stronger with you beside me in the wilderness. A jug of wine, a Buick and thou . . ." But she ignored the temptation, and he went back to Carmel alone.

They closed up the Queen's Castle, drove to Los Angeles in three days, picked up old Mrs. Bellows, put the Buick on a flat car, and spent an agreeable month in Santa Fe with the Henris. Kroll was there and a strange and stimulating countryside. The communal pueblos fascinated Bellows as much for their social organization as for their picturesque qualities, and he painted them many times.

Henri thought Bellows ought to see Mabel Dodge's experiment in primitive culture at Taos. Emma disdained the long dusty ride, so the Buick departed, stuffed with male artists all intent on their much-talked-about objective. They found it so interesting that they lingered longer than they had intended. Kroll, who had a late afternoon train for New York to catch, began to fidget, but George rallied to the challenge. Over the dry hills and arroyos he forced his Buick with skill and without mercy, enveloped at every bump in an impenetrable cloud of yellow dust. This caused the party to swathe their faces in their bandannas, and by the time they neared the station one and all were coated with a thick ocher layer. Radiator cap steaming and screaming, George swept up to the station to find the eastbound train about to depart. Everyone began to yell hoarsely from behind their masks as the Buick rocketed up to the platform. The brakeman and conductor automatically raised their hands in token surrender, for the hold-up tradition was still strong in that part of the world. The car's brakes held. Kroll swung aboard the train. George Bellows had had a good day.

Other traditions were revived in Santa Fe. Anna Bellows mistrusted the Indians. Once, when some approached George, she cried out: "Stay away from them, George, they're dirty." She and Emma disliked living amid so many Papists who were always crossing themselves as they passed the churches. A great many people talked together in Spanish. In their dual opinion Santa Fe was not a proper environment for Anne and Jean. Late in October, George tagged the Buick for shipment and deposited his paintings at the new local museum for show. Then the whole family entrained for New York.

A fortnight later Bellows was writing Henri about the events in the metropolis. His class at the League, largely female, was progressing satisfactorily. Luks and Kent were both scheduled to lecture and criticize during the next two weeks, and he was battling with Emma who insisted that he dress properly for these occasions.

"The Thomas Eakins exhibition," George continued, "proves him to be one of the best of all the world's masters. The greatest one man show I've ever seen and some of the very greatest pictures. Unfortunately the catalogue reproductions are very bum, but otherwise this show seems to be becoming of very great importance. The photographer got all the details and none of the values. This is deplorable as I like to keep such things when they're good.

" 'Mrs. Frishmuth,' the musical instrument collector, is the most monumental work I ever looked at. 'Dr. Gross' Clinic' must equal 'The Night Watch.'

" 'Man at a Table' good as the best of Renoir and Cézanne. Something here also to remind me of Manet and Titian."

He joked about a current exhibition of contemporaries: "You won't see any of my pictures as Birnbaum will sell them all.

Started off immediately. Showed one in his much discussed exhibition—sold at once. 'The Fisherman,' $2000.00, 1500 to me (joker).

"Buick hasn't come yet, lost on the railroad. War is hell.

"A new star has arisen in the field of art analysis. Jay Hambidge, late illustrator, comes forth as a John the Baptist proclaiming the coming of a new understanding and the key to the Greek mysteries. I am attending a little class of his once a week and think we're on the trail of something which may be worth while. Too new a student to give critical judgment yet." Later he added: "Want you very much to *get in* to Hambidge."

The meeting with Hambidge had been engineered by Kroll who, one evening at the Salmagundi Club, had said: "There's an interesting little guy who gives weekly lectures uptown at his studio. You ought to hear him." They went together, and Hambidge remembered his first meeting with Bellows: "He seemed to forget he was in a very crowded room. Finally at some point he stood up and interrupted. 'Do I understand you to mean——?' He hesitated, and then added, 'Perhaps I could make that clearer if I went to the blackboard.' He pushed his way through the crowd in front of him and, taking the chalk, repeated the diagram on the board without hesitation. Upon being assured that it was correct, he said: 'That is what I wanted to know. Now I understand.' "

Jay Hambidge has been described by people who knew him as "a dignified and dedicated fellow" and as "a pompous little squirt." However others saw him, he became the most important single influence on George's work for the rest of his life.

The doctrine preached by Hambidge was called "Dynamic Symmetry." It consisted of a series of geometric formulae governing the relationships of squares and rectangles within a composition. These involved ratios and roots and elementary mathematics that appealed to Bellows' mind. He came to regard Dynamic Symmetry as "probably more valuable than the study of anatomy. It comes within the range of positive knowledge . . ." To those who protested that it brought art into the realm of science he retorted: "If a thing is made easier by technical understanding, then by so much is it true that having this particular phase made easier, your strength is conserved for those things which remain superbly hard."

Dynamic Symmetry seemed to George an answer to the puzzle

the Cubists had presented, a demonstrable relationship between flat planes. As far as his own work was concerned, although he insisted that most of his late production was based on it, he seems to have used it as affirmation of what he had known from the beginning. In some of his drawings one can see that the lines of the formula have been applied on top of the initial sketch.

Mrs. Story, study for "The Studio," 1919.

All winter long he sat, rocking away with a cigarette in hand and the ratios of Jay Hambidge interlocking in new formations in his mind. "The universe," he wrote, "is made up of a certain number of elements, less than a hundred. The 'period and law' of these elements is *metrical*. They are arranged, not haphazard or in groups, but by number; and those of like quality appear at fixed and regular intervals." When civilization seemed bent on its own destruction, the contemplation of a simple and well-ordered cosmos provided a welcome refuge.

Between these bouts of theory, George and Emma made the usual rounds of theaters, operas, concert halls, and exhibitions. But the war was always with them. It shouted from the headlines

and the recruiting posters on the walls. "Johnny Get Your Gun,"
"Tipperary," "There's a Long, Long Trail A-Winding," drives for
the Red Cross and the Fatherless Children of France and the
Y.M.C.A., railroad stations jammed with troops—George ran
across a copy of the Bryce Reports, those eye-witness testimonies of
German atrocities from the early days of fighting, and was absorbed and horrified by their contents. Man's inhumanity to man
was a challenge to which he always rose. As his rocker creaked back
and forth beside his empty easel the ghastly images evoked by the
reports began to merge with the roots and ratios of Dynamic
Symmetry.

In April, 1918, the Kaiser's armies began their final desperate
drive at the heart of France. Again civilian refugees clogged the
roads with their pitiful belongings. The uncertain terrors of
enemy occupation were resumed. One day, early in the month,
Bellows picked up his lithographic crayon and began an astonishing series of prints, the twentieth-century version of Goya's "Di-
sasters of War." The Spanish master had long been one of his
favorites, but this new portfolio would have been created in any
case. The scenes simply exploded onto the stones.

Each day and far into the night George sat over his sketch board
and his lithographic stones. George Miller, his printer, came in for
long sessions and Emma, from her sitting room on the floor below,
could hear the turning of the press and their excited voices, sometimes cheering, sometimes swearing, as the proofs rolled out, brilliant or blurred or not quite deep enough in tone.

By the end of May Bellows had produced sixteen prints and two
variants of these, an amazing record of more than two designs a
week. Even more astonishing is the variety in the compositions. A
central triangle is common, and Hambidge's Root Five rectangle
provides the basis for "The Enemy Arrive," "Sargeant Delaney,"
and "Massacred." The parallel plane limitations of Dynamic
Symmetry he varied with designs in space, and in "Sniped" he laid
the basis for the composition of his "Crucifixion" painted five
years later.

These eighteen stones produced a grim indictment of war,
sometimes as moving, often as revolting as that of Goya's or of his
French predecessor, Jacques Callot. Violence is there, and tension,
melodrama, and tragedy. George's "Massacred" lacks the instantaneous impact of Goya's "Madrilenos," but his "Last Victim" out-

does Daumier in its stark intensity. The simple dignity of Bellows'
"The Murder of Edith Cavell" appears in the work of neither of
his precursors.

From the start of his print-making activity, Keppel's Gallery
had been Bellows' main outlet. He now deposited them there.
William H. Allison, assistant manager, looked at the record of
atrocity in some dismay. "I *had* to draw them," protested George.
"Oh then," said Allison calmly, "We'll *have* to show them."

Interspersing this six weeks of concentration, the ordinary business of life went on. Two of Bellows' paintings, lent to a new
Philadelphia Gallery, disappeared with its directors and were
never recovered. An indignant female artist accused the Mac-
Dowell Club of discriminating against women, and he had to give
her a reprimand. He even dashed off an amusing little fantasy
entitled "Procrastination Is the Thief of Time" to his nephew
Howard Monett. Its theme was later popularized by Monroe Leaf
under the title of "Ferdinand the Bull." From this kind of leitmo-
tif he would plunge back to his balcony and the revolting starkness of such a print as "The Cigarette."

His earlier lithographs had begun to find a market, sometimes
appreciative as the following note, written by a fellow member of
the Salmagundi Club, shows: "I didn't lose any time going after
that print [Stag at Sharkey's]. I picked that fight theme, and
Gosh! I can't wait to get it home and on the wall. This drawing
has more bowels, entrails and guts than anything I've seen in
many a day and you bet I'm proud to own it."

This adulatory letter, mailed in June, came to an empty house,
for the Bellows family had already established summer quarters in
Middletown, Rhode Island. They had driven down in the Buick
with the Speichers, now their most intimate friends. George and
Gene's long association had been close, but the stress of war and
the conflicting emotions it aroused had drawn them even more
firmly together. Now with millions of Americans straining every
nerve and muscle to end the war across the Atlantic, neither of
them was content to sit idly by with draft cards in their pockets.
The more they read of trench warfare, the less they wanted of the
infantry. Both were romantic to the core. Despite the protests of
their wives they applied for the Tank Corps, then in the process of
organization.

The family settled down in a comfortable farmhouse, surrounded by barns, herds, gardens, and clucking poultry, but George was indifferent to his bucolic surroundings. His mind was still occupied with themes he had explored the past spring. He had brought along four big canvases that he had started in New York, and after some trouble trying to get his easel in a good light he started work on them. In July he produced "Massacre at Dinant," and followed it at one-month intervals with "The Germans Arrive," "Edith Cavell," and "The Barricade." Only when he had finished the last of these in October did he do some ten sketches out-of-doors on his favorite twenty by twenty-four-inch panels, scenes of the farm, of a life-saving station, and of the Newport Hills.

Returning to New York, he found an unexpected fame awaiting him from his war prints at Keppel's. There they came to the attention of Bellows' one-time hero, Charles Dana Gibson, who called them "the finest things that have been done anywhere" and sent them on to the Committee on Public Information in Washington. Later, when he was trying to coax some cartoons from George to use in the original *Life,* Gibson added: "I hope [the lithographs] hang in the room when they discuss peace terms . . . It is a pity these pictures were not made when the war started."

In August, Bellows had sent the freshly finished "The Germans Arrive" to the show window of Scott and Fowles on Fifth Avenue. One E. C. Babcock wrote him: "I don't hesitate to say that to me it is the most impressive thing on Fifth Avenue," and the critic, Frank Crowninshield telegraphed: "Picture at Scott and Fowles immense. Best Thing on avenue."

"The Murder of Edith Cavell" was exhibited at the Anderson Galleries in space set aside for a charitable organization known as the "Allied Salon." As he had caught the perfect expression of physical violence in "Stag at Sharkey's," here he presented the anticipation of violent death with tragic calm.

No single episode in the war so aroused public indignation against the Germans as did their execution of Miss Cavell, a British nurse, before a firing squad. Nothing incidental or momentary entered into George's interpretation of the scene; rather, he gave it through its quiet restraint a timeless universality, relying on vivid contrasts of values to stress the drama of the episode.

Royal Cortissoz of the *Tribune* saw the painting and almost forgave the artist his past sins, including the print "Reducing." He saw in "Edith Cavell" a piece of "circumstantial realism."

"It is quite the finest thing Mr. Bellows has ever done, really rich in that deep tenderly felt beauty which as a rule he would appear to disdain. The scale of colors used in this canvas is not very broad. But the play of light and shade exploited within it is so subtle as actually to enrich the artist's tones. His tragic theme to me is enveloped in an unearthly loveliness."

Joseph Pennell, who had arrogated to himself Whistler's mantle as an etcher, thought otherwise. He told Bellows that he had no business to paint such a scene since he had not been present at the execution. George politely responded that he was not aware that Leonardo da Vinci had "had a ticket to the Last Supper."

He was hard at work on his last war canvas, "The Return of the Useless," when the false Armistice gave place to the real Armistice, and a veritable orgy of peace followed. The shooting war was over, the Allies were victorious, and the final outlawing of war was at hand. Duveen, subsidized by Helen Frick, asked Bellows to immortalize the event in two huge panels, ten-feet high, "Hail to Peace" and "The Dawn of Peace," at $500 each.

In these paintings George embedded all the aspiration of America after the Armistice. The Red Cross nurse had become the personification of healing and of quiet, replacing the slightly motheaten angel that had played the role for so many centuries. The dove, cast in the part of hope since Noah's ark, remained. Doughboys and civilians completed the cast. Allegory was not Bellows' forte, and these subjects gave no scope to the dynamic qualities of his genius. His products are certainly bolder and more universal than Sargent's smoky murals in the Widener Library at Harvard, but for the audience of today they are as dated as the Harding Administration, the W.P.A., and Mussolini's Italy.

With these pictures he put the war behind him, except for a tiny lithographic version of "Hail to Peace" that he printed for his Christmas card. His final painting of 1918, "Portrait of an Old Lady with a Bonnet," showed how desperately he was trying to resume his old stride. In this respect he mirrored the nation's mood—the determined "return to normalcy," the quest for the familiar, the plunge into the bosom of the remembered past, not realizing how that past had withered in the interval.

Tennis at Newport; *lithograph, 1920.*

REORIENTATION

» *1919 - 1921* «

» VIII «   *"What the world needs is art, art, and more art."*
George Bellows

The Peace Conference in Paris began to fit together the jigsaw puzzle that the war had left behind, while the citizenry of the United States attempted to deal with the millennium in its own inspired way. Emotions generated by the recent havoc floodlit all the facets of reform. Abolishing the saloon, even the "demon rum" itself presented no problems to a Congress acutely aware of its starry-eyed constituents. The recent splendid and well-publicized actions of the fair sex on the fringes of the shooting made it easier to crown the efforts of Carrie Chapman Catt and her followers with equal suffrage. The nation clamored to mend a world obviously in need of drastic repair.

These two pending amendments to the Constitution struck George Bellows quite differently. He approved "Votes for Women" because of its egalitarianism; but although virtually a teetotaller himself, he looked on the Volstead Act as an infringement on those individual rights he had always championed.

His professional reputation had never been higher. Writing for *Shadowland,* critic Holger Cahill likened him to John Sloan as "an American of the Americans," to Sandberg's poetry in his "sometimes terrific disorder," and to Whitman for his feeling of awe in commonplace things. Bellows' work, he thought, maintained a healthy respect for any tradition that remained alive, but he did not believe the pursuit of beauty to be "the sole aim of art, particularly when it condemns the artist to a quavering lyricism."

As for George himself, the year began calmly enough. He sparked his classes at the League, picked out pictures for exhibitions, teased his father-in-law, and vied with Speicher on the squash courts and with Henri at the pool table, letting the tensions of the war relax and his own imagination reorient itself. In February he began to paint again, turning to the factuality of portraiture as an antidote for the speculative violence contained in his war portfolio: "The Old Pioneer," "The Little Red Frenchman," "Old Lady with Blue Book." In March he translated the design of his lithograph "The Studio" into an oil, bringing the ages and action of the children up-to-date and studying the subtle gradations of light as it spread over walls and ceiling. He shifted from elderly models to his eight-year-old daughter Anne, painting her blonde charm sheathed in blue-green silk. Then came April, whose sudden sun and showers reflected themselves in his own fortunes.

A big exhibition of his work at Knoedler's attracted an appreciative public, and his pictures began to sell. Four of the little Monhegan panels went at $500 apiece. His larger compositions were finding permanent homes: "The Golf Course" at $2,000, "The Circus" at $2,500, and the once-maligned "Crowd at Polo" at $3,000, his biggest price to date. Even deducting the dealer's commissions, it was a handsome net indeed.

To counterbalance this success, Mrs. Chester Dale began sittings for her portrait. The Dales were already amassing what would become one of the finest collections of contemporary art in America, and success or failure in this assignment might have special consequences for the artist.

Mrs. Dale sat and sat and sat—in April, May, and June. Perhaps the necessity of moving his equipment into the unfamiliar atmosphere of the Dales' apartment bothered him; perhaps he tried too conscientiously. Mrs. Dale complicated matters by insisting on having her dog included in the painting. He may have sensed that Mrs. Dale, for all her admiration of his artistry, did not entirely approve of him—"a bit vulgar, a bit too loud," she confided to others. For whatever reason, two versions of the picture would not oblige either the sitter or the painter, and luncheons at 146 were gloomy affairs as George bolted his meal between angry growls and the children made themselves as inconspicuous as possible. The problem was still unresolved when summer began and the Bellows family reembarked for Rhode Island.

Middletown had not changed during the past eight months, but George saw it with new eyes. The year before he had been entirely absorbed by the war. Now he looked around him and relished everything in sight. He painted the beach under a canopy of luminous clouds, the meadows at Seconnet with Anne, Jean, and the farmer's boy Joseph sitting reflectively in the sun while full-blown foliage warmly enveloped neat white buildings. One day Emma returned in triumph from a shopping expedition with a length of purple silk that exactly complemented one of her favorite blouses. Her quick fingers—she made all her everyday clothes—transformed it into a long, full skirt, and George immediately swept her into a chair and began work on "Emma in the Purple Dress." He wrote Henri: "I think I have painted my best portrait of Emma and a rare picture to boot. A hand and an eye, the width of the shadow side of the head are still in question."

His letter continued: "Mrs. Dale, who has been facing me for two months from the model stand has appeared on my trail in Newport . . ." Maud Dale, dissatisfied with the first versions of her features, had stepped into her limousine one morning determined to settle down on the painter until he gave her satisfaction. He made two more attempts, each without benefit of dog. Once she posed in a purple dress, much simpler and much more expensive than Emma's. Then she wore a white skirt with a red jacket, a broad four-in-hand tie, and a furled umbrella. Chester Dale was delighted with the results, paid $3,000 for the pair, and urged Bellows to rework the first version (with dog). It remained a failure.

He painted Emma again in a new black print dress, using a very restricted palette and modeling her fine features in a full, sculptural light. "On the Porch" grouped his daughters with their cousin Margaret Story, the small forms relaxed within the rigid architectural framework, the warm and casual foreground marked off from the meadows by abstracting rectangles of light and shade.

It was wonderful to be in the open air again. His sketches bore a freshness and a spontaneity that he had denied himself for a year. Even the long-promised visit of Joe Taylor and his family to New York could not tempt him to leave Middletown, although he turned his house at 146 over to them, and gave them complete lists of what to do. The galleries they should see were Montross, Knoedler's, Daniel, Kraushaar, Keppel, Macbeth, Bourgeois, Durand-Ruel, and Ehrich. The restaurants he listed were National Arts Club, Players Club (stag only), Still's and Allaire's on Third Avenue, and the Café Français. At the mention of Petitpas' he added: "When you go there you will probably see an old man with a white beard surrounded usually by several people engaged in talk. This is John Butler Yeats, father of W. B. Yeats, the Irish poet. In his prime he was a great portrait painter. George Moore says he's the greatest conversationalist he ever met. I think so. Go up and introduce yourself to him and tell him I told you to. You'll probably have a fine evening with the old man if he's feeling fit."

One trip to New York, however, Bellows could not avoid. It involved the final arrangements for an exhibition he regarded as of prime importance to international relations. In the spring, full of the postwar enthusiasm that had fairly smothered General Joffre when he visited New York and had nearly cracked President Wilson's pince-nez on his arrival in Paris, the French Ministry of Fine Arts had made a handsome gesture. It proposed an exchange of paintings, the American group to be shown in the Luxembourg Gallery in Paris in the late fall. George found himself along with Henri and a large number of staid academicians on the committee of fifteen to select the American entries. It was obvious that if the choice of the remaining exhibitors were left to a majority vote the progressive elements among contemporary artists would be ignored, and this Bellows was determined to prevent. His proposal, backed by Henri, was revolutionary.

The democratic process of "majority," Bellows urged, should be replaced by the equally democratic doctrine of "representation." The committee should remain an executive committee, but would enlarge the membership of the whole by two simple devices. Each of the original fifteen would submit a list of names of the artists he felt should be represented, and any name that appeared on all the lists would automatically be elected. The remaining choices should be consolidated into a single list from which each member, in order determined by lot, would select one name, this process continuing until the full complement of one hundred painters and twenty sculptors had been chosen.

The proposal was so manifestly fair and its presentation so persuasive that the conservatives were caught napping and accepted it unanimously. But when Bellows' first choice turned out to be Max Weber, the arch disciple of Cézanne and Matisse, eyebrows were raised and Tory heads began plotting evasions. Blissfully unaware of this, George wrote a triumphant article for *The New France,* extolling the plan and exulting in the demise of the old jury system. "And now," he stated, "France and America have come together as never before, and arm-in-arm, the process of intimacy goes on. With kindly curiosity we reach for each other to know and to understand." Before the year was out, his optimism was to be shattered by duplicity on both sides of the Atlantic.

Back in Middletown, George picked up new enthusiasms. During his stay at Crehaven in 1916 he had brought domestic animals into his pictures for the first time. Here they were all around him again commanding his serious attention: "The Young Horse Grazing" was painted with bent neck while the wind combs his mane and chickens scatter around the yard like raucous bits of tumble weed. It was the cattle, however, that claimed most of Bellows' attention: their bulky bodies, heavy shoulders and broad, flat backs moving monumentally over field and hill. "Five Cows," "Boy and Calf," and "Bull and Horses" are titles that wove in and out of the record of his late summer work, interspersed with landscapes, portraits, and tennis tourneys. Whenever the bovine theme appeared it dominated the setting, sometimes blending with it or linking the planes together, usually contrasting arbitrary colors with cool foliage, as grazing beef munched placidly under quiet skies. "The Black Bull" is an exception to this rule. He stands majestically in a clearing, dominating it as surely as the finest beast that ever faced a matador in Madrid, the dark, breathing focus of a little universe bounded by rocks and trees, sun and shade.

Color was very much on his mind again and "The Red Sun," if not entirely successful, is worthy of Bierstadt at his most extravagant. He experimented with atmosphere in "Fog Curtain" and with light in "Dark Day." Through all these canvases he was reliving, refining, amplifying a decade of his own discoveries made fresher by their hibernation during the year just past. Many of his new ideas were incorporated in two versions of tennis games at Newport, where he often went to watch McLaughlin and other stars of the day perform in a game he knew and loved. Yet here, as always, the swift actions of the players were only part of the scene. In these paintings the sport became almost incidental within its environment of late afternoon: creeping shadows, parasols glowing with the sun, and arching elms interlacing with arching galleries and knitting each picture into an entity rather than an incident.

Anna Bellows was with them as usual for a good long stay. Her son called her "the biggest mother in captivity," and her vast bulk made posing a congenial occupation although the rigidity of the model's chair was not as agreeable as the comfortable curves of her rocker. In "Grandma Bellows," George gave her large-featured head the forcefulness that had become his trademark, but in the vibrancy of her hair and throat he embodied a new textural sense he had begun to experiment with in "Old Lady with Bonnet." His "return to normalcy" was proving as progressive as it was satisfying.

The Bellows family was back in New York by the first of October with a thousand things to do. The Luxembourg Show was already on the high seas with its mission of international cordiality; but there were other exhibitions to plan for, Anne had to be started in school, and stock-taking was an event of annual importance. He looked unfavorably at "Fisherman's Family," just returned from a summer in the galleries of England, and destroyed it.

Buffalo had opened a dual show of Bellows' works and those of John C. Johannsen. Within a month these pictures were to move to Chicago and he with them on a special appointment to the Art Institute at $1,000 a month for two months' work. By vigorous application George and Emma achieved a miracle in new clothes, supplies, and arrangements for the winter exhibitions. They survived a round of farewell parties to arrive in Chicago for the opening of his first major exhibition in the Middle West.

Praise from Buffalo greeted his contributions: "George Bellows sets a standard of excellence, neither elusive nor poetical, but direct. In his work is seen strength—a great, broad, muscular strength—with all its imperfections and crudities, its advantages

Cartoon to the Children from Chicago, 1919.

and disadvantages, but above all its apparent sincerity of purpose. George Bellows is a painter of democracy, and a clean, hard worker, however much you may disagree with his methods and his vision."

He had included three of his war paintings: "Massacre at Dinant," "Edith Cavell," and "The Return of the Useless." The commentator found the last of these "horror inconceivable except through the medium of art." Of his two big panels "Hail to

Peace" and "The Dawn of Peace" it was merely noted that they were included in the show. America had almost forgotten the catharsis of the Armistice. The country had taken the peace negotiations in an assured stride, and was now lending a very sympathetic ear to the rising voice against further involvement in European struggles. Isolationism's core had always been the Middle West, and in this atmosphere George and Emma spent the last two months of 1919.

Chicago entertained them regally and exhaustively. They enjoyed themselves thoroughly although they missed their children and their friends. George sent plaintive cartoons to his children; to his friends he sent a shower of letters from a newly acquired typewriter, and these were returned in kind. His large and eager class at the Art Institute, with some defiant exceptions, found him as stimulating an instructor and critic as he himself had found Henri fifteen years before. He deluged his pupils with his philosophy of painting: "You don't know what you are able to do until you try it. Try everything that can be done. Try it in every possible way. Be deliberate and spontaneous. Be thoughtful and painstaking. Be abandoned and impulsive. Learn your own possibilities. There is nothing I do not want to know that has to do with life and art." Or: "As a work of art is a document of the human mind and spirit, we don't care to see the documents of empty heads or hearts. The work of art should be a document of the wholeness of man, not of one single part."

The Institute was holding its thirty-second exhibition of American painting, and George was pressed into duty on its jury of awards. To his delight he found his colleagues unanimous in choosing Leon Kroll's "Leo Ornstein at the Piano" as the outstanding painting in the show. When they discovered, however, that Kroll's price was higher than their purchase prize, it was Bellows' pleasant duty to telegraph his old friend:

"INSTITUTE LIKES YOUR ORNSTEIN BUT DOES NOT LIKE TO ASK FOR REDUCTION. ARE YOU WILLING FOR ME TO SOUND YOU ON SUBJECT OF AWARDING YOU LOGAN PURCHASE PRIZE OF FIFTEEN HUNDRED DOLLARS AND LOGAN MEDAL AS PURCHASE PRICE? I HOPE YOU ARE FAVORABLY INCLINED."

Kroll accepted without reservation.

There was little time in Chicago for independent painting.

George finished two nudes, one with a bowl of fruit, the other with a white shawl over her shoulders. Then, at a reception, he was enchanted by a very old lady, Mrs. Mary Brown Tyler. She, in turn, took a fancy to him and consented to pose in some of the dresses she had worn a half-century before. The first of these was a full-flowing, wine-colored gown with a broad lace collar fringing a low neckline. The tone and texture of the costume delicately enhanced the brittle vitality of the little face, reflective under a flowered cap. Mrs. Tyler, pleased with her first experience as a model, returned to sit again, this time in the tightly laced wedding dress she had worn in 1863. Its creamy tone and shimmering surface provided fascinating contrasts to the softly wrinkled flesh tones of her features. These two are among the finest Bellows' portraits; but Mrs. Tyler's relatives did not approve of them and insisted that they should not be associated with the family name. They consented to the Victorian anonymity of "Mrs. T.," not realizing that the sitter would never lose an opportunity of relating her experience to any one who would listen.

The holidays found George and Emma in the family circle at Columbus. Anna Bellows was as hale as ever, but half-sister Laura Monett, nearly sixty, supported her pretty head with a frail, palsied body. Nephew Howard Monett was short, lively, and a good companion. George found himself homesick for his daughters in New York and sent them the following, complete with sketches:

"Daddy is sitting in Grandma Bellows' lap and printing you another letter.

"We have only had time to receive Christmas presents. I got a shirt and two pairs of socks, and some beautiful drawings from Anne and Jean, also half of a story by the well-known authoress, Miss Anne Bellows.

"Besides this I received a box of cigarettes, a box of matches, a free ride on a street car, a free ten dollar bill, some fresh air and a drink of water.

"I gave Mommy an ostrich for Christmas. She thinks it's a fine bird, but I don't think she will let any little girls play with it.

"You must go to bed very early and go to sleep very quick so you will be strong enough to give Mommy and Daddy an awful *big hug*. But when we get home you can sit up all night."

. . .

For all these promises of a quick return they would have seen the New Year out in Columbus except for catastrophic news from the Luxembourg Exhibition. Rumors from Speicher and Henri had reached Bellows in Chicago that not all the pictures chosen had been hung, that the French authorities had exercised a censorship of their own, that the "moderns" had been rejected out of hand. No authoritative source was willing to comment. The two American artists in charge were unavailable for quotation. In this morass of gossip Henri sagely wrote: "I have no feeling that if this thing has been done, the French authorities have done this of their own volition. Why should they? It does not seem reasonable that they should take it on themselves to interfere in the matter of our selections. The French are too experienced in art matters. Some influence from American sources must have been brought to bear to make them omit pictures from the show." He guessed that "our home town has been very recently disturbed by the introduction of the same plan of jury as was employed for the Paris show."

By December 27 the American officials were back in New York, and a showdown was in order. Henri arranged it for the last day of the month and sent George a frantic appeal for support: "They know you are not due until after the date set. I am afraid I will be all alone in the fight to have a full and public repudiation of all concerned in the matter . . .

"It will be hard for *one* to extract the facts. I need help from another to whom personal interests can make no difference.

"The names of those whose pictures were not hung are: Bouché, Gussow, McFee, Maurer, Sheeler, Stella, Max Weber, Zorach.

"Can you imagine a greater comtempt than the fact that Max Weber, whom we worked so hard to place on the committee so the 'Modernists' would have a square deal in the representation, should himself be refused place in the exhibition . . . ?"

To this explosive cry George responded as he always did when the master was in need. On New Year's Eve he sat with the other members of the Luxembourg Committee and helped to wrench as much of the hocus pocus out of the embarrassed officials as he could. No formal statement was ever published; but the specific affront to Weber sufficed to indicate bitter and devious hostility to him and all he stood for. In retrospect, the episode becomes the more fantastic in that Bellows and Henri had determined to show

Europe how strong French influence was becoming in America, while some of the French connived, at least, in suppressing it. The year 1919 evaporated in a cloud of disgust and suspicion.

George began the New Year with a fervent letter to the editor of *The Arts,* outlining his grievances over the Luxembourg debacle and urging the magazine to take up the torch against injustice. Then he rocked furiously for a few days in his study, raging at an invisible target. He wanted an opponent whom he could challenge directly, and it was not long before he found one.

Henry McBride of the New York *Sun* patted his reviewing pencil reflectively against his lips as he looked over Knoedler's exhibition for the French Art Fund, studied more than a dozen Bellows' offerings, and found them not to his taste at all. His paper printed his opinions on January 11. George read them with utter disbelief and then realized he had not only found an adversary, but one who led with his chin. The critic had the temerity to write: " 'The Red Sun' is apparently painted in aniline dyes, and 'The After Glow' also has a scheme in yellows which can scarcely endure. Perhaps the artist deliberately used dangerous colors in order to see what would happen to them in a month or two."

Three angry drafts sufficed to produce a letter to the *Sun*'s art editor: "Mr. McBride has endeavored, by the use of the words 'apparently,' 'scarcely,' and 'perhaps' to avoid a direct false and libellous charge on which appropriate action could be based; but I submit that his intent is plain and that he intended to charge me with dishonest practice of my profession as an artist, wherein the permanence of the material used is a fundamental thing, and of offering for sale paintings painted in fugitive colors. [This] is an exceedingly damaging and malicious act if allowed to go unchallenged and disproved. I have always sought to use only colors of the highest standard of permanence. I have always held it as a high ideal that working for permanency was to the joy of the workman."

At the same time he scribbled a number of blasts directly to the critic. The first of these, one he certainly did not send, included a reaction to another of McBride's phrases. Speaking of the work of a certain Mr. Nave, which he did not like, the critic had added: "But as he at least uses legitimate colors, his canvases are already more bearable than those of a better known pupil of Mr. Henri's." Pride as well as rage went into George's retort: "As I am the only Pupil of Mr. Henri's mentioned and well known as such, this is taken as an additional reference to me—whether intended or not— and I think it was so intended. The connection is inescapable . . . The accusation that you make in my case is so serious that it amounts to calling me a liar and a thief."

McBride took this on the chin he had left so open and went quietly down to the mat. His apology was printed directly under Bellows' letter in the *Sun*. He weasled cleverly on the point at issue, saying that his "impressionistic" passage had been misinterpreted, but his regret was stated clearly, pacifically, and with dignity.

Stephen Clark, whose collection ultimately became one of the finest in the United States, had already bought Bellows' "The Skeleton" and "Anne with a Parasol." He now wanted "Margaret," but decided that three Bellows' were too many and made George an offer of exchange. His answer came within a week:

"I have made it a principle not to allow myself to get into the business of exchanges as it is most unsatisfactory. I feel that when I sell a picture it is a good one, and carries a value that can be realized upon in the Art market, if for any reason the owner wishes to dispose of it.

"Generally we artists need ready money, and our patrons are not usually so situated. If you are disappointed or tired of the Portrait of Anne, I am very sorry and really surprised. I suggest that you offer it for sale through one of the dealers. It should in due time return to you your investment and possibly also with interest . . ."

George knew his man. Stephen Clark bought "Margaret" for $1,500, but he kept coming back and never dropped the hope of some day making an exchange.

The portrait of "Mrs. T. in Cream Silk" remained unfinished, while Bellows put it aside and executed another version of it that pleased him. Off it went promptly to the National Portrait Painters Association where Harry Hewes, the New York correspondent for the Chicago *Blade,* admired it and invented an extraordinary background for the sitter: "It happens that Mrs. T. is a neighbor of the painter, and often of an afternoon drops into the studio to make tea for him and his friends, among whom she has some staunch admirers. Back in the days when Forty-Second Street was on the edge of the country almost, Mrs. T. was a belle and one of the loveliest, if such contemporary report as is obtainable is to be believed, as ever came to the metropolis from Dixie . . . A hundred years from now it is conceivable that this 'Portrait of Mrs. T.' will still keep the memory of George Bellows alive and fragrant . . .''

In February, robust and bearded, Waldo Pierce occupied the model stand. He and Bellows were old friends, and the resulting big bluff portrait, full of a sound knowledge of the great Venetian painters, bespeaks a pleasant, relaxed atmosphere. George sent it to the Corcoran Gallery in Washington. When the catalogue of the exhibition was printed he wrote a whimsical letter to the compiler:

"I see in the catalogue just sent me, that my 'Portrait of Waldo Pierce' is described as being lent by Mr. Pierce. This is not the case, as my entry will show. It is for sale, and not a rejected portrait commission painted for fun. The vast numbers in Washington who would like to buy my work are led to think by the catalogue that Mr. Pierce would not part with the canvas for any price; and he wouldn't if he owned it. But as he is a good artist like me, he has to sell pictures before he can buy them. 'Lent by Mr. Pierce' looks well in the catalogue, but it isn't true, and is false pretense, and is in the way. Therefore I suggest you print a new catalogue and have the error corrected, or sell the canvas privately."

March found him working and reworking the tennis theme, but new ideas eluded him. He felt cramped and unable to settle down seriously to anything. When the Speichers asked George and Emma to visit them in their comfortable new house in Woodstock at the foot of Mount Overlook, they accepted with alacrity. Leaving the children in the Storys' charge, they enjoyed an exhilarating drive up the Hudson, bright with early spring, and moved in on their friends' hospitality.

The change of scene and pace worked wonders. George and Gene spent every day painting out of doors; in the evening there was either a lively bout of conversation or a game of poker to round out the hours before bedtime. April gave way to May, but they lingered long enough for George to turn out a half dozen more panels before cranking up the Buick for the return to New York. Meanwhile, he and Emma had rented the broad-eaved Shotwell House on the mountainside for the summer, and with this transaction in mind George immediately sat himself down at his desk and addressed himself to his Aunt Fanny in San Diego:

"Emma tells me that she wrote you a letter the other day in which she invited you to visit us this summer. I suppose you were pleased with the spirit of the note and proceeded to think no more about it. This letter is being written to make you think more about it . . .

"I am aware, my dear Aunt Fanny, that you have not been blessed with the best of luck. I have — Therefore I think it would be a nice idea to try and strike something of a mean proportion . . .

"Further than this I want you to feel that you are not needing to worry about the future. As the chances are, it would not be a very available plan to leave you something in my will. I think I will leave you something right away. My mother is going to do exactly what I am proposing for myself, and between us you are to have a regular income of a thousand dollars a year which, added to what income you have of your own, should make the days comfortable for you.

"We are going to a wonderful mountain country, famous among artists and where I have procured a wonderfully fine estate, a very large house in the center of a farm on the slope of the second highest mountain in the Catskills. We are also fortunate in having a good maid at last so that your visit would be as easy as pie. We will send you a round trip ticket and expenses on the train . . .

"I feel like adding that if I can paint another picture with you as a model, as good as the one I have done, that everything will be paid for. You did not see the canvas as completed. I worked a great deal on it when I got to New York. I chose it to represent me in the great exhibition in the Luxembourg, Paris."

Just around the corner from 146 East Nineteenth Street, Gramercy Park spread its broad block of fenced-in trees and shrubs, an attractive place for the Bellows daughters to skip rope and play with the neighborhood children. From time to time their father would walk them there for an airing, usually to find an agreeable crony with whom he could argue while keeping an inconsistent watch on the antics of the little girls. The setting reminded him of his pleasant visit in Woodstock with the Speichers. One day he tackled the subject of the park on a good-sized canvas, the composition with a central figure in white against a big tree reminiscent of the scene Kroll had painted of the Bellows family four years earlier in Camden. A hint of Kroll also appeared in the glow of sunlight on the leaves and something, too, of Renoir in the vibrant streaks of light along the pathway. The firm angular bulk of the building in the background with its luminous window panes was entirely his own.

Thus far, 1920 had been a poor year for sales, so when a letter arrived from Cincinnati, where he had sent "Sun Porch," he hoped it might contain some good financial news. The first sentence raised his interest: "To me the most alluring painting in the Cincinnati Museum is your 'Sun Porch.' " But what followed was disappointingly familiar. The writer wanted the painting for his Moosehart Institute for dependent children, which he extolled at length, ending with: "Wealthy and influential men would rejoice to buy your masterpiece for an institution that is an honor to America. Senator Harding is a Moose . . ." This final sentence probably provoked profanity, for Warren Gamaliel Harding would never have become President of the United States had George Bellows had his way.

In June he painted Emma at a window and a portrait of a dark-faced woman, "Miss Ruth." Then came vacation and the Shotwell house in Woodstock, exactly what they wanted, including the company; in addition to the Speichers, the Henris were there and Kroll and any number of other artists and their families whom they had known for a long time. The village was at the foot of the hill, the baseball field in its midst, the studio was everything George desired, with plenty of room and a good north light. Gram Bellows arrived from Columbus, and Aunt Fanny arrived from San Diego. Laura Monett and her son Howard looked in on their way to Sag Harbor. The family cast of characters matched the perfection of their setting.

Except for the ball field and frequent excursions into town for meals, Bellows saw little of his surroundings for the next three months. He promptly sat Anne down in a low rocking chair, wearing a simple white dress, a Japanese fan in her lap, her fair hair sweeping gracefully over her shoulders, and painted another of his inimitable summaries of childhood. He followed this with two nudes and a portrait that he later destroyed. In August he kept his promise to Aunt Fanny to surpass her portrait painted in Carmel, placing her in a Windsor chair so large that it emphasized her tiny frame. Her long, wizened face and work-worn hands stood out vividly against the geometric lights on her black silk dress, while a low vase of purple flowers behind her right shoulder provided almost the sole element of color. He called it "Old Lady in Black."

Encouraged by this success, he tried a more ambitious design and, in September, painted "Elinor, Jean, and Anna."

He worked a long time preparing this big four-and-a-half by five-and-a-half foot canvas, basing his whole design on a simple root five triangle from Hambidge's "Dynamic Symmetry." Excitedly, he placed every center and every contrast within the rigid but intricate geometric framework. Yet the outcome of the group portrait gives no suggestion of such contriving, and it seems certain Bellows' mind had already grasped the fundamentals of the composition before he ever subjected it to a mathematical formula. He placed Jean, a small white triangle, in the center. The turn of her head to the left was just enough to set the hunched little body of Aunt Fanny in balance with the monumental bulk of Gram Bellows. Probably no finer expression exists of the exquisite contrast between childhood and old age.

Stories linger around the painting of this picture. The old ladies loved to sit, and George probably insisted that they pose separately because the clacking of their busy tongues would have been a violent distraction to him. On the other hand Jean, only five, could imagine no more congenial but no more uncomfortable an occupation, and Marjorie Henri played victrola records to her to hold her attention for a few minutes at a time. Still, when it was done, he knew that it was good.

Then his older relatives made their way back to the west, the children returned to 146 with the Storys, but George and Emma stayed on and on. He shipped "Elinor, Jean, and Anna" off to the New Society show, its second under that name, and then with the

Speichers renewed the charm and relaxation of the spring before, the same pattern of outdoor sketching and the type of cosy evening that only very close friends can know.

The outside world impinged on this rustic idyll from time to time in various ways. A Miss McCaulley asked Bellows his opinions on "national art," to which he replied: "I am still of the opinion that Art is not very thrilling when looked at nationally . . . Some day when I have time I may travel and see the world. I would not expect to find very many better pictures than have been brought to me here . . . It is not a very original observation that all great creative genius has dealt with its own life, its own ideas, in its own time . . ."

The Henris, who had left early for New York, regretfully declined an invitation to return. "I am avoiding the Nat. Arts billiard room," wrote the Master, "because I do not think it would be fair to myself to destroy my health by playing in that air before you come. I will reserve all my vigor to use up on playing with you.

"I am told, however, that great improvements have been made in ventillation etc. There are electric fans, and I noted that the walls have been painted. They are overly cheerful now . . .

"Lord! And I never mentioned your boils! Excuse the oversight —I wouldn't have hurt your feelings for anything. How are they?"

The reds and golds of October fell before the November winds, but George lingered long enough to produce fourteen small panels, including "The Hudson at Saugerties," before they rejoined their children around the Thanksgiving board.

The forthcoming exhibition of the New Society was very much on Bellows' mind. The organization, formed two years before, had been the result, in part, of his own hard planning to give greater opportunity to younger American painters. In an article for *Vanity Fair,* he outlined some of its aims:

"The New Society of American Artists was organized through spontaneous combustion. It starts with youth, although some of its members bear title to venerable. Its motive is to retain youth or desist altogether. It will remain significant just so long as it succeeds therein. Its only honors are respect, its only funds the work it has to show.

"Great artists have often flourished in the poorest communities. The gods plant their philosophers, seers, discoverers without counting conditions or noting an audience . . . An artist can exist in a country that buys bad art; his situation is more difficult in a country which buys none . . . But however much or little an artist may require the material support of his neighbors, the neighbors are in vastly greater need of the artist, a need greater still because they have, almost universally, no suspicion of it. Where such suspicion is aroused, a great period of culture is sometimes born.

"A final merit of the Society is its catholicity. Pigeon hole critics will find the names in the catalogue to be those of the most diversified personalities, names they have been in the habit of identifying with all sorts of 'schools,' 'enemy camps,' 'movements' and 'nonmovements.' It is very satisfactory to find here a manifestation of the fact that the Real Thing is neither conscious of or interested in classifications . . .

"To us, living in the present, it is important that the present, not the future, shall be great. A great present is the best assurance of a great future. It is not necessarily ridiculous to have faith. It is, however, very important to have it. Among some of our artists sometimes the great genius of America will arise. Some of him is probably here now.

"Look!"

Bellows' entry in the exhibition was "Elinor, Jean, and Anna." He need have added no more, for within a few days of the opening he received the following:

"I must drop you a line about the picture. I feel like going and selling everything I have to buy it . . . It's a national landmark and monument . . . It's a very great thing . . .

[signed] John Jay Chapman"

With this sentiment Willard Huntington Wright agreed in *Hearst's International:* "In this painting Mr. Bellows has accomplished a difficult feat. He has lifted portraiture out of the status of a mere profession, and conferred upon it a genuinely aesthetic distinction . . ."

The picture caused such a sensation that in the February, 1922, issue of *Vanity Fair,* a retouched photograph of George appeared on the page headed "We Nominate for the Hall of Fame" with the following citation:

"Because he is one of the most forceful and distinguished of American painters; because he is a master in four graphic arts; because he has recently exhibited one of the greatest portrait groups in modern art."

George's fellow nominees in that issue were: H. L. Mencken ". . . because he had taken his place as one of the most important living critics and has become a sort of godfather to the younger generation of American writers"; Maude Adams ". . . because she is soon to introduce us to a wholly new development in moving pictures"; Bernard Berenson ". . . because of the pleasure we have in signalizing his present visit to America"; and Albert de Kossah ". . . because he has come to America to paint a portrait of General Pershing."

The United States was the happy hunting ground for European portrait painters, and nothing irritated the native-born artists more. George must have viewed rather wryly the bracketing of his name with that of the latest of these "invaders" of whom little had been heard before—and nothing since.

"Elinor, Jean, and Anna" moved on to the Pennsylvania Academy's annual show where it earned the Beck Medal, and provoked some sour remarks from the editor of *The Arts*. He looked primly down his critical nose on all awards and medals, but grudgingly admitted that in the case of the Bellows painting there had been "no great miscarriage of justice." "Who are we," he continued, "that we should presume to render today the verdict which the centuries alone can give? A hundred years from now those who come after us will be able to judge the relative merits of George Bellows and Arthur Davies. In the meanwhile the best of us are groping in the dark." With this somber reflection on his own profession he returned to his office in Manhattan.

In the same issue of *The Arts,* a reviewer spoke disparagingly of Bellows' lithographs, then on view at Keppel's: "Unless he is doing portraits George Bellows is making illustrations for his titles. His figure studies . . . are not as clever as most of his lithographs. They are striking enough, but they lack real solidity of drawing."

With these unenthusiastic comments grumbling in his ears Bellows showed the portrait of "Old Lady in Black" at the National Arts Club and was rewarded with the first prize of $600. Then

Ossa piled itself on Pelion when a gentleman from Des Moines bought the painting for $3,000, of which the Club retained a nominal 10 per cent. All this was welcome income in a year still suffering from the severe "recession" that followed hard on the postwar boom. It also caused a minor public sensation, and Bellows commented wryly: "The papers are asking for my picture . . . I was approached by the movies who suggested that I don a velvet jacket and plush hat and stand in the attitude of Creative Fancy. I received letters and telephone messages of congratulation. A man over in Egypt wrote to ask if by chance I was related or descended from the famous Edward Bellows who built the Suez Canal."

The most serious consequence of his good fortune was a summons to address the annual meeting of the National Arts Club, an organization composed of artists and business men interested in art. With this dual type of membership in mind, he began his speech in a half-jocular vein by suggesting that if the purpose of the Club was the fostering of artists and their work, then it should not take up their valuable time by demanding orations from them: "Of the conditions necessary to creation, the lonely, long and solitary periods of contemplation are perhaps the most important."

He then advanced a challenge to the lay members of the club, those who patronized the theater, concerts, and opera, bought books which they sometimes read, hired chauffeurs, clerks, lawyers, doctors, and architects, and yet put such money as they had for painting into European Old Masters, "the normal human tendency to find all greatness among the dead." To remedy this situation, he suggested that application blanks for lay membership contain the question: "Do you possess any sculpture, paintings, prints, drawings, even good reproductions of works of art by living American artists other than in the servants' quarters?"

He pointed out that $20 to $100 would buy almost any of the best drawings by contemporary Americans and that "for the price of a theatre ticket or so one can buy the proof of an etching by John Sloan who, in my humble opinion, is the greatest living etcher and a very great artist."

Prophetically, he foresaw a future in which progressive government would eliminate large fortunes altogether and the artist would have to find a different and more modest market for his wares. He predicted the renting of pictures and suggested that wealthy patrons might make part-time jobs available to young artists so that they could have the means to go on with their creative work.

In conclusion, he extolled the work of Homer, Eakins, and Ryder over and above "most of the antique and foreign masterpieces"; noted that some of the artists present at the dinner were quite the equal of their European contemporaries for "they produce, not American Art, but Art"; ended with the insistence that "Modern Art is on a par with the great things of this century. Art is like Love; it can never be better than the best."

The lithographic stones in the balcony at 146 had rested virtually untouched for nearly two years. A sudden fever of drawing overtook Bellows, and in three months' time, before the end of March, 1921, he completed sixty compositions ranging over various subjects and moods. There were four nudes; eight scenes of sports: polo, pool, boxing and bathing; twenty-eight of his family and friends; one of the critical profession. There was a restudy of "Sargeant" Delaney from the war series, and a Daumier-like rendering of a hold-up.

Among the most interesting were three extracted from his fabulous memory. "In the Subway" recalled a passing glimpse of an immigrant couple's happy faces. "The Snow Storm" reproduced with extraordinary fidelity an oil he had painted years before and destroyed in a moody moment. "Sunday Morning, 1897, Going to Church" was a vignette of his boyhood when his parents had squeezed two neighbors into the family surrey and left almost no space for him. The flick of the horse's tail and the flutter of the fringe poignantly recall an age already made obsolete by the automobile.

He changed printers that winter, and it was now Bolton Brown who came in to ink the stones and run them through the press while George hovered about, chain smoking, studying every proof minutely and fidgeting when the inking process began again. He also used a new type of paper, abandoning the less absorptive quality of the Chinese for a very soft Japanese product. Collectors disagree as to whether the earlier or later prints are the finer, although the majority prefer those turned out by Brown. The dissenters find Brown's efforts fuzzier and duller with less brilliant contrasts, but Bellows thought the new relationship an harmonious one, and Bolton Brown signed the proofs along with the artist.

In March, he began another portrait of his mother. It was, perhaps, inspired by his lithograph of "Sunday Morning," for he pictured her sitting in her rocking chair in the house on East Rich Street where he had been born. He had no need of her in the studio, for his painter's eye had photographed her big-featured head with its thoughtful eyes and humorous mouth, her large ears, full chin, and the wrinkles above her eyebrows. A round-topped mirror reflecting the latticed windows, the old-fashioned pen in its stand, even the pattern of the carpet rushed fondly onto his brush as the stateliness of his subject moved into the intimate focus of its presentation.

He found time to write an article entitled "What Dynamic Symmetry Means to Me" for the June issue of *The American Art Student* and interspersed his discourse with some sparkling comments on education in general: "The study of dynamic symmetry is probably more valuable than the study of anatomy . . . It comes within the class of positive knowledge . . .

"The manifestations of the laws of dynamic symmetry are as infinite in variety as the manifestations of living forms or combinations possible in music. Recently I heard the Philadelphia Orchestra, directed by Leopold Stokowski. The entire evening of music was nothing but a source of pleasure because my ears were enjoying the strains of great music while my eyes were enjoying the movements and the inspired gestures of its great conductor. Every movement of his hands, his arms, his body—every changing expression of his face invoked by the music fitted perfectly into the interpretation of the selection being played; he was literally a fine bit of Greek sculpture in motion.

"Nearly all art teaching today is a highly personal affair,—giving out by the instructor of his personal knowledge; and it largely results in an imitation of the teacher's work and methods.

"Dynamic Symmetry is an impersonal, general, universal law. The understanding of its manifestations is a key to knowledge just as mechanics are based on the laws of gravity and of the lever. Knowledge is power,—knowledge gives freedom.

"The first thing a student should learn is that all education that amounts to anything is self-education. Teachers, colleges, books—these are only the opportunity for education. They are not education *per se* . . .

"Inspiration and emotion [are] the spark that sets man's mind thinking at its keenest pitch. Love of beauty is the spark which causes its creation."

In the spring of 1921, Bellows was talking more easily than he was painting. An enterprising interviewer from *Arts and Decoration* penetrated his studio and came away with some revealing observations:

"If ever there was an iconoclast in art it is George Bellows, but he does not destroy from the wanton motive of a doubter . . . We asked Mr. Bellows why he had not drawn on the work of men like Rembrandt and Titian. 'Oh, but I have drawn on them . . . I wish to understand the spirit and not the surface . . . For instance, I don't think that Bouguereau amounted to much, and it might surprise some if I claim an influence from Botticelli.'

"Every great master has put his heart and his own life on his canvas: he has fed on both art and life. It is easy to imitate, just as it is easier to enjoy inventions than to make them. If an artist has a sincere will to express his own life, he will not need to bother about his originality . . ."

Outdoor activities were resumed in May. At frequent and regular intervals, tall George and Gene Speicher would take on small Leon Kroll and William Glackens in spirited doubles matches on the excellent tennis courts at Ninetieth Street and Park Avenue. When one of the men could not appear, Emma filled in for him, holding her own and often outplaying her opponents. All this was by way of a prelude to their coming transfer to another summer in Woodstock, again in the Shotwell House.

There the Bellows family settled down quickly under the shadow of Mount Overlook, but George left almost immediately for Tuxedo Park where a portrait commission waited for him. Mrs. Montgomery Hare had wanted a likeness of her small son Meredith, but knew not where to turn amid the swarm of European portrait painters then hovering over every possible sitter.

Mrs. Chester Dale took the problem efficiently in hand. She believed that George Bellows was a *great* artist, and she knew that he would produce a *great* portrait of her son. Very few people, including her husband, argued long with Maude Dale.

As he had accustomed himself to luxurious living in San Mateo, so George fitted himself comfortably into the rural grandeur of Tuxedo Park. Work progressed, as usual, at a rapid pace, and within a week he could report to Emma:

"Today I am going to try no. 3 in a new uniform which sounds fine: Eton jacket, grey pants, hat etc.

"Mrs. Hare is a peach. Mr. Hare is like my late brother Ben [Monett], but not such a kidder. I have met four Mr. Hares and they are all corkers . . .

"The boy is an awful nice kid, but god, what an itch. I am glad we have girls. I love you. So you married me after all . . .

"If it was fifty miles here I'd come back every evening. Think of it anyway. But it is almost to N.Y. This is really a marvelous valley.

"Well, old lady, I could keep this up for a long time. I love you. Dinner is served . . ."

He did not mention the usual obstacles thrown in his way. Mrs. Hare *knew* how her son should be painted—a stiff white collar around his neck. "That's no way to dress a boy," George protested later to Emma, but he had the tact not to say the same thing to Mrs. Hare. He executed a portrait with the starched linen and then one with a soft open-shirt collar. Mrs. Hare, confused, rather liked them both, but could not make up her mind. When he tried a third version he completely clouded the issue, so that Mrs. Hare took none of them and salved her conscience by buying some of his lithographs from Keppel's.

He returned to Woodstock briefly to turn out some drawings for the *Century Magazine,* and then at the behest of Herbert Bayard Swope of the *New York World,* he was off to cover a much-publicized prize fight at Boyle's Thirty Acres in Jersey City. In 1919, Jack Dempsey, hailed as the "Manassa Mauler," had toppled big Jess Willard into oblivion. Promoter Tex Rickard had lifted the ugly business of pugilism up to a level entitled by W. O. McGhehan "The Manly Art of Modified Murder." The public was agog, largely because Dempsey's opponent was to be a Frenchman and the *entente internationale* at the moment was wildly pro-French. Georges Carpentier was a built-up light heavyweight with singularly regular features, great personal charm, and a lively taste in dress. Herbert Bayard Swope believed that the only artist in the world with a reputation for boxing scenes should "cover" this international bout.

In the steaming July heat, Boyle's Thirty Acres packed in eighty-thousand fans and $1 million. Bellows, sitting in the press row with many old acquaintances, watched every moment from the time the crowd began to pack in until the referee dramatically counted out Georges Carpentier in the fourth round. Then Bellows took the first train back to Woodstock, milling over in his mind what moment had been the most dramatic in the fight, and produced "Introducing Georges Carpentier."

Mr. Swope had not envisioned such a picture when he offered the commission, yet George spotted the moment of real triumph. Dempsey was not popular. The American Legion had called him a draft dodger; someone had produced an ineptly staged photograph of the champion of the world stripped to the waist but wearing striped cutaway trousers. The public had gone to the fight to see Carpentier win, and its hero's only victory had been his introduction in the ring when Boyle's Thirty Acres erupted into a cliff-shaking shriek of acclaim. From that moment on, the image of the overmatched hero was chopped down remorselessly by the "Manassa Mauler" until it went limply to the canvas and stayed there for ten seconds.

In Woodstock again, he immediately recaptured the mood of the summer before. All the fullness and sensitivity and skill that he had distilled in "Elinor, Jean, and Anna" met again in a magical synthesis when he painted the portrait of Katherine Rosen, daughter of his next-door artist neighbor. Here he used the absolute minimum of means from his palette and his maximum skill in the delineation of texture. The sheer gold of the fair locks against the Victorian sheen of black horsehair, the lovely, vital curves of ripening adolescence against the firm brown frame of an old-fashioned chair—everything he knew he poured into this, the finest portrait of his life. Stephen Clark, when he saw it, was not content until it was his own.

Otherwise, the summer of 1921 was entirely normal. Baseball and tennis worked their way into the studio routine, and although the habits of the Woodstock group were largely unaffected by Prohibition, late hours took their toll. One Sunday morning the Bellows children slept very late, but their parents had the misfortune

Nude Study, Woman Kneeling on a Pillow; lithograph, 1924.

to wake early, neither feeling at the peak. George growled around morosely for a while and then, racquet in hand, tramped a profane path down the hill to the courts. Emma decided that what she needed was a long walk, too, with a Christian Science Church as her objective, miles away. Presently, George returned after a disappointing match, a long up-hill trudge, and the Woodstock sun bringing every ray it had to bear on his throbbing head. The children were still asleep; his mother and the Storys were nowhere to be found. He needed Emma, who presently appeared, struggling hot and tired up the long, winding drive.

"Where the Hell have you been?" roared George. "For God's sake don't tell me you walked to Church on this hot day?" Emma had him there. "Exactly! To Church, *for God's sake*—and *I* feel perfectly fine!"

Drawings for the *Century Magazine,* retouching the portrait of his mother, another portrait of Anne in a purple wrap, all these kept him indoors through September.

He propped up wriggly Jean in a pink dress only to find that his adoring model, now aged six, could not sit still for very long. To help out George, Emma took a back seat in the studio and read "Black Beauty" so eloquently that her small daughter burst into tears. "That's a Hell of a book to read to her while I'm trying to paint her!" roared George. The painting suffered nothing from the explosion, largely because the artist knew his subject so well.

Kroll, the Henris, and the Speichers provided the consultations, opposition in games or at the poker table, and the good companionship that Bellows always sought. When his household of old people dispersed and the young ones with them, George roamed the countryside again, but produced only two small sketches. His eyes were alert, not for subject matter, but for building sites. He inspected any number of possible locations on the slopes of Mt. Overlook and in the valley and then settled for a small triangular lot in the Speichers' backyard. It was a snug bit of land bounded by brooks on two sides, close to the ball field, the links, and the courts. Emma was content; George was enthusiastic. As they packed up their belongings, plans began to form vividly in his head, for he had always wanted to build a house of his own.

My Family, No. 2; *lithograph, 1921.*

THE HOUSE THAT GEORGE BUILT

» *1921 - 1925* «

» IX «   *"A great school is where a great teacher is."*
                         George Bellows

George had already expressed his ideas on architecture in an interview with a representative of *The American Architect:* "I am sick of American buildings like Greek temples and of rich men building Italian homes. It is tiresome and shows a lack of invention . . . All living art is of its own time . . . Few architects seem to grasp this. The Bush Terminal Sales Building is expressive of our needs. Greek temples with glass windows are foolish.

"I do not believe in period style. It seems second hand . . . Original styles of the present period would be desirable and could vary with their locality . . . These styles could be as flowing, as virile, as truly fine as any we now worship, for they would be of our own time. We would understand them."

Except for reworking the portrait of Jean in a pink dress, he painted very little before Christmas. News came from Chicago that "Old Lady in Black" had won the First Harris Prize and $500. Aunt Fanny Daggett had definitely proved his most lucrative sitter, paying for her cross-country trip many times over.

The year 1922 began auspiciously. Chester Dale decided it was time for Bellows to paint his portrait and, in contrast to his wife's which had gone through three versions and consumed many months, his own took no time at all. He and the artist were so well acquainted by now that George had no difficulty in setting down the bright incisiveness of the sitter's small head, and Mr. Dale paid him $1,500 with great satisfaction. He never bought another Bellows during the artist's lifetime, but later he paid a great deal more for many of his paintings.

In the January issue of *The Arts,* Mrs. Mary Roberts took issue with its editor on the position of Bellows as an artist. Mr. Field had written disparagingly, penning such phrases as "seeking formulas to prop up his art," "using other men's theories as a crutch," "having been created by a cruel divinity without the artistic instinct."

"I do not find," wrote Mrs. Roberts, "that 'little questions trouble Bellows and keep him from the great question of life.' . . . Let us observe that extraordinary excursion into the very heart of life, George Bellows' painting of Edith Cavell. It will especially illustrate this point of view. There is no more profound, heroic, deeply touching incident of the war than the sacrifice of Edith Cavell. The unutterable beauty of the last few hours of her life are beyond words moving and splendid. This Bellows felt deeply. But when he transferred this tragic moment to canvas he did it very quietly; eloquently, but without display. It takes genius to do an epic in paint as it would in poetry . . . In this study of a terrible fact, Bellows has not drawn one sentimental line.

"Mr. Field uses Steinlen as an example of a man who knows how to paint a crowd as a mass and as individuals. He does; but so does Bellows. In a Bellows crowd people are presented with a large impersonal vision, yet each individual with definite peculiarities and interests.

"He is, as Mr. Field says, 'a man full of energy'; and fortunately for his art this energy is held in leash by a rich imagination, a delicate sensibility and always a rare equilibrium. This, Mr. Field does not say."

She also spoke her mind on "Elinor, Jean, and Anna": "The technique is at once powerful and tender, with a knowledge of color, of tonality, that leaves the composition enveloped in a curious velvety atmosphere, something almost too spiritual to characterize . . ."

A few months later, the Carnegie International Exhibition expressed its agreement with Mrs. Roberts' opinion of "Elinor, Jean, and Anna" by awarding it the first prize, as the outstanding picture in the show, and the $1,500 that accompanied this distinction.

Late in January, George was pestered by a feather-headed female who wanted his support for her proposal that the public should choose the pictures purchased for the Montclair Art Museum. He finally replied:

"Does the public also vote on disease in Montclair?

"The foolish purchases of works of art notoriously made by nearly all public galleries is not due to the fact that the authorities are prejudiced or foolish; or that the neglect of *Vox Populi, vox Die* is the trouble . . .

"Each Museum employs a curator or active head who is supposed to be chosen for his or her knowledge and appreciation of art. Such a person lives and thinks his business, and there is some hope of his living and thinking straight; and if such a person is worth anything he is worth confidence. Otherwise a change should be made . . .

"Pleasing the public and pleasing the Board of Directors is a timid performance which gets nowhere. Education is showing people something they do *not* know."

With education on his mind, he let his eyes rest a while on the portrait of Dr. William Oxley Thompson, president of Ohio State. It still hung prominently on the west wall of the studio where he had placed it many years before. Then he put his thoughts into a letter to Professor Taylor:

"When I was in college, I, being a youth of experience unknown, subscribed to the legend that Dr. Thompson was a great man. I had a personal reason for feeling kindly, even a great affection for him. It seemed to me that if, when in later years I was busy painting in Columbus, I could get him to pose for me I might, through this feeling, have been able to paint a very fine thing. When the opportunity arose, however, the romance seemed to have fled. But I did find a picturesque figure, an affable, more or less kindly man with the usual egotism, a practical mind—finis. The model stand is the most searching place in the world.

"Now this sentimentalizing over authority is one of the things about university life which I remember with disgust . . . The real life of the spirit, culture, is almost left out, for the first essential is honesty, and complete, disinterested effort for truth and beauty. Sentimentality takes the place of philosophy, and pseudo-science usurps the entire fund of energy . . . The University should describe itself as the Cog Wheel Mfg. Co., Maker of middle class minds for middle class jobs.

"A great school is where a great teacher is, and where he meets with a great pupil."

After this diatribe on the educational process, Bellows added a topical note:

"An itinerant painter of portraits [Ignacio Zuloaga] has come to our shores. He is said to have a name in far places, and to have spoken to Kings and Princes. We will judge if he pleases us."

During the late winter the *Century Magazine* knocked on his door again, offering him his first big illustrating commission: fifteen drawings and a portrait for a serial they planned to run of "The Wind Bloweth" by Donn Byrne, the popular Irish author. Each drawing would pay $100. He read the story, liked it immensely, and went to work with his customary intensity.

The tale was a romantic fantasy, not unlike Ibsen's "Peer Gynt" in the wide range of its settings: Ireland, the Near East, and South America. Although he had never been abroad, he knew New York's "Shanty Irish" immigrants from his student days, and the types still existed on the fringes of Manhattan. He looked them up and restudied them. He pored over prints, "rotogravure" illustrations, and the French academic-romantic paintings of Arab countries still prominently displayed on museum walls. Six weeks later all sixteen drawings were complete.

In these big compositions he used all kinds of media: crayon, pencil, and ink-and-wash, never hesitating to cut out sections he did not like and rework them on skillfully inserted repairs. He maintained throughout the fantastic mood of the story and the swift changes of pace that the script implied. Yet during this orgy of design he still found time to give lectures at Miss Dow's and the Brearley Schools.

In March he painted two portraits. Samuel Knopf was well pleased with his likeness, one that combines the firmness of Bellows with the suavity of William Merritt Chase. Mrs. Walter

Richter, whose husband avidly collected Bellows prints, was less satisfied, and the likeness remained in the storage racks at 146 when he died. Perhaps he found her artificial and dull, as demanding as Mrs. Chester Dale. His mind was already centered on spring and the building season in Woodstock.

Just before he left painting in New York for carpentry in the country, Marie Sterner, the dealer who had handled many of his paintings in the past, found a permanent home for the picture which, above all others, had made him famous. "Stag at Sharkey's" went to Cleveland for a net to the artist of $1,500, half the sum that "Old Lady in Black" had brought him the year before. With the sale went a change of titles, for "Club Night" had identified the big, powerful oil through its previous exhibitions. Ultimately, the city that had the first opportunity to buy a prize-ring Bellows at its Athletic Club in 1909 found a bargain in his best.

April came and with it the only entry in his record book until August: "For four months built house in Woodstock, N.Y."

Bellows had already proclaimed his ideas on contemporary architecture, and he had now to put them into practice. He had watched his father design and execute many buildings in Columbus and had helped him with his drafting and in the actual building process. With theory and practice in his pocket, he now designed and erected his own house.

On or about April 6, 1922, he began to turn his sketches of the house into three-dimensional reality. Dynamic symmetry shepherded his initial studies, but it played little visible part in the finished product. With the part-time help of a local carpenter and mason, he put in the foundations, fitted the framing and the sheathing and the rafters as the story-and-a-half home assumed solid shape, its plain exterior enlivened only by a small gable over the front door. Whatever the theoretical geometry involved in its design, the house was palpably planned from the inside out, conforming to George's utilitarian theory of architecture. Sawing, joining, nailing, planing—he had loved these simple manual skills since his childhood. Some of his artist neighbors contributed with a variety of talents and improvisations. John Carroll, painter, found that a pillow strapped to the front of his pants made shingling more comfortable and persuaded George to imitate him, thus giving great amusement to the plentiful sidewalk superintendents.

The plan of the house is compact, almost sparse, reflecting in some ways the amenities of the Federal style in which he and Emma had lived for a dozen years at 146. A long living room with an arched fireplace balances a kitchen whose high screen cuts off a breakfast room in a manner not unlike that of the basement of their city house. The stairs are steep and narrow, opening onto a short hall lighted only from the doors of three bedrooms. The daughters shared the room in front; the maid adapted herself to the cubicle in between; and George and Emma occupied a small dressing room and a generous screened porch at the back. There was room for everyone, yet the frugality of the over-all design is reminiscent of George's father.

Every cranny under the eaves, every inch flanking the fireplace and windows of the living room was cubbied off and fitted with swinging doors. One of these, hinged from the top, pulled out to act as a table for the typewriter it usually concealed. In the girls' room, George adapted the sloping space above the stairs into a closet for their dresses. "Just the right height," he observed with pride, unaware that within a few years the length of the girls and of the clothes they wore would have changed. Emma had the interior painted white throughout. It suited her particular standards of housekeeping and served as a fine foil for the orange color of the chests of drawers, tables, and benches George was turning out as furnishings.

There was no electricity or refrigeration. Butter and milk were kept in the nearer brook. An oil stove in the kitchen warmed that room during the cool fall months when the children were with the Storys in New York and their parents delayed their own departure as long as they could. George chose to keep his water tank filled by man power, and installed a huge hand pump like those used on old-fashioned railroad hand cars. "Wonderful exercise," he explained, demonstrating it to his family and to curious visitors. He fitted up a string gauge through a hole in the ceiling under the tank, similar to Thomas Jefferson's device for telling time in Monticello, that marked "full" and "quarter full" on the wall. This measuring diagram worked well, but after the first summer Emma abolished it with the firm statement: "Every time that tank needs water, you're out painting."

By August the house was sufficiently complete to contain the family. It was a little cramped at first, compared to the spacious Shotwell House, especially since monumental Anna Bellows was with them again.

This was Gram Bellows' last summer in Woodtock. Her direct, fishing-village manners and her habit of saying the first thing that came into her head were something of a cross to Emma, but her good humor matched her physical proportions, and at heart she was kindness itself.

When Gram and Mrs. Story were together they got along very well as old ladies often do, but they had difficulty in finding topics of common interest other than their children, their grandchildren, and their religions. In this last field they were politely poles apart, except on the Bible. Here they never disagreed and had many friendly competitions in a game of quotations. It was the fiery Old Testament for Gram and the peace of the New Testament for Mrs. Story. Gram knew all about both Heaven and Hell, and also a great deal about her acquaintances who had gone to one or the other place. Mrs. Story did her best to explain Christian Science, but with very little effect since Gram invariably said, "It's real nice," and promptly took a cat nap.

Gram's strong ideas on profanity disturbed her son not at all. One Sunday dinner, when George was having trouble carving a rather tough roast, he exploded, "God Damn It!" whereupon his mother looked at him severely and said: "George, I ought to take you right over my knee and spank you." George replied with a mischievous grin: "That, Mother, presupposes that you have a knee?" and she fairly laughed her chair to pieces.

At eighty-four, Gram's girth would have dismayed any life insurance expert, yet her appetite remained gargantuan, and her favorite topic of conversation was the Ladies Birthday Club of Columbus and its recipes. At one party that summer, when she had baked a cake according to the club's formula, she caused Emma a great deal of embarrassment. A tall, wide young woman who had played "The Powerful Katrinka" in the movies and did not like to be reminded of the fact hove into view. Gram, with a gasp of admiration, remarked in a stage whisper: "Well, now I *never* saw mor'n that! Why she makes me look like a *flea!*"

As part of his building program, George had dammed up the brook outside the kitchen and lined its sides and bottom with concrete, and there his daughters and their friends found bathing an invigorating hardship. Every day they splashed in it noisily, skittering little handfuls of water at each other and shrieking with joy at every splash. Sometimes the tumult disturbed Bellows in his studio, and he would drop the problem in hand, fling open the door, thrust out his bald head and roar: "Shut up, damn it! I'm painting." The subsequent quiet lasted very briefly.

He painted very little, however, until the summer was over—a small panel and a single portrait. There was always one more thing to be done to the house, some detail he had overlooked in the building's perfection. Not until October when he and Emma were alone again did he start sketching in earnest. Then he executed eighteen panels, while the oil stove in the kitchen worked overtime and the ashes in the fireplace built higher each day and into the night.

One of the last of the year's paintings was "The White Horse," an admirable example of the romantic poetry and warmth that he brought to his work in the open air, as warm and yet utterly unlike the rigidly disciplined pictures he produced in his studio such as "Katherine Rosen."

The end of the year found him absorbed in the studio at 146 with twenty-seven drawings illustrating H. G. Wells' new book, *Men Like Gods*. Hearst's *International Magazine* was planning to run it as a serial and offered him $3,800 for the assignment. Time was short, for the first installment would appear in December. He had all the drawings at least sketched before Christmas.

The series offers an amazing variety from the comedy of "The Reception," the rococo charm of "The Garden of Growth," the tragedy of "The Christ of the Wheel," and the outright drama of "The Fall of the Quarantine Crag." They have been criticized for prudery, but in the early 1920's it was a skilled artist who could even dream of bringing naked Olympians and clothed Earthlings together without creating an uproar.

Stephen Clark now reappeared on the scene, still dissatisfied with "Anne and Her Parasol" and still determined to make a trade. He had seen "Katherine Rosen" at the Rehn Gallery. This was the Bellows Clark had been looking for, and this time he had his way. The two paintings were exchanged with a net profit to George of $1,300; and many years later Emma gave Anne the rejected portrait.

Just before the New Year, the *Century Magazine* ordered a drawing on lynching. Bellows remembered an account of such an outrage reported graphically during his days at Ohio State. The scene had so burned itself into his mind that he recreated it with no trouble and no loss of its tragic savagery. Into it he pressed all the concentrated protest he had expressed in the most violent prints of his war portfolio.

The first six months of 1923 were absorbed by drawing. As color had enveloped him on Monhegan a decade before, so sheer draftsmanship took him over and held him fast until June. Poised over his lithographic stones he reworked his designs for "Men Like Gods" and "The Wind Bloweth," punctuating them as the mood directed him with such topics as "The Dead Line," a scene in which miners' families cloud the mouth of a mining shaft waiting for the bodies of their men to be brought up; "The Law is Too Slow," a restudy of his lynching picture; a rehash of "Billy Sunday"; a portrait of fellow-shingler John Carroll; "The Plaid Shawl"; "Mary." There were pleasant satires too: "A Married Couple" sniped at the penchant of some old men for childish brides, while "Spiritual Potentate" skewered vested bishopry as painfully as ever Goya poked the point of his brush at the King of Spain.

Emma suffered all winter from a series of migraine headaches, more easily surmounted by staying in bed, and George, who usually slept late, found himself saddled with dressing his daughters and seeing them off to school. He solved the problem by making a game of it. The objective was to have as much fun as possible without disturbing "Mommy." His role was simply to be as funny as he could, and the childrens' roles were to keep their giggles down. He would start out by putting a dress on the wrong way round. Then his fingers would lose their fabulous dexterity and fumble over the tiny buttons. "Where'd you get all that spinach," he would suddenly demand as he combed their soft straight hair. The girls treasured these moments, for they rarely had their father completely to themselves. The discipline was particularly hard for impetuous Jean but no serious breaches of the rules disturbed Emma as she wrestled patiently with error in the room beyond.

In the spring, Bellows' correspondence took on an international flavor. William Nicholson, painter, wanted to use George's lithographs in a new publication, *The Owl*. Bellows made his own copyright problems clear at once, offered some unpublished prints, and wound up with a thumping endorsement of Bolton Brown, his printer: "Mr. Brown would like to be in England . . . Like most creative men Mr. Brown is not rich, and it would be necessary for him to create some kind of an income when he is abroad . . . There is a complete series of Mr. Brown's lithographs in the British Museum which can be seen for reference . . ."

The same day he wrote directly to H. G. Wells, to whom he sent all the lithographs for "Men Like Gods" and a complimentary print for him to keep. "They are," he conceded, "full of faults, but I have tried like the devil to make them do the finest thing I am capable of."

Nothing came of his hope to have his illustrations incorporated into the first bound edition of "Men Like Gods." At the same time, however, his sales of lithographs in 1921 and 1922 had brought in more than $1,000. In 1916–1917, they had netted him less than one hundred. Five years had seen him lift up the art of lithography with a single hand.

Shortly before he moved to Woodstock for the summer, Bellows pulled out a relatively small canvas, covered it with paper, and painted "Introducing John L. Sullivan." Twice before he had used the "introduction" theme, always with the crowd as an essential foreground feature. Now he swept away aesthetic distance and brought the spectator directly into the ring. The "Boston Strong Boy" met him there, a double-breasted suit wrapped around his beer-barreled body, as he smiled fatuously at the announcer. The fight fans on the far side cloaked themselves in boredom. In one corner the reigning champion, Jefferies, lounged on his stool and offered a languid hand to an admirer. In the other corner three other celebrities, young and old, chatted among themselves while they waited for the spotlight. John L's vanity, forgotten by the mob, begged for forgotten plaudits, and so underscored the theme of the transience of fame.

Early in June, George was in Woodstock with the family. It was wonderful to return to *his* house, to see how the planting of apple and lilac had survived the winter, to move with assurance through the spaces that had seemed so unfamiliar a year before. The Henris visited them briefly, for they were spending a year in Spain, and Marjorie's later letter of thanks to Emma brought strangely urban echoes to their ears:

" 'The Follies' were great, and it seemed funny that my curiosity about bananas was satisfied. Eddie Cantor sang it at least ten times, with the house joining in; so now I'm singing it and my Señor is going to before long. When I went off to see Mother yesterday I couldn't keep from saying: 'Yes, we have no bananas—bananas' until she said I was not myself.

"Tell Elsie: A Book that is making a great stir is 'Batonala' by René Marin, in French. The Boss is reading it—it is the last and most primitive word . . ."

This sophisticated chit-chat found no answering response in George Bellows. He had planned to add a room to his house for his mother, but Anna Bellows' rugged constitution was disintegrating in Columbus. Howard Monett kept him in touch, with gloomy news. Only one portrait, of fellow-shingler John Carroll, found its way into Bellows' record book for July.

By early August there was no evading the certainty that his mother was dying. He and Emma took the long train ride to Columbus in the stifling heat, having turned the children over to the practiced hands of the Storys. All went well during their absence, for Anne wrote "Aunt Ethel" Clarke that: "Marmee and Daddy are in Columbus because Gram Bellows is passing on. I'm sorry, but we are having a lot of fun with Gramma and Grandpa Story. They say we must enjoy ourselves. So we do."

The days of waiting for the end were terrible for George, sitting in the quiet, shuttered house on South Monroe Avenue. Always the man of action, there was nothing specific for him to do here. When Anna Bellows was finally released by "senility and a cardiac condition," he followed her coffin out to Green Lawn Cemetery to join his father's with dolorous thoughts in mind. He had shared his mother's joviality, her heartiness in everything; he had admired her patience although it was no part of his inheritance. Only his ailing sister, Laura, and her son remained as ties to his Columbus, Ohio, birthplace.

News of the funeral prompted a letter to Miss Clarke from eight-year-old Jean: "The swimming pool is low and Gram Bellows' funeral was yesterday. Now I will say something *cherry* [sic]. When are you coming up to teach us to swim? You had better, because we might get drowned."

A very sobered George and Emma returned to Woodstock to find excellent professional news. "Emma in the Black Print" had sold to a Boston collector for $3,000, while "Elinor, Jean, and Anna" had gone to the Albright Gallery in Buffalo for a net of more than $6,500. These sales were encouragement for the further work he wanted to do.

Uppermost in George's mind at this time was his own family. He had tried a grouping of his wife and daughters when they were in Ogunquit in 1915. Later he had revised the picture to bring the children into contemporary focus. Now he discarded both of these experiments, giving one of the drafts to John Carroll, who was so desperately in need of funds that he could not even buy supplies. A fresh canvas, five-and-a-half feet long, was stretched, and a whole new design was begun for "Emma and her Children."

He placed Emma off-center to the right with Jean on her lap. Anne took a place at the opposite end of the sofa, and Dynamic Symmetry nodded its approval. The painting occupied him for the better part of September.

His younger sitters were troublesome. Jean, for once, presented relatively few problems, for she had an entirely comfortable seat all through the five days of her posing. Anne, however, was obliged to perch herself in a thin white dress on the horsehair of the sofa. This tickled and scratched and made her squirm and fidget, so that an extra ten days were required to achieve exactly what he intended. Both girls had long since gone on his payroll at professional model wages, $1 a sitting. When Jean discovered that her sister was collecting $10 more than she was for the same painting she staged so effective a tantrum that her silence had to be bought with an extra $10. This bribe made for poor relations with Anne for several days.

It was during this period of coolness that Jean decided to test her will again. Emma had found the perfect maid for the summer, one who liked to work and did not miss the city. One day, Jean tentatively kicked her in the stomach and then kicked her a second time. The indignant servant protested to Emma that she would have to leave if this happened again. Emma spoke sternly to Jean, who could hardly wait to escape her lecture and try her acrobatic skills once more. In this emergency Emma called on George, painting or no painting. Jean panicked, and rushing up to her room where Anne was quietly reading a book, shrieked, "Don't tell Daddy where I am. He'll murder me!" A minute or two later George, furious because Emma had been irritated by someone other than himself, charged up the stairs. "Where's Jean?" he roared. "In the trunk," said Anne with a careless gesture of betrayal.

No trace of the perpetual turbulence in the Bellows household appears in "Emma and her Children." The atmosphere is one of quiet reflection, entirely removed from the lively prettiness that pervades Renoir's "Mme. Charpentier," so often cited as its prototype. The picture has the rich reserve, the intimacy that invests "Elinor, Jean, and Anna" and the "Portrait of Katherine Rosen." No one else could have conceived and executed so personal a masterpiece.

In the middle of his work on "Emma and her Children," Bellows made a hurried trip to the Polo Grounds in New York to cover an assignment for the *Evening Journal.* He described it tersely to Henri: "I was also interrupted by having to go to the fight between Dempsey and Firpo. When Dempsey was knocked through the ropes he fell in my lap. I cursed him a bit and placed him carefully back in the ring with instructions to be of good cheer. I made a good drawing for [*The Journal*] which the printers' strike prevented from publication."

The Dempsey-Firpo match, brief but violent, has been called the fight of the century. Since his victory over Carpentier two years before, the Champion's unpopularity had undergone a sharp revision. His opponent, aggressive and powerful, was almost unknown outside his native Argentina. Paying customers packed the

Polo Grounds, and it was apparent from the opening bell that the mayhem they had paid to see would be worth the price. During the first round, the Champion floored the Challenger seven times and was himself knocked flying through the ropes and into the press box. Back in the ring, Dempsey then proceeded to knock out Firpo in the second round.

Bellows chose for the drawing the climactic moment when 190 pounds of flailing prize fighter plummeted out of the ring, a magnificent three-dimensional composition charged with a vibrancy no other artist could equal. At variance with the story he had written Henri, he put himself in the design at the extreme left of the front-row spectators.

By late September, "Emma and her Children" was complete, and Bellows turned to a wholly different theme. The year before he had drawn "The Crucifixion" to illustrate a story in Hearst's *International Magazine*. "I Saw HIM Crucified" by Arthur Conan Doyle, purported to be a letter from a Roman soldier who had heard the story of Christ's death from the Centurion. The recent death of Anna Bellows had brought her son's mind onto the subject of religion with remarkable poignancy.

Since his emancipation from the hallelujah Methodism of his youth, he had subscribed to no fixed creed. The group in which he lived and worked belonged to the "emancipated," the intellectual agnostics, the determined atheists. It believed in a mind free from superstition of any kind. In his mature years George attended church only when duty to his parents or his own curiosity prompted him to do so. His lithograph "Spiritual Potentate" allied him squarely with Goya as a satirist on organized religion, and "The Sawdust Trail" spoke candidly of his distaste for revivalism. Yet there was something basic in the Christian theme of redemption through suffering that he could not dismiss. As Bishop Hobson said of Robert Frost, "His religion was utterly unorthodox and yet profound."

Into his "Crucifixion" he put something of the robustness of Rubens, the emotion of Tintoretto, the mysticism of El Greco. The two-dimensional planes of Dynamic Symmetry he developed into three, the great crosses marking off the sides of a central cube. He placed onlookers against this solid core in frozen attitudes of awe: Adam covering his face in remorse, the Centurion starting forward with a gesture of hope, the Virgin embracing the foot of the cross in a great sweeping curve of grief.

Critics have objected to the stiffness of these figures, forgetting their fundamental purpose in the whole: the moment of stunned revelation, while, in contrast, the rigid lines of the Christ define simultaneously despair and exaltation.

Bellows described the new technique he had used on this canvas in a letter to Henri: "I painted the Crucifixion complete in two colors, setting mixtures of a semi-neutral blue and a semi-red-orange with the intermixture and using nothing else until all the picture was finished thus. Then it was easy to sway a cool color a little cooler or warmer with glaze, and the same for warm. Then . . . by holding to the established form with a third color, a perfectly marvellous full coloration was developed in texture strikingly like certain of the best old masters."

Still in Woodstock, Bellows ran across a photograph of a painting, "Fisherman's Family," executed after his stay on Monhegan a decade before and later destroyed. He decided to try the same design again, keeping the composition with Anne on his shoulder and Emma by his side, the group framed by rugged hills and a quiet cove. This second version sublimated the vitality of the first with a new-found massiveness and luminosity. He put the finishing touches on "Emma in the Purple Dress," begun at Middletown four years earlier. When this painting was sold nearly thirty years later, *Time* magazine commented: "As one of Bellows' best, 'Emma in a Purple Dress' ranks high among U.S. portraits."

Late in the fall came the stunning news that Kroll, the perennial bachelor, had married—and a French girl at that. George immediately wrote:

"Dear Husband,

Your news was a great blow to some of the girls here, and very pleasant and delightful news to others. Among the men it was received with general and genuine enthusiasm. I am sorry to say that except for my daughters the news was received among the children with some indifference.

"We had a wedding breakfast for you on the 18th and other

celebrations at which we were addressed by recent visitors from France, at which it was agreed that the bonds between the two countries were more thoroughly knit than ever.

"So now you are married everything is all right, and now all we have to do is to go on living. My fondest wishes to you both, and may the best man win . . ."

A copy of Henri's recent book, *The Art Spirit,* was acknowledged as follows:

"This evening game you taught (not without my help) to the artists of Woodstock, this gambling business, has been the death of nothing to do at night except read, write and draw. We now draw cards.

"However most everybody has left, and I have come to a stop in the daytime, called it a summer, taken stock, showed the work to everybody, and am ready to pack up, go to New York, and start arguing with Pennell.

"Your book is a beauty. I read it often. It seems to me a very unique thing in literature and increasingly valuable . . ."

Chicago awarded Bellows' "My Mother" its Logan Purchase Prize, $500, and $1,700 more to meet the price he had set on it. This was highly satisfactory, but Peyton Boswell,. recently appointed editor of *Art News* came up with a suggestion that made George Bellows angry. In brief, Boswell proposed to sell space in his magazine to artists for the reproduction of their wares. In reply, George wrote:

"I am not interested in even subscribing to what is now totally an advertising and not a news stand. In conventional ethics, paid-for data is at least supposed to be marked 'ADV.' What becomes of the news if honest artists refuse to subsidize [and] what becomes of the artist without funds, which is the classic condition of many of the best?

"I may be wrong in all this. I am possibly very old fashioned . . . But starting myself as a poor unknown young man, I have for years received publicity for which I spent neither time, money nor attention; and in my innocence have supposed this the perfectly reasonable and natural interest of the newsgatherers . . ."

Editor Boswell had a bear by the tail, but he could not let it go:

"The proof of the pudding," he wrote smugly, "is in the eating. The *Art News,* under my management, has more than doubled its circulation . . .

"The two publications of which I am the Editor are doing more to promote an interest in art and a love of beauty in the American people than almost any other agencies that can be named. You, with whom gruffness is an obsession, ought to be square enough to admit that.

"I shall not publish your letter. If I did I should have to turn right around and sue you for libel!"

George ended the matter in characteristic fashion:

"The proof of the pudding is in the eating as the little boy said when he had swallowed some delicious rat poison. As a writer you should be careful of the felicity of your metaphors . . .

"A bought press is perhaps the worst menace a country can suffer from . . .

"I have not lived without luck, and could best serve my private interests by fitting snugly into the routine of things. I suffer, however, for this very reason from a bit of a responsibility complex, and hence the trouble I take in this matter.

". . . You know perfectly well there is no libel contained or intended. Libel is falsehood, and one who libels is given a sharper title.

"Awaiting therefore your thanks rather than your enmity, and thanking you for pointing out my obsesssion which I might well hope to cultivate further,

"I remain

"Yours gruffly,"

The Corcoran Gallery in Washington awarded "Fisherman's Family" its first prize. Bellows lectured at the Masters School and the Art Students' League, wrote and received innumerable letters on all kinds of subjects and, like the rest of his group, waited with curiosity the arrival of Leon Kroll with his bride. From Madrid, Marjorie Henri characterized the general suspense in her Christmas letter to Emma: "We finally got The Word from Leon and the Boss read it to me from his bed; and I was sure he was making it up. I wouldn't believe it until I had it in my own hands. I want a rough idea of her looks, Em—you know. Also does she speak English?"

The Society of Perfect Husbands and Wives had reason to be concerned over Leon's choice. These artists, visionary in politics and unconventional in speech and dress, were knit together by a thoroughly Victorian sense of family life and responsibility. Harmony among the members of the distaff side was quite as important as among the painters.

A radiant Kroll presented his wife at a dinner party in the Bellows home and showed the society that it need not have worried at all. Viette Kroll was a very beautiful woman—they would have expected that of Leon. She was also brilliant, warm-hearted, and quite as devoted to her husband as were the wives of the other members. What the prospect of her induction into this closed circle may have cost her remained her secret. The veteran members shortly found themselves wondering how they had ever got along without her—and her English was as charming as she was herself.

With the Henris away there was no New Year's party to welcome 1924, but the New Society's opening was set for January 3, and every one connected with it was busy over the holidays. George's entry was "The Crucifixion."

Not since "Elinor, Jean, and Anna" had New York been so excited by a picture. Henry McBride of the *Herald* headlined it the following Sunday:

NEW SOCIETY'S SUCCESSFUL OPENING

GEORGE BELLOWS' CRUCIFIXION IS
SENSATION OF EXHIBITION

"In such a hubbub, of course, criticism ran to extremes. I heard one lady say, for instance, that Mr. Bellows' big 'Crucifixion' was 'the greatest picture ever produced by an American.' Mr. Bellows' picture was the rallying point all afternoon for those who love to argue, and doubtless will be the most talked about painting in the collection.

"As in all Mr. Bellows' painting there is something to be said for it and something to be said against it. The points in its favor may be stated first. It is vigorous and ambitious. An artist who has his living to make doesn't undertake a religious picture in these days without considerable preliminary thought, and that Mr. Bellows finally decided to risk all the necessary time and energy is a high testimonial to his courage . . .

"But there is a reverse to the medal, and there will always be those to look at both sides of a coin.

"Is Mr. Bellows' work truly great, either in feeling or in workmanship? Ah, there we get down to business. I cannot feel religious ecstasy anywhere in it, but on the contrary a continual reaching out for theatrical effects . . .

"In color, draftsmanship and composition the painting is the reverse of commendable. Color has always been a trial for Mr. Bellows and he does not seem to improve . . .

"At the reception I heard the ominous word 'Goya' continually rising above the choruses of praise, but to me there was far more Greco than Goya in the picture."

On the other hand, Robert J. Cole, under the heading of "Young Progressive Who Became an Elder Statesman," declared:

"It is only a few years since George Bellows, Henri, Luks, Glackens, Sloan and a few others were the progressives of American Art. Now they are almost the Pilgrim Fathers or Elder Statesmen, or something of the sort.

"To identify this painter too closely with a group, however, would be a mistake. He stands by himself, and his work needs no signature. For there is marked individuality in both color and design. If he has a kinship, it may be with such an earlier artist as Winslow Homer . . ."

Thus the experts elegantly thumbed their noses at each other across the critical ring, while Bellows and Bolton Brown continued their ritual around the lithographic stones on the balcony at 146. By March they had turned out thirty-three designs, ranging in editions of 8 to 103. The subject matter was amazingly diversified as always, although the proportion of portraits increased remarkably: Anne and Jean, of course, in a variety of costumes, and Gene Speicher. Many others, however, were drawn on a commission basis.

Bellows made eight careful and diversified nudes. He dipped into the past and redrew studies for "The Wind Bloweth" and "Men Like Gods." It was an election year, and in his semisatirical "Appeal to the People" the only seriousness is shown by the candidate who bears something of a resemblance to his hero Woodrow Wilson.

The best known print of this series is "Dempsey and Firpo." The original drawing had never been published, and the composi-

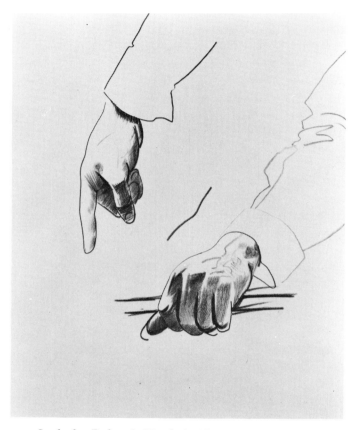

Study for Referee's Hands in "Dempsey-Firpo," 1924.

tion was far too good to lose. He tried it twice. The first version was printed in the very large edition of 103 proofs, priced at the unprecedented figure of $60 each. It sold well immediately, at a time when he was asking only $15 for some of his finest prints of nudes.

A long and rather lonely epistle came from Henri in Madrid:

"Thank you for the snap shot which is now decorating the wall of our studio and smiles on all that I do whether is it good or bad. I have a regular collection on the space on the wall, the said portrait which is the best yet of G.B. being in the place of honor. Flanking it are reproductions of the portrait of Emma and her Children, a faint newspaper cut of the Crucifixion, etchings by John Sloan, and a cut of a plump little girl putting on or off a stocking on a handsome leg, a head by Speicher from the New Society in Greek stillness, and whatever else has come our way, of the doings of you folks at home in these times of our absence . . .

"I used to say that when a man gets beyond fifty he almost invariably says 'the Country is going to the dogs.' Well here I am well in that age, and if I don't say the country is going to the dogs, I do say that there shall have to be a general awakening or we will find ourselves living in one of the backshifts of progress . . . We are affected by our environment. It seems as though there were waves and backwashes. The waves are when the artist is dominant in human affairs, the backwash is when the puritan, the prohibitionist, the commercial gets the upper hand. Dark days. When the wave is on it isn't so bad for the poor—there is romance anyway. When the powers of the backwash have the rule, poverty exists just the same if not much more, and it is grim, hideous and hopeless . . ."

The Bellows children were growing rapidly with that capacity all children have of doing so without their parents being aware of it. One evening Anne was bidden to a party at the Haggin's, miles uptown in the fashionable residential quarter, and when George went to fetch her he decided to walk home. Although she had on party slippers, Anne skipped gaily along beside him, block after weary block, treasuring every minute of time with this father of hers whom she adored but saw so seldom. Another night that winter, when Emma was grappling firmly with another headache and they had two tickets to John Barrymore's "Hamlet," George easily persuaded Anne to take her mother's place, dress the part, and come along. He squired her through the evening as proudly as if she had been Emma herself.

Ever-generous Gertrude Vanderbilt Whitney gave the Bellows

her box for "La Traviata" at the Metropolitan Opera House and they promptly arranged a dinner party with the Speichers, just returned from Buffalo, and the newly married Krolls. Then Laura Monett appeared unexpectedly from Columbus, and Emma dutifully gave her the hostess' seat. This proved unfortunate, for "Lollie" Monett, shaking with palsy and as frank as her stepmother Anna had been, made it quite plain that she and "foreigners" had *nothing* in common. The atmosphere in the Whitney box became thick with embarrassment, but George's friends rallied to his leadership, while "the foreigner," Viette Kroll, passed off the provincial slur with graceful dignity.

A Dr. Watkins of Montclair provoked from George some interesting comments on great painters: "My habit of mind as well as my opinion does not take any account of the subject matter treated by artists. It is, therefore, not my habit of thought to refer to certain painters as landscape painters or portrait painters, but just look at them as artists.

"All the men you mention are beyond doubt great painters, great artists as well. Of them, Winslow Homer is my particular pet. And one other American or better, two, stand on the same pedestal with him, in my mind, neither of whom you mentioned: Thomas Eakins and Whistler . . ."

Jay Hambidge died, and Bellows was deluged with requests of all kinds of information on Dynamic Symmetry. Among the appeals for information, letters, and lectures came one from Mrs. Hambidge herself who needed help in arranging for the publication of a primer on the subject. Bellows worked out a tri-partite division of the material for her and then, in turn, appealed to Lacey Caskey, the distinguished Curator of Classical Art at the Boston Museum. Caskey, who had been a close friend of Hambidge's, without being a believer in the universality of his dogma, must have been amused to read George's statement: "If Mr. Hambidge had been more practical, I feel he would have better proceeded in this sort of order [George's] and it is very unfortunate that he did not create this particular work himself."

Henri heard of Hambidge's death and poured out the finest eulogy the deceased ever received:

"The news of Hambidge's death was a shock. What a loss! What a friend who could be a friend because he knew so much. He gave us a lot, could have gone on giving and could always appreciate. My grief is mixed with anger. I can't help but think of those despicable dogs who went out of their way to bark their criticisms at him . . . I believe he would be alive now and working if these people had not killed him . . . Now we have lost him before he was finished. The absence of such men creates a great loneliness."

With the memories of his last experiments with color and technique strongly in mind, George took to his easel long before the first real spring days came. "River Front," a subject he had dealt with ten years before, was now tried out again, using an underpainting of green and red-orange, with blue, purple, and yellow added later. The background seems curiously to press toward the front, the tugboat and the overlapping sails almost huddled against the pier, giving a spatial effect not unlike that of the neo-Impressionists.

In April, civic jury duty took the artist out of his studio for a fortnight. Then he launched into a smaller, more complex design: "The Picnic." The mood was entirely different, reverting to some of the more poetic fantasies produced for "The Wind Bloweth." In a fairyland of summer sky and glassy lake, mountain, and steep hills he arranged his family: Emma at the tablecloth, himself with a fishing rod, and Anne pursuing Jean down a slope and Speicher sleeping limply under a bush. The configuration of the hills, the radiant light from the foliage, even the theme of the fishing rod were reminiscent of the Bellows' summer at Carmel, although both drawing and painting were simpler and more direct.

The May 3 issue of *Collier's* appeared, and George, opening to the story entitled "The Chins of the Fathers," could not believe his eyes. He had worked hard over an illustration for this sentimental story of the prize ring, and was so pleased with the composition that he had already begun to turn it into the canvas entitled "Ringside Seats." *Collier's* had taken the drawing, spread it out over two pages, and had cropped pieces from the right edge, the top, and through the center! Bellows let out an enraged howl, and Emma, on seeing the evidence, agreed that this was a desecration.

He addressed his objections to the offending magazine in the form of a bill:

"George Bellows to

"Colliers Weekly, Dr.

"Two drawings illustrating Chins of the Fathers $800.00

"If there were any way of suing you for libel on the reproductions I would do so. To trim, cut, and otherwise mutilate an artist's work is quite analogous to misrepresentation before the public, in this case going as far as criminal libel . . .

"Proportion among the many elements is almost everything in a work of art, and proportions of size and shape are fundamental in a fine thing, and must be held sacred. It is time for publishers to be taught a lesson on this score for their guidance on the rare occasions when they deal with the work of serious artists."

Writing this paragraph brought his rage to a fine boil:

"Not only have you shown the worst of taste, and a total lack of consideration for me, you are also guilty of [a snide trick.] Sanding the sugar, watering the milk, stretching one into two. Instead of appearing then before the public as having created one beautiful drawing, in which the proportion of light and shade was basic, I am shown by you as having made two rotten drawings in which [with] your trimmings and cuttings light and shade is completely destroyed. I therefore intend at least to be paid for the 'two' rotten drawings, as per contract . . .

"Kindly return the original to me at your earliest convenience. It will revive my spirits again in its virgin loveliness. I hope only the photo plate has been raped; otherwise you will be in for trouble."

Collier's response was necessarily pacific. It found the artist in a calmer mood, but no less adamantine.

"Your letter, I am sorry to find, shows a practiced hand at avoiding the point.

"I am not challenging or criticizing the reproduction of my work. It was not 'reproduced.' To reproduce means to duplicate. I am stating that my work has been changed, cut up, deleted, edited, and spoiled, and all without asking any permission from me. It is quite as bad as if I had written a fine poem and your office had chopped out lines ad. lib., destroying all metre and all reason for being. Mutilated is an exact description, the only possible further step is total destruction . . .

"The question is far more important than this single incident. It is enlarged by being party to a great principle . . ."

That same day he looked around for a lawyer, found one in Judge Van Slyke, and instituted legal proceedings against *Collier's*. His report on the matter to Henri is characteristic:

"Emma was furious and ordered me to war. I have gone.

"I hope you don't think of me as Don Quixote for butting a stone wall. I know you are with me on the question."

All through this ethical tussle he had been hard at work on "Ringside Seats," exacting satisfaction from every brush stroke as he thought of the indignities the original drawing had undergone. Then he painted a portrait of Leila Kalman, which he called "The Violinist," experimenting with the linear pattern of the instruments and the folds of her blouse in an almost cubist vein. The picture was slow to develop, and he took it along with him to Woodstock when the time came.

Plans for the summer were uppermost in his head by the end of May. He wrote his occasional handyman-mechanic, one Albert Cashdollar:

"I am coming to Woodstock on the 23rd, sure. I am sending by mail the number plates for my car and also the check from Brown's Garage in Kingston where my battery is stored. Will you get the keys to my garage from Griffin Herrick, get out my car and fix it up in any way you feel necessary or advisable. It probably needs a good deal of cleaning inside, and the rack which holds the battery is badly broken . . ."

To *Good Housekeeping*, which wanted a piece on the Salvation Army and was willing to take anything he offered, he wrote asking for the manuscript because "it might suggest something to me," and requesting a number of photographs of Salvation Army equipment. Salvation Army lassies would be hard to find in Woodstock. To Concord, Massachusetts, he sent an acknowledgment of the prize it had awarded his "Miss Ruth" six months before. He dashed off a brief gem to Mrs. John Carroll in Woodstock:

"Dear Inez:

If you were a bee
I would be glad to have the hives."

He kept his half-sister, too ill to come East, abreast of all his plans and added a significant line or two:

"Two weeks ago it was all arranged for me to paint Paderewski, the well-known Polish politician, for Mr. Steinway. Like most sitters, however, he didn't show up. Had a fit, cancelled all dates, and went home to fight . . ."

The Bellows family had a fine summer in Woodstock. George began at once to turn his drawings and prints of the Dempsey-Firpo fight into an oil, underpainting it entirely in Indian red and building it up with other colors. This technique accounts for the extraordinary warmth of the canvas, catching in its tone the wild excitement of the episode. The subject suited him entirely, for the battle with *Collier's* had reached the courts, and on Bastille Day he received the following telegram from Judge Van Slyke:

"Defendant's motion of Judgment denied, Judge holding that your picture was mutilated, its artistic merit destroyed and that our action for libel is maintainable. Congratulations!"

The first round of combat having been decided in his favor, George now entered the ring again with a wholly different opponent, his nine-year-old daughter Jean. She adored posing for her father, but was always an impatient model. This time she found her complex, old-fashioned costume hot and uncomfortable, and the effort of standing still completely boring. He did his best to make the process easy, letting her sit at every opportunity while he worked on the details of the cuffs, the pattern of the skirt, the hat. When the ordeal was over he could point with pride to another of his penetrating studies of childhood, Jean's grave little face surveying the spectator above a quaint gay dress, the whole painting flooded with a rosy tonality. He called it "Lady Jean."

In many ways the summer was normal enough. There were the usual Sunday baseball games and George, always the captain, kept up his witty chatter, although his years and added weight made the stealing of bases harder than usual. Once he managed to stun himself on the way to the sack and his daughters, seeing their father unconscious on the ground, raised such an hysterical display on the bleachers that he was far more embarrassed by their behavior than by his own ineptitude.

Poker games began after supper and lasted far into the night, heavy with talk and laughter and the smell of cigar smoke, all penetrating ultimately to the girls' room directly above. As the play went on, Anne and Jean invented lively games of their own, becoming so noisy that their father would finally throw back his head and howl: "Stop having so much fun up there!"

The annual Maverick festival in August, with its weeks of preparation, called out the finest costumes in Woodstock. Every artist's house was cluttered with trunks of gay garments, and the ladies always took weeks to prepare for the event. George preferred to dress according to the fancy of the moment, going one year with a drooping moustache, another as an over-stuffed brunette, and another as a Nubian slave. In whatever guise he chose, there was never a more persuasive master of ceremonies than George Bellows.

Yet something was very wrong about the summer of 1924. Nothing quite fitted its accustomed place. When George reached for an infield fly, a sudden cramp took his attention from it. His diet inherited from his mother, began to play him false. Roast beef, fried chicken, stewed tomatoes, pie, or cake. One of these must be to blame, but which?

He took his troubles to Dr. Downer, a general practitioner with none of the patter of a New York specialist. He had a way of prescribing castor oil when really needed and of asking an artist if the photograph of a fifth-century Greek sculpture hanging in his hall was "some of your work?" The cognoscenti laughed at him behind his elderly back and called him an "Old Dodo."

Doc Downer prescribed no castor oil for George. Instead, he talked to him like a Dutch uncle: "You've got chronic appendicitis and you ought to get yourself in good enough shape to have it out. It's a perfectly simple operation now-a-days, but you're overweight, you eat too much, smoke too much, and you must give up violent games for a while to get ready for the operation. Nobody's indestructible, you know."

Doc Downer went as far as professional ethics would allow, giving orders to his patient. The real problem was not the disease, but its host. George had always believed he could lick any illness by himself and the lonely, regimented week in the San Francisco hospital over his tonsils had given him a horror of operations.

He made one concession to the doctor's admonition on smoking. He gave it up for a while, much to Emma's delight. "Giving it up" amounted to cutting a cigarette into thirds, and slipping over to see Charlie Rosen, Katherine's father, in his studio next door to puff a fragment into its ultimate shred, safely removed from Emma's observation.

George Bellows was a sick man, but he concealed his weakness from everyone. He spent his days in the studio, producing "Nude on a Hexagon Quilt," which he called "Venus" until Emma changed his mind. The picture is obscurely reminiscent of the "Figure in Motion" that Henri showed at the Armory in 1913. Henri had sought for sudden effect; Bellows probed into the subtle problems of weight and texture, exploiting in more graphic form Matisse's absorption with geometric pattern.

He tried several portraits, but the only one that really pleased him was of his country neighbors, Mr. and Mrs. Philip Wase. In this canvas the starkness of his boyhood Methodism found its mark, for the picture is conceived in cool tones with only incidental touches of brilliant reds.

Bellows tried one last big picture in 1924, a recollection of Titian's "Sacred and Profane Love." He gave it that title at first, and later amended it to "Two Women," partly because of Emma and also with a piquant eye toward Anthony Comstock's "League of Decency." The painting has a thoughtful look without the sensual contrasts of the great Venetian. Bellows was painting as a Victorian American, not as a Renaissance humanist. A curious sense of distance and reflection, not unlike that of "Emma and her Children," a strong feeling for texture and for shape mingle in this scene with its startling prediction of Picasso's "Woman Before a Mirror."

George and Emma sent the children back to the Storys and school as usual, and then spent a generous autumn with the Speichers. George rambled about the countryside, cursing the intermittent clutches at his midriff, and painted familiar spots such as "Risley's Barns," "Jim Twadell's Place," and "My House, Woodstock" before garage-mechanic Albert Cashdollar drove them in the Buick to the station and another winter in New York.

A mass of new and unfinished business greeted Bellows there, and he tackled it with something less than his usual ardor. Chicago had planned a joint show of his and Kroll's work. Everybody wanted his pictures for exhibition, and several people were actually buying them. The flooring of his studio was badly in need of repair. The case against *Collier's* had come to a standstill. Laura Monett lay dangerously ill in Columbus. He himself was in no condition to cope with things. But he did.

Forty-two paintings went to Chicago. He lined up more for a big exhibition at Durand-Ruel and dealt on a fairly regular schedule with the other business that pressed against his door. He typed more than forty letters between the middle of November and Christmas and wrote a number in longhand.

He declined offers to lecture on Dynamic Symmetry. He generally accepted invitations to join various organizations, although when the American Association of Mural Painters' bid arrived, he felt compelled to write: "Although I am not denying that I have wished to do so, the fact remains that I have never in my life created a mural decoration, and I cannot see how I can qualify."

Kroll and Bellows had been garnering Chicago awards at frequent intervals. This year the prize went to Leon, and George responded to the news at once:

"This is an uninspired note to congratulate you as the recipient of the distinguished honor, from the distinguished Art Institute of Chicago in the matter of the distinguished prize for the distinguished amount of money. It gave me fifty percent as much pleasure as if I had received the money myself,—nay, I will say sixty percent, because I can't help but feel that you appreciated getting it yourself." [It was the only money Kroll had made in his first year of marriage.]

"We received a long letter totally without French accents from your adorable wife, and Emma let me read it. I liked it very much.

I hope that after she gets a dull letter from Emma in reply, that she will try again in the same exalted spirit, realizing that I am going to read the letter as well as Emma . . ."

Nephew Howard Monett kept him informed of his sister's condition and urged him to come for a visit. Perhaps because George was fighting his own battle with ill-health, he covered his worry as lightly as he could with the phrase: "If we come out to Columbus, it would be fine to see the Illinois game, which I suppose is the Saturday before Thanksgiving."

Repairs to the flooring of the studio would normally have been made by the artist himself, but he felt too wretched to undertake the work alone. He opened negotiations with his Woodstock carpenter, Mr. Herrick, who had helped him build his house, saying that he wanted someone in whom he had confidence, "not these rare birds around New York." Budging a country carpenter from his home base has long baffled more influential men than Bellows, but nothing shook his confidence in his ability to get what he wanted in the end.

As the weeks wore on he felt increasingly wretched, but despite professional warnings to get rid of his appendix before it gave him serious trouble, he declined. Every concession to his doctor cost him dearly in pride as well as in diet. "Why the Hell!" he protested when confronted with milk and yeast cakes for lunch, but he got them down.

Bolton Brown, his printer, was laid up with rheumatism. To him the painter gave the wisdom he would not take himself:

"I hope the right doctor will give you the right advice and return you to your characteristic energy. For God's sake don't get the feeling that you are an old man.

"I certainly do not want to let the winter slip by without making some more lithographs with you . . . at least through January and February."

In San Diego, Aunt Fanny's indomitable spirit returned to its Maker. George wrote:

"Aunt Fanny will always remain to me the most beautiful and important vision of my babyhood . . . One of the beautiful things about Aunt Fanny was her characteristic treasuring of beautiful memories. It gave me a great sensation, I recall, to have her bring me on her visits some drawings which I had made as a little boy.

These drawings are, of course, the earliest evidence of my tendencies to be an artist . . ."

Zuloaga, the Spanish portrait painter who was limning every fashionable head from coast to coast, turned up again in New York. He had been presented with a Bellows lithograph by one of his admirers, and George had met him twice. Given a third opportunity, he wrote his hostess:

"I was greatly disappointed to be forced to cancel my engagement with you. I was taken with a whale of a cold and could not speak above a whisper, and as history tells us that our father, George Washington, lost his life by going outdoors with a cold [and] since I am evidently one of his descendents, I felt I must profit by his example."

He completed his last major oil: "Jean, Anne, and Joseph." The theme recalled a summer in Middletown; the three children are spaced lightly in the foreground. The characters remained the Rhode Island cast, but the setting, dominated by Camden's rounded hills, was drenched in the radiance of California's early morning.

He toyed for a while with another sketch, "Summer Fantasy," and then left it unfinished to deal with other problems. Mr. Herrick, that "reliable" carpenter in Woodstock, had done nothing about the floor repairs. George wrote: "Your note is very disappointing. I have practically promised Bolton Brown to make lithographs with him during January, and I should hate to change this arrangement . . ."

Like a shopkeeper taking his year-end count of stock, he called in all his paintings that were in dealers' hands. Instinctively he was putting his house in order. He asked his photographer for more prints of his latest photograph, making some suggestions about the shape of the picture.

Laura Monett lay at the point of death. Bellows wrote his nephew: "We are at a total loss in knowing just what to do, or to plan to do, as it would be superfluous to come to Columbus just now if your mother is unable to see us or even understand our presence. There is, of course, always hope; and if she brightens up again (which we pray for) I feel that we should come at once. Otherwise I suppose it is the final act. There is nothing more I know to say here.

"I am sending out a bright little landscape which I spoke about in my other letter. I see no reason to hold this, for if good luck turns it may help to brighten the room, and if it is useless in this way I hope that you and Marie will enjoy it for yourselves.

"Count on us to come at the moment you say the word."

It is doubtful if Bellows could have made the journey, although he would have tried if "the word" had come. His household was full of Christmas talk, but he sometimes could hardly rouse himself to speak. There were large-lettered signs at the table: *"Eat Slowly!" "Chew!"* but he never noticed them except when Emma called them to his attention. The doctors had told him to eat and smoke less. He had almost abandoned any form of exercise because he was not up to it, and he was seriously overweight. On the major issue of an operation his attitude was: "Doctors! What the Hell do they know about it?" Alone with his family his moods shifted freely from gloom to impatience, but with none of his usual quixotry. In the evenings he would start to sing and then break off to lie down on a couch.

To the outside world he maintained a magnificent front. He sounded like his normal self in telling a gentleman from Virginia that: "It is impossible for me to consider an effort to create a portrait from a photograph." To Kroll, arranging their show in Chicago, he quipped:

"It is an awful thing to be cursed by prize money, especially if it is the only money you have at the time. Prizes and success are generally, of course, an awful thing, and great artists have succeeded (maybe in spite of them); but the paradox remains that the greatest masters of the past have, in as many cases as not, been successful, and have all received the plums in the pudding of their generation . . .

"All I want you to do about my exhibition at the Institute is to prevent me from having any success with it."

One evening he felt well enough to escort Emma to a performance of "Desire Under the Elms" at the Greenwich Village Theatre. When it was over he wrote Kenneth Macgowan:

"The play is magnificent. I felt I was under the spell of one of the world's greatest dramatists.

"I wish I could paint the portrait of Gene O'Neill sometime. As I told you, we were kids together when I was a young art student in New York, but I haven't seen him to talk to for sixteen years, I suppose. The talk was very high, or very low, in those days."

Just before Christmas he propped up one of his unfinished summer sketches on the easel, "The Picket Fence." It offered an extraordinary synthesis of many things he remembered—a quiet,

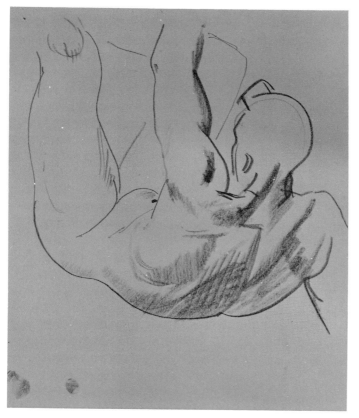

Study for Dempsey in "Dempsey-Firpo," 1924.

isolated home, bright with sun and cosily unlike his "Shore House." He incorporated an insistent diamond pattern of shadows under the eaves, recalling his interest in the Cubists at the Armory Show and his study of Dynamic Symmetry. The rounded shapes of the Camden Hills and Mount Overlook loom over shrubbery lit by the fog-filtered sunlight of Carmel. The long-limbed shadows recall his studies of tennis at Newport. It is a strangely calm, orderly and reflective design. There was much to do on it still, but very little time.

He remembered to invite a fellow Woodstocker to join his Squash Club, acknowledged a lady's poem, fended off a request from Mark Van Doren to cooperate in a series of articles about the environment of American artists, sent off an autographed photograph to Minnesota, reaffirmed his decision not to lecture on Dynamic Symmetry, and requested the return of some of his lithographs from an itinerant dealer whom he heard was in town. Then came Christmas Eve, the tree, the holiday and, after several days of acute discomfort, the Henris' annual New Year's party.

The Henri studio blazed with light and cheer to welcome in 1925. Will and Effie Glackens, Gene and Elsie Speicher, George and Emma, and a handful of others gathered for one more of those evenings that meant so much to them all. The men held forth on the latest of their paintings; on books and plays recently seen or read; and on politics, for Coolidge would be inaugurated in another two months, setting back the Socialist cause for another four years. Lively quips and humorous incidents laced more serious discussions. George, briefly recovered in health and spirits, provided the spark as always. When the party broke up long after midnight, every one remembered his great laughter booming out in the street below.

On New Year's Day, Ethel Clarke came in to find George lying on a couch in the studio. "He won't eat anything," protested Emma. "I *can't* eat," he retorted listlessly. Emma went down to the door with her friend. "I'm worried," she said. "You know *I* can't call a doctor, and *he* won't. I don't know what to do."

The morning of January 2 Bellows roused himself impatiently. His studio was stacked high with the new flooring that awaited Mr. Herrick of Woodstock; he decided to start the job himself. After all, the best cure for any ailment, he maintained, was hearty exercise. He climbed up to his elaborate tool chest in the balcony, picked out what he needed, and getting to his knees began to rip up the worn floor boards. He was hard at work when the great pain struck him. He doubled over while it lasted. Before he could stumble down the stairs to the telephone, Emma, her principles cast to the wind, was frantically trying to reach a doctor.

There were comings and goings and a general commotion at 146. Then two frightened little girls, looking out their window, saw their father, wrapped in a heavy overcoat, walk heavily down the short front steps and into a waiting taxicab.

The operation was a success. The ruptured appendix was removed without killing the patient although his whole system was charged with accumulated poison. Early reports from the hospital were optimistic, even in the days before wonder drugs, for Bellows' constitution was already a legend. On January 5 Emma appeared at the opening of the New Society's exhibition, looking as cool under her new red hat as if nothing at all were the matter. Thereafter, ignoring "Science," she virtually lived at the patient's bedside. George smiled at her when he was conscious, although he was delirious a good part of the time. Then, early in the morning of January 8, the telephone rang on the dark landing below his studio. George Bellows was dead.

Self-Portrait; lithograph, 1921.

THE AFTERMATH

« *1925 -* «

» X «   *"A great present is the best assurance of a great future."* George Bellows

Nobody believed it at first. It was impossible to imagine the robust vitality of George Bellows cut off bluntly at the age of forty-two.

A man's death presents his family and friends with three problems. The first and most pressing is the disposal of his body. The second is the disposition of his assets. The most protracted of the three involves healing the great wound inflicted on the lives of the survivors. In the case of George Bellows, problems two and three blended; problem one remained inexorably in the foreground for immediate resolution.

Emma, her mistrust of the medical profession now bitterly confirmed, returned to her home in a state of shock to find that her father had incurable cancer and required an immediate operation. William E. Story, merchant of fine linens and laces, had long subscribed to Christian Science to please his wife, but now he demanded surgery. In this emergency, the funeral of his distinguished son-in-law devolved upon George's friends. Emma chose the church and the music, but the other details were left to them, and they seized gratefully on any activity as a focus for bewildered minds.

George Bellows had married Emma Story fifteen years before in the simplest possible ceremony. He was buried with all the pomp that those closest to him could command. The setting was the celebrated Church of the Ascension on Fifth Avenue at Tenth Street; and there, two days later, he lay in his coffin under John LaFarge's Peruginesque mural, so vastly admired by the critic Royal Cortissoz. Twenty-four pallbearers included Speicher, Henri, Sloan, Glackens, Prendergast, and Lawson from the original Eight; and Bolton Brown, the printer. The seats were crowded with a brilliant and assorted assembly of artists, musicians, authors, dealers, collectors, fellow townsmen from Woodstock, and hundreds of other men and women whose lives had touched upon Bellows'. Zuloaga was there; and the President of the National Academy of Design; Charles Dana Gibson, his old idol; and Joseph Pennell, his old antagonist.

A selection from Handel opened the service. There were readings from the Scriptures, and the choir included one of George's favorite spirituals, "Listen to the Lambs," among its numbers. The service ended with Emma's choice, Grieg's "Ase's Death." Then the mourners dispersed and Emma found herself alone with the Speichers and the Henris following the hearse through a drizzly Brooklyn to the Story family lot in Greenwood Cemetery.

Some days later Speicher reported to Kroll in Chicago: "I know you will understand when I say that since poor George's death I have been in a daze and am only now getting out of it. I have done only the things that actually had to be done. Each day I realize more and more what a terrible thing has happened and the vast emptiness that is getting longer and longer. I don't think I can ever be reconciled to the injustice of George's going. To think of all the little 5 cent characters hanging around and painting 2 cent canvases . . .

"The service they all say was impressive. To me it was the longest twenty minutes I ever hope to put in. I saw no one, heard nothing, and then there was that trip through Brooklyn . . .

"Emma, poor girl, is holding up her end amazingly. She of course has her minutes of depression, but with her C. S. and her character I think she is coming through beautifully. The kids of course are what help enormously.

"Poor Henri is terribly cut up. The two days immediately after he heard the news he sat round with a handkerchief which he never put down. I of course always did realize that he and George were pretty close, but after hearing him talk about George I saw that he held him as a god. Henri, of course, has acted all his life in a sincere way and never said 'yes' when he meant 'no' in matters of right or wrong. That kind of decision brings with it very staunch friends and many enemies, and I know that he realizes that one of his staunchest props and sympathizers is no more. He was wonderful and beautiful through it all. He is a great warm human being. Marjorie and Elsie were equally great and came through in every way."

Kroll, holding the fort in Chicago and besieged by that city's press, found an outlet for his confusion and grief in a violent diatribe on critics and their ways. Standing in the great gallery of the Art Institute with George's pictures all around him, he blasted a crowd of reporters for their cavalier treatment of the exhibition, for their blindness to excellence in art, and especially their hostility to the work of a great American painter. This explosion brought him momentary relief before the loneliness crept in again.

Elsie Speicher and Ethel Clarke handled the scores of letters from enthusiasts, cranks, and autograph hunters, while Emma personally answered the hundreds that came from people she knew and those she recognized as having been important in one way or another to George. And as her firm, small, vertical handwriting, so different from George's profligate slant, repeated the familiar phrases, her mind was already reaching out reluctantly to the larger decisions that had to be made. Her own altered way of life could wait a little while. Her responsibility for George's reputation could not. Press and public had reacted to his death in a wholly unprecedented fashion. She never quite understood why; but George had been her life, and she would prove worthy of him.

On the day of his death the Columbus papers reorganized their front pages to accommodate two-inch banner headlines: "GEORGE BELLOWS DEAD."

In New York the *Sun* editorialized: "This country has lost one of its foremost artists and the most eminent of the younger academic painters. [The younger generation] looked upon him as the Ajax who was to defy for their benefit the too conservative traditions of the older schools. The intransigents revered him as their leader, although he seemed free from what his elders are disposed to regard as the heresies of the most modern school . . ."

The *Times* probed more deeply: "It is a misfortune not only for his many friends but for America and art that George Bellows should have died before his work was done. He had the experimental temper from first to last . . . and in all his ventures and speculations he was consistently himself. Time can only enhance the effect of his sound craftsmanship and personal vision. He was a valuable driving force and his talent was great . . . There will be an appreciable lapse of expectation and interest [in art exhibitions] with nothing more to look forward to from that bold and skillful brush, that orderly and eager mind.

"No man is born an artist. To the initial impulse must be added the essay so hard and the sharp conquering. It is good for the enduring fame of this artist that the conquering followed swiftly upon the essay in one method after another, in one medium after another; and it is good for those who have studied under him that he taught no less gladly than he learned. There is no one to fill precisely his place in his generation, so there is more than customary significance in saying that his loss is one to be mourned."

Since the death of Michelangelo, no artist's memory had received so sudden and spontaneous an accolade. It remained to see what would follow it.

Into the immediate spotlight of publicity stepped Ignazio Zuloaga, the visiting celebrity from Spain, with an offer of $5,000 to start a subscription for the purchase of "Two Women" for the Metropolitan Museum of Art. The Bellows entourage, in its inchoate state, regarded this as outrageous presumption. The infiltration of fashionable foreigners had always been a major irritation, and the suggestion that George Bellows be first immortalized by an alien aroused instant hostility. No direct statement was issued to the press, but two months later the *Herald Tribune* reported various members as using freely the accusation of "advertisement" and "publicity," "bad taste," "ill-advised," and "bad judgment." Henri was cited as having communicated with Zuloaga's sponsors, since when the $5,000 offer "had not been renewed." The reliability of the article is open to question since it included the amazing statement that: "Bellows did not visit Europe until he was a finished craftsman."

Zuloaga's gesture was of small consequence compared to the immediate problem of exhibitions. The New Society's exhibition was about to close, and on its heels, in February, the last of the shows that Bellows planned himself was due to open at Durand-Ruel. This "temple" of French Impressionism had never before given over its walls to a single American, and the event was to provide something of a minor earthquake in the rapidly growing ranks of the Francophiles. For it, the painter had set aside ten of the pictures done in 1924 including the colorful "Lady Jean," dramatic "Dempsey Firpo," and monumental "River Front." The chill formality of "Mr. and Mrs. Philip Wase" contrasted with the romance of "The Picnic" and "Jean, Anne, and Joseph." Portraits of the violinist Leila Kalman and Elizabeth Heerman shared the honors with "Ringside Seats" and "Nude on a Hexagon Quilt." Only two earlier canvases were included, one of his 1923 portraits and the spacially conceived "On the Porch" from 1919. Variety had always been a Bellows characteristic, but this concentration on his most recent work showed that when he planned the show he was engrossed in his new approach to form.

Forbes Watson was still smarting from the blast George had aimed at him ten years before during the dispute over the Olney portrait. He had been accused of "two-faced caution" then. The rightness of this rebuke he proceeded to demonstrate in his review of the Durand-Ruel exhibition: "In the younger generation of painters who have begun to make their ideas felt since Bellows first won his place in the eyes of the public there is a distinct reaction from the kind of brilliance Bellows had in such unusual degree. Disparagement of what he stood for has not been lacking. One wonders how far the pendulum will swing back . . .

"The present is not the moment to dwell on the defects of his qualities. The point is that Bellows had positive and exceptional gifts. Among them were energy, courage, love of life and enormous natural facility."

A fortnight after the exhibition closed, the *Times* took a broader view: "Each time Durand-Ruel show their French paintings they seem to change a little in the light of the work that immediately surrounds them. After Bellows, Pissarro and Sisley are gentle and contained . . ."

Ever since 1916 when the first lithograph was pulled from the press at 146, the Frederick Keppel Gallery had been the principal outlet for Bellows' prints. In April, Emma tested her independent judgment by arranging for a major showing of the whole series and some of the drawings at that gallery. Henry McBride of the New York *Sun* was refreshed by his visit to the show:

"There is one item in the present exhibition that emphasizes anew the tragedy of the sudden taking off of the artist. This is the original drawing for the lithograph of the Firpo fight . . . the immense artistic superiority of the drawing over the lithograph shows the direction of the artist's study and hints of the added richness he could have given his prints had he lived.

"As it is they are handsome; and, of course vigorous. Bellows loved force and forceful doings, and even in his portraits he meant to hit you hard . . . The blacks, which at the beginning were so inveterately black, were beginning to take on mystery and color. Nevertheless, one of the early lithographs, the one called 'Stag at Sharkey's,' is such a rhapsody of enthusiasm for the drama of pugilism that it must remain one of the favorites on the entire Bellows list."

In this last statement, history has borne out Mr. McBride, for "Stag at Sharkey's" has become an indispensable requirement for every serious collector of American prints.

After the first shock of Bellows' sudden death was over, and the long road ahead appeared in sharp focus, Emma kept her head. She had been gratified by the exhibitions at Durand-Ruel and Keppel's, especially since they netted her a useful income from the sale of an oil and a number of prints. One-man shows have always pleased an artist and his family. Yet it was increasingly apparent that some more significant demonstration of Bellows' genius must be organized.

A great retrospective exhibition had been inevitable from the moment of George's death, and the demand for it came not from family or friends but from the public. Three days after the funeral, the Grand Central Galleries tendered the use of their exhibition space without cost for a memorial show. It was perhaps unfortunate that their invitation contained the inducement: "Mr. Zuloaga was here last week and stated emphatically that they were the best exhibition galleries he had ever seen and finer than any he knew of in Europe." To this gesture Emma responded with veteran tact: "Your very kind and generous offer was received by me with great appreciation . . . eventually I hope to do the wise thing. At present there are so many immediate and pressing decisions to make that a definite answer is impossible . . . Thanking you for your sympathy and consideration . . ."

Talk of a grander setting was already abroad. Speicher hinted at it in his letter to Kroll. Before January was over Henry McBride came right out with it in the *Sun:* "Storm clouds have always hovered over the head of George Bellows. He has always been the center of dispute. Therein lay great merit, too frequently misunderstood . . . He was in love with force. That made him a hero to the young. He was also a born intransigent . . .

"Because of the influence Mr. Bellows exerted on his fellow artists, because of the bright light that constantly beat upon his endeavors and because of the differences of opinion in regard to his attainment, it seems to me imperatively necessary to do something publicly for his memory."

In April the trustees of the august Metropolitan Museum of Art offered their galleries for a comprehensive exhibition of the work of George Bellows.

The Metropolitan, in 1925, enjoyed a unique position among American museums. Boston pressed some of its departments hard and was actually superior in its collections of Oriental art and French Impressionism, but a never-ending succession of New York collectors and philanthropists decanted their treasures and their trusts into the Metropolitan's receptive maw. The Museum's policy was derided as "conservative," especially by the apostles of the "new learning" from Europe whose vociferations would result, four years later, in the foundation of the Museum of Modern Art. Still, the Metropolitan had bought the first Cézanne ever owned by an American institution and purchased it from the Armory

Show of 1913. It had also performed a service, unique in the history of American art, of holding nine posthumous one-man shows by American painters.

The list of these native painters is a compendium of what the museum, in its fifty-odd years of existence, had considered important. There were Whistler and William Merritt Chase, the French-trained painters of elegance; Homer and Eakins, the uncompromising homespun realists; Abbott Thayer, who had apostrophized the pre-World War I American womanhood; Frederick Church, the reporter on Nature's wonders at home and abroad; and J. Alden Weir, perhaps the most accomplished advocate of Impressionism that America ever produced. All of these men had had at least a quarter-century more of working years than Bellows to ready themselves for the honor. None had been recognized so quickly after his death.

To organize the exhibition the museum wisely appointed a committee of twenty-five, including its own director and curator of paintings, the president and other members of the National Academy of Design; Henri, Glackens, Luks, and Sloan from the Eight; Mrs. Whitney and Mrs. Hare from the artist's patrons; and Kroll, Davey, and Eugene Speicher from his immediate circle of friends. Yet although the committee met at least once—an appropriate gesture—the choice of paintings, drawings, and prints devolved upon Emma who measured her judgment with that of Henri and Speicher in coming to the final decisions. By the end of the summer of 1925 they had made up their minds.

On the night of October 11, hundreds of the elect in evening dress swarmed into the Metropolitan's vast halls principally to check on who else was there, whom they were with, what they were wearing, and to decide which lions should be met and which ignored. Yet before the evening was over a great many of these, after the initial amenities, muscled their way through the crowds to look at the lifetime work of George Bellows.

It was there in incredible abundance: sixty-three oils, twenty-four drawings, and nearly sixty lithographs. Two decades of American life, personalities, and thought had never been so broadly nor so penetratingly displayed. The range of subject, design, and color was unique, the effect was overwhelming.

Henri himself squired Emma through that tremendous opening, an exhausting experience for them both. When it was over he turned to her, very close to tears, and said: "I always gave him my most severe criticism because I thought he was my best pupil. Now I am sure of it."

In her private life Emma Bellows faced widowhood at first with bewilderment and sorrow. For fifteen years she had lived, loved, and battled with a singularly vital man. She had now to prove to herself and to his memory her own capacity. Her daughters found her one day, shortly after the funeral, lying prone, her eyes red from weeping, and realized for the first time that despite their parents' tempestuous and frequent quarrels they had been inexorably in love with each other. But Emma had strength and fortitude as well as sentiment. She knew nothing of finance in general and nothing whatever of the state of George's financial affairs. Her romantic concept of the condition of an artist's wife, earlier expressed in her choice of a serviceable wedding dress, reminded her now that an artist's widow must be even poorer. Her entire capital as she then conceived it consisted of six hundred paintings and thousands of drawings and lithographs that still remained unsold in their racks and portfolios at 146. These, she determined, would see her through the rearing of her daughters.

Her first major decision was to manage everything herself. Marie Sterner, her husband's favorite dealer, was in charge of the Durand-Ruel exhibition that George had arranged for months before his death. It would be well worth the notoriety for an American painter's work to be shown in the shrine of the *avant-garde* French, and Bellows had chosen the paintings, largely his latest work, and presently on view at the New Society. Emma thought the forthcoming show ought to be cancelled. Her imagination had already leapt ahead to the concept of a full-scale retrospective. Her whole being, warmed by George's enthusiasm over his last paintings, was disinclined to let the public become too familiar with them too soon. She could not break the contract with Durand-Ruel, but she dispensed with the services of Marie Sterner as soon as she could after the exhibition was over.

In assuming the responsibility for disposing of her husband's work, the "Titaness" of Upper Montclair discovered the career she had once dreamed about before she discarded it for matrimony. By the end of 1925, Emma could record sales amounting to $60,000, three times as much as George had ever realized in a single year. There would be periods to come when popular response to his sudden death had waned, when World War II sent dollars into projectiles instead of paintings, but she stuck to her instincts and her pride. In 1942, when great museums were evacuating their treasures to rural caves, she built a storehouse for her own in the isolation of her Woodstock property. She never cut her prices unless she had been prepared to do so before the bargaining began. She never sold a picture or a drawing unless she was certain that the buyer understood it and would appreciate it. She became in her own contained way something of a holy terror to museum directors if they hung a Bellows too low or in the wrong light, and to the salesmen on Fifty-Seventh Street. The legend of her acumen and personality still lingers with many dealers even now as they progressively move their galleries northward in the direction of Parke-Bernet and the Metropolitan.

Emma was determined to publish a photographic record of George's work for all the world to see. In 1927 she had Alfred Knopf and Company reproduce all of George's lithographs, one hundred and ninety-five in all, in a handsome, cloth-bound volume. This she followed two years later with a numbered, two-thousand-copy edition of one hundred and forty-three photographs of his paintings prefaced by a color reproduction of "Mrs. T. in Wine Silk."

More than this no one could be expected to do, but Emma Bellows did do more. She avoided the complexities of direct merchandizing and found that the preliminary services of a professional middleman were not only a buffer against the initial impact of a sale but a comforting source of advice as well. She personally looked to the condition of the canvases and saw to their framing. For years she kept a small stock of George's pictures at Frank Rehn's on Fifth Avenue, and this arrangement worked well enough, although the paintings were always shown with the work of other artists and she rather wanted to see them grouped together, at least from time to time. In the back of her mind she envisaged a small gallery dedicated to the art of George Bellows. This concept was on a scale quite worthy of her husband. It was also unique.

In 1940, the Keppel Gallery, which had handled all the Bellows lithographs from the beginning, decided to merge with Harlow. Genial and knowledgeable H. V. Allison, who had been Keppel's specialist in the Bellows field, now proposed to set up a gallery of his own; and his son Gordon approached Emma for the privilege of handling the Bellows prints. She graciously assented with the phrase, "Where the Allisons go, there will go the Bellows!" Once the gallery was established she made it the display case for the Bellows oils as well. From that time on, H. V. Allison and Co. has been the sole outlet for the estate of George Bellows, holding a small exhibition almost every year, presenting always a little unfamiliar material and some that is better known. Before she died in 1959 Emma had disposed of four hundred oils. Moreover, the Bellows market never suffered the eclipse that the works of Eakins, Homer, and Sargent experienced after their deaths, but has shown a steady growth in demand and in price.

Emma herself expanded with the years. In the first days of disbelief following her husband's death, her thoughts were fixed upon retrenchment. All four floors at 146 seemed a profligate amount of space to house an impecunious widow, however large and variegated her family. She promptly installed her mother on the ground floor and turned the second floor into a rentable apartment. The studio had been George's domain and into it she now centered her grief and her determination. Quarters became somewhat cramped, especially when her widowed sister Lillian moved in to give her unneeded strength. Emma converted the balcony into a bedroom for herself and her daughters, keeping the big painting area for a living room and the basement for herself. For the rest of her life she retrenched as befitted her idea of the status of an artist's widow, although to the outward eye she was careful to preserve George's image in an expensive mink coat which she felt gave the proper impression of a *successful* artist's widow. At home, except for his paintings glowing on the walls, her needs were minimal—a space to sit and chat, a kitchen, a sparse bedroom with a Bible.

As the years went by and customs changed, Emma kept a firm hand on herself and on her emotions. When her daughters reminisced about their father in a sentimental vein she remarked firmly: "It's a good thing for your memories that your father isn't alive, because . . ." When daughter Anne's wedding mushroomed from "a few friends and family in the garden at Woodstock" into hundreds who would not be kept away, Emma could only remind herself of the casualness of her own marriage. She embraced daughter Jean's stage career as though it had been her own, yet when her youngest elected matrimony she staged it in the studio at 146, insisting on the "Wedding March" and champagne. She had, after all, surrendered her own independence and found the capitulation good.

Drawing of George Bellows painting a landscape, by George Luks during a session of the Committee for the Memorial Exhibition at the Metropolitan on May 21, 1925.

Through more than thirty years Emma reviewed her image of George and polished it to suit herself. She had never really approved of his background, especially his raffish friends from the playing fields of Columbus. When a curious visitor politely asked her the origin of the nickname "Ho," she had her own version: "It was short for H_2O, the formula for water. You see, he was a teetotaler." When *Life Magazine* cited Bellows as "the last of the Ash Can School," she riposted that the painter of "Elinor, Jean, and Anna" and "The Crucifixion" could not possibly be given that association. *Life* apologized at once, but did not print its retraction.

At the same time she never lost her objectivity in recalling major facts. The ugly rumor that she, with her Christian Science, had been the cause of George's death went the rounds for many years, but when it appeared in print she promptly replied that *he* had always relied on doctors. In doing so she had publicly to admit her failure to convert him.

Yet for all her refinements on her memories of George, Emma's personality unconsciously took on much of his unique character. Deprived of her adored target, her mind blended its memory with her own blunted arrows. In her later years she seemed much taller than her modest five foot six inches, and in her voice and in her laughter, always loud and clear, could be recognized much of George's invigorating boom.

Emma Bellows established a record in her management of her husband's estate which she never fully understood. She could not have done this without the incomparable material he had bequeathed her. George Bellows has been dead for forty years, yet his fame has gained luster as decade after changing decade of taste has showered his work with increasing admiration.

The impersonal judgment of the American public on the work of George Bellows in the years following his death has no parallel.

In evaluating the reception of the memorial exhibition at the Metropolitan one might dismiss it as influenced by immediate personal emotions. Thus Frank Crowninshield's introduction to the catalogue carried an expected adulation. It nevertheless managed to incorporate in its text a prophecy: "We believe that the work of this painter—when the whole panorama of it has been unrolled and estimated—will take its place beside the poetry of Whitman and the marines of Homer, and that the three will then be seen to constitute the most inspiring, the most native and the most deeply flavored performances in American art."

Twenty-one years later (1946) the Art Institute of Chicago opened a second major Bellows exhibition. Eugene Speicher supplied the catalogue with a mine of reminiscence and an immaculate eulogy. Unbiased Frederick Sweet provided the bulk of the text, including invaluable notes and observations. At the end of his account he wrote: "What is important for us today is that [Bellows] caught the brute force of the prize fighter, the ruggedness of the country pasture, the dignity of old age, the essence of childhood and recorded them appropriately not only for his own generation but for all time."

In 1957 the National Gallery of Art presented the first one-man show in its history—George Bellows. The introduction to the catalogue was written by Henry McBride, one of the artist's old-time severest critics, and one who had endured the full force of the Bellows rage when the permanence of his colors had been questioned. Three decades had drained the acid from McBride's pen: "But tragically, just as it began to be acknowledged by the world at large that there was a 'Bellows influence,' death cut it short. Just when professional opinion had agreed that Bellows was the chief ornament of the contemporary school he died . . . leaving a void that somehow has never been filled . . . For Bellows was not among those easily hypnotized by foreign fashions . . . When he gazed at the tenements he made you aware of how they could spill out their thousands into the streets at a moment's notice . . . But in the doing of them he put no trace of rancour; no criticism of society as such."

McBride continued: "The portrait of 'My Mother' is acknowledged by most experts to be a masterpiece and can be shown in company with Eakins' best portraits without sense of incongruity. It has the Eakins intensity and monumentality that springs, I suppose, from the implacable Americanism characteristic of both men . . .

"Transcribing a pretty scene, for this artist, was not enough. For him something had to be doing. Stupendous clouds threatening the very mountaintops, a fierce crack of lightning, perhaps one of our own famous hurricanes—and the artist's attention was enchained. The picture had to be painted. The difficulties were nothing. For sheer courage Bellows challenges any artist we have so far produced."

In 1963 John Gruen reviewed the current Bellows exhibition at Allison's for the New York *Herald Tribune.* He wrote: "If one were to ask 'What makes American landscape paintings different from European landscape paintings,' the answer would be quite simply: 'The light, of course!' It is the light from American skies. [Bellows paintings] have both vitality and psychological penetration and an unmistakable American ambience—the sort of painting that could not be duplicated in any other part of the world."

If George Bellows at the age of twenty-two had elected a career as shortstop he would, in 1925, have left behind him a bust in Baseball's Hall of Fame and a scrapbook of yellow clippings. Instead, he chose the artist's life and he left a bust, a scrapbook of yellow clippings, and a multiple inheritance of powerful yet sympathetic commentaries on the scenes of yesterday, today, and tomorrow in America and beyond its borders.

Robert Frost unwittingly wrote Bellows' epitaph:

"Two roads diverged in a wood and I—
  I took the one less travelled by,
    And that has made all the difference."

» Plates «

Clifton Webb, 1905

The Cross-eyed Boy, 1906
»306«

Private Collection

George Bellows, Sr., 1906

»307«

River Rats, 1906
»308«

Collection of Mr. Everett **D. Reese**

Dance in a Madhouse, drawing,
1907

The Art Institute of Chicago,
Charles H. and Mary F. S.
Worester Collection
»309«

A Knockout, 1921; lithograph
after the drawing of 1907
»310«

Dempsey and Firpo,
1924, oil

*Collection of Whitney Museum of
American Art, New York*

Forty-two Kids, 1907

Club Night, 1907
»312«

North River, 1908

Up the Hudson, 1908
»314«

*The Metropolitan
Museum of Art,
Gift of Hugo Reisinger, 1911*

Excavation at Night, 1908

Steaming Streets, 1908
»316«

In the Woods—Waterfall, 1909

The Lone Tenement, 1909
»318«

The Bridge,
Blackwell's Island

»319«

Stag at Sharkey's, 1909
»320«

Stag at Sharkey's, 1909
(detail)

*The Cleveland Museum of Art,
Hinman B. Hurlbut Collection*

Blue Morning, 1909

Summer Night,
Riverside Drive, 1909
»322«

*The Columbus Gallery of Fine
Arts, Columbus, Ohio*

Both Members of This Club,
1909

Polo at Lakewood, 1910
»324«

The Warships, 1909

Beach at Coney Island, 1908-1910
»326«

Shore House, 1911

New York, 1911
»328«

Men of the Docks, 1912

The Circus, 1912
»330«

Dr. William Oxley Thompson,
1913

A Day in June, 1913
»332«

Cliff Dwellers, 1913

Evening Swell, 1911　　　　　　　　　　　　　　　*Private Collection*
»334«

The Big Dory, 1913

Emma at the Piano, 1914
»336«

Judge Peter B. Olney, 1915

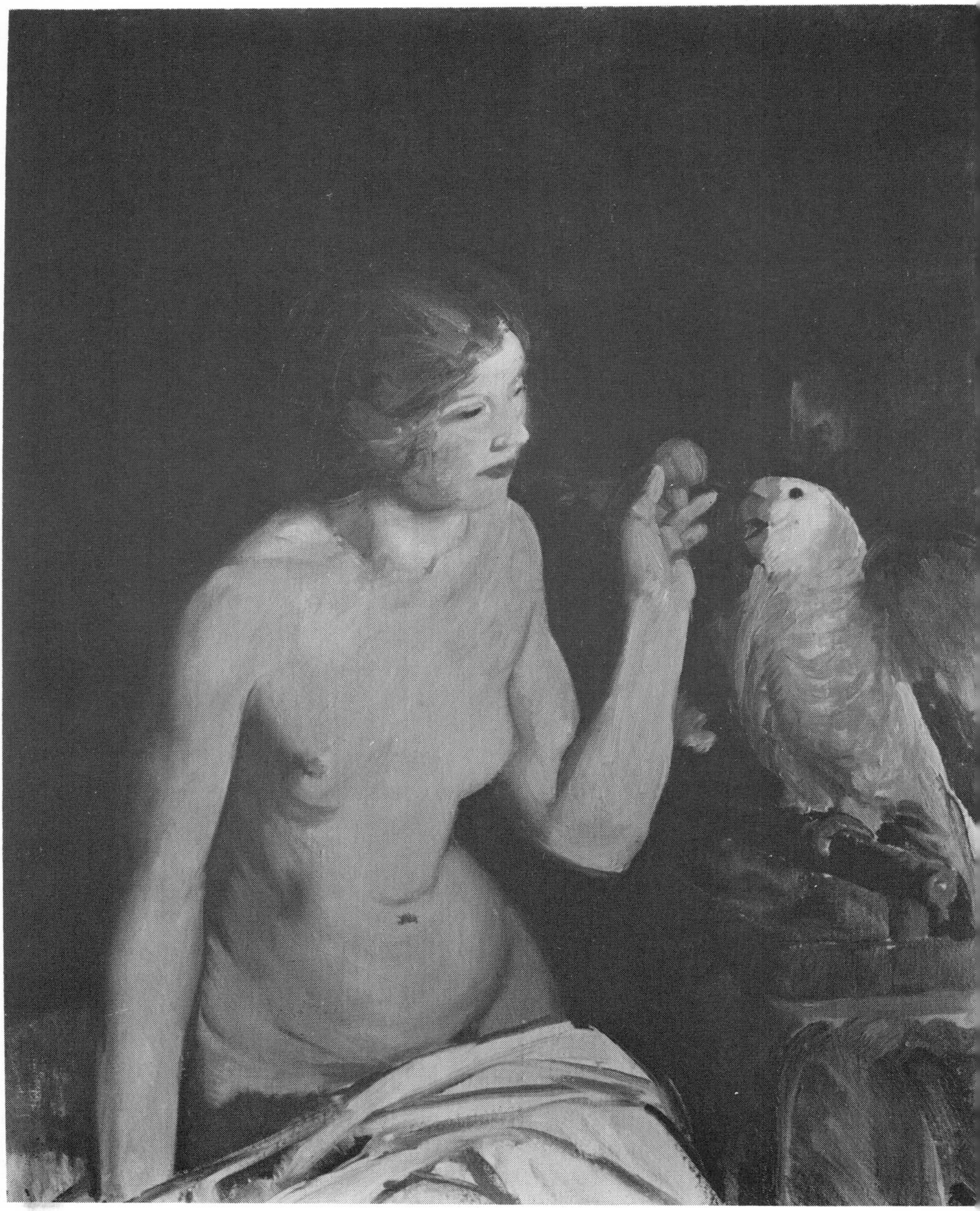

Nude with Parrot, 1915

»338«

Collection of
C. Ruxton Love, Jr.

The Sawdust Trail, 1916

The Rope, or Builders of Ships,
1916
»340«

In a Rowboat, 1916

The Pig and His Sty, 1916
»342«

Collection of Mr. and Mrs.
William Wickham Hoffman

Fisherman, 1917

The Sand Team, 1917
»344«   *The Brooklyn Museum*

Anne in Black Velvet, 1917

Edith Cavell, 1918
»346«

The Studio, 1919

The Black Bull, 1919   *The Bellows Estate*
»348«

On the Porch, 1919
»349«

Aunt Fanny, 1920
»350«

Anne in White, 1920

Katherine Rosen, 1921
»352«

*Yale University bequest of
Stephen Carlton Clark, B.A., 1903*

Katherine Rosen, 1921
(detail)

Yale University bequest of
Stephen Carlton Clark B.A. 1903

Elinor, Jean and Anna, 1920

Gramercy Park, 1920
»354«

Mrs. Eleanor Searle Whitney

Nude with Blue Ostrich Fan,
1920

Mrs. T. in Cream Silk, 1920
»356«

Jean in the Pink Dress, 1921

Cornfield and Harvest, 1921
»358«

My Mother, 1922

The White Horse, 1922   *Worcester Art Museum*
»360«

Emma and Her Children, 1922

The Crucifixion, 1923
»362«

The Bellows Estate

Ringside Seats, 1924

The Picnic, 1924
»364«

Jean, Anne and Joseph, 1924   *Mr. and Mrs. Jack L. Warner*
»365«

River Front II
»366«

The Picket Fence

Lady Jean, 1924
»368«

Lady Jean, 1924
(detail)

»Index«

(Titles referring to paintings are in small capitals. If the painting is illustrated, the page reference is in italics. References to periodicals are italicized.)

Adams, Maude, 241
A DAY IN JUNE, 151, 170, 206, *332*
Aitken, Robert, see *Frontispiece*
A KNOCKOUT, 76, 77, 128-129, *310*
Alexander, John W., 126, 185
Allaire's Restaurant, 226
Allison, Gordon K., 297
Allison, William H., 219, 296
Allison, William H. and Company, 197
American Architect, The, 251
American Art Student, 244
American Magazine, The, 153
Anarchism, 21, 153-155, 169, 201
AN ISLAND IN THE SEA, 137, 138, 171, 181
ANNE IN A BIG CHAIR, 195
ANNE IN A PURPLE WRAP, 249
ANNE IN BLACK VELVET, 211, *345*
ANNE IN BLUE GREEN SILK, 224
ANNE IN WHITE, 238, 351
ANNE WITH THE JAPANESE PARASOL, 203, 234, 258-259
APPROACH TO THE BRIDGE, NIGHT, 170
Armory, The, 161, 162, 163, 165, 167
Armory Show, The, 12, 42, 66, 165, 166, 167, 168, 171, 174, 192, 278, 293
ARNOLD, MRS. HAROLD, 160
ARRANGEMENT, EMMA IN A ROOM, *112*
ARTISTS JUDGING WORKS OF ART, *84*
Art News, 266-267
Arts and Decoration, 245
Arts, The, 233-241
Art Students League, 42, 77, 111, 117, 124, 213, 214, 215, 224, 267
Association of American Painters and Sculptors, 150, 151, 155, 158, 161, 163-164; see also Armory Show
AUNT FANNY, 18, 20, 212, 213, 236, 237, 239, 240, 241, 242, 247, 251, 252, 255, 280-281, *350*
AUTUMN FLAME, 172

Baker, Ray Stannard, 154
Barnard, George Gray, 197
Barrymore, John, 54, 271
Baseball, 22, 23, 28, 29, 34, 42, 44, 53, 54, 58, 59-60, 68, 133, 138, 139, 140, 237, 276-277

Basketball, 23, 24, 27, 29, 34, 42, 66, 77

Bayard, Lucie, 191

BEACH AT CONEY ISLAND, 102, 326

Beaux, Cecilia, 94-95

Beck Medal, 241

Beer, Thomas, 48

Bellows, Anna, 17, 18, 19, 20, 26, 31, 34, 64, 67, 75, 89, 97-98, 121, 160, 166-167, 191, 199, 211, 215, 228, 231, 237, 257-258, 261-262, 264

Bellows, Anne, 144, 145, 146-147, 159, 171, 173, 184, 185, 189, 191, 201, 205-206, 211, 213-214, 215, 228, 231, 236, 259, 262-263, 271, 277, 298

Bellows, Emma, 42, 43, 48, 49-56, 59, 60, 63, 66, 78, 79, 86, 87, 92, 93, 94, 97, 98, 99-100, 101, 103, 108, 113-115, 116, 117, 118-122, 127-128, 132-133, 134-143, 145, 146, 147, 156, 157, 159, 160, 170, 172, 173, 179, 184, 186, 188, 189, 196-197, 200, 201, 203, 204, 205, 207, 209, 211, 213, 214, 215, 217, 218, 228, 230, 231, 235-236, 237, 238, 245, 248-249, 256, 258, 259, 260, 261, 262, 263, 265, 271, 273, 275, 278, 279, 280, 282, 284, 285, 287, 288, 289, 292, 293, 294, 295-299

BELLOWS, GEORGE, bust by Robert Aitken, Frontispiece; cartoon of by Luks, *298*

BELLOWS, GEORGE SENIOR, 17, 19, 25, 31, 75, 89, 114, 121, 157, 160, 166-167, *307*

Bellows, Jean, 188, 189, 191, 203-204, 206, 209, 211, 213, 214, 215, 238, 249, 260, 262, 263, 276, 277, 298

Bellows, Laura, see Monett, Laura

Berenson, Bernard, 241

Beta Theta Pi, 27, 28, 32, 152

Billy Sunday, *144*, 177, 186-187

BLUE MORNING, 93, *321*

BLUE SNOW, THE BATTERY, 125

Borglum, Gutson, 151, 161, 162

Boswell, Peyton, 266-267

BOTH MEMBERS OF THIS CLUB, 101, 104, *323*

Botticelli, Sandro, 245

Bouché, Louis, 232

Bouguereau, Adolphe William, 43, 72, 245

Bourgeois Gallery, 226

BOY ON A DOCK, *106*

Boyensen, Bayard, 153

BOY WITH BARE CHEST, 88

Brearley School, 254

Brown, Bolton, 243-244, 260, 280, 281, 288

Brownies, The, 23, 24, 29, 31, 67, 157

BUILDERS OF SHIPS, 200, *340*

Burlingame, Charles C., 189, 192, 193

Burroughs, Bryson, 73

Byrne, Donn, 254

Cafe Francais, 226

Callot, Jacques, 218

Camden, Maine, 199-203
CANFIELD, JAMES, 95
Carmel, Calif., 209-214, 273
Carnegie International Exhibition, 47, 96, 132, 169, 178, 252
Carpentier, Georges, 246-247, 263
Carroll, John, 255, 262
Cashdollar, Albert, 275, 279
Caskey, Lacey, 272
Cassatt, Mary, 159
Catt, Carrie Chapman, 48, 223
Century Magazine, 249, 254, 259
Cézanne, Paul, 72, 73, 96, 159, 164, 215, 227, 293
Chamberlain, Joseph, 127
Chanler, Joseph, 146-147
Chapman, John Jay, 240
Chase School, see New York School of Art
Chase, William Merritt, 13, 38, 39, 40, 42, 66, 68, 69, 90, 106, 127, 254, 294
Chicago, Art Institute of, 228, 229, 266, 279, 289, 299-300
Chicago, Ill., 228-231, 299-300
Christie, Howard Chandler, 29
CLARK, PAUL, 211-212, 214
Clark, Stephen C., 234, 247, 258-259
Clarke, Ethel, 55, 56, 66, 87, 99-100, 118, 119, 148, 188, 196-197, 261, 262, 284, 289
CLUB NIGHT, 9, 76-77, 78, 89-90, 255, *312*
Coleman, Glenn O., 42, 68, 82, 107

Collier's Weekly, 152, 198, 273-275, 276, 279
Comstock, Anthony, 45, 100, 278
Corcoran Gallery, The, 97, 267
Cornell, Fred, 44, 47, 51, 56, 59, 60, 63, 65
CORNFIELD AND HARVEST (Woodstock), *358*
Cortissoz, Royal, 166, 204-205, 221, 288
CREAM SURF, *171*
CREHAVEN (Bellows' spelling), 203, 227
Criehaven, Maine, see Crehaven
CROWD AT POLO, 125, 127, 131, 177, 224
Crowninshield, Frank, 220, 299

Dabo, Leon, 171
Daggett, Fanny, see AUNT FANNY
DALE, CHESTER, 14, 225, 251-252
DALE, MAUDE (Mrs. Chester), 14, 224-225, 246, 255
DANCE IN A MADHOUSE, 67, 70, 207, *309*
Daniel Gallery, 226
Daumier, Honoré, 86, 197, 219, 243
Davey, Randall, 95, 133, 134, 135, 136, 142, 188, 198-199, 200, 202, 206, 214, 294
Davies, Arthur B., 12, 73, 81, 107, 108, 110, 128, 130, 151, 155, 158, 159, 161, 162-163, 168, 202, 241
Debs, Eugene, 74, 208
Degas, Edgar, 126, 127
Dempsey, Jack, 246-247, 263

DEMPSEY-FIRPO, 263-264, 270, 276, 283, 291, 310
Delineator, The, 152
DOCKS IN WINTER, 129
Dr. Downer, 277-278
Doyle, A. Conan, 264
Drew, John, 66
DuBois, Guy, Pène, 14, 162, 168, 170, 203
Duchamps, Marcel, 165, 176
Duncan, Isadora, 195-197
Durand-Ruel Gallery, 226, 279, 291-292, 295
Duveneck, Frank, 13
Dynamic Symmetry, 12, 216-217, 218, 238, 244, 255, 265, 272, 279

Eakins, Thomas, 58, 66, 104, 215, 243, 272, 294, 297, 300
Eastman, Max, 169, 176, 209
EDITH CAVELL, see THE MURDER OF EDITH CAVELL
Ehrich Gallery, 226
Eight, The, 80-81, 82, 83, 85, 96, 102, 107, 128, 130, 151, 294
El Greco, 264, 269
ELINOR, JEAN AND ANNA, 238, 240, 241, 247, 252, 262, 268, 353
Emerson, Ralph Waldo, 41
EMMA AND HER CHILDREN, 262, 264, 271, 278, 361
EMMA AT THE PIANO, 180, 195, 336
EMMA IN THE BLACK PRINT, 225, 262
EMMA IN THE PURPLE DRESS, 225, 265

EVENING SWELL, 146, 334
Everybody's Magazine, 152
EXCAVATION AT NIGHT, 88, 315

FAMILY GROUP, 180
Fauves, The, 163, 172, 202
Ferrer School, 153
Firpo, Luis, 263-264
FISHERMAN'S FAMILY, 180, 228, 265, 267
Fitch, Clyde, 28, 48
FLANNIGAN, JIMMY, 75, 82, 88
FLANNIGAN, PADDY, 88, 93, 195; see also BOY WITH BARE CHEST
FLOATING ICE, 167
FOOTBALL, 27, 140
FORTY-TWO KIDS, 55, 76, 83, 97, 99, 104, 186, 311
Frick, Helen, 221
Frick, Henry Clay, 123
Frost, Robert, 264, 301

Gauguin, 159, 169, 172
GEORGE BELLOWS PAINTING A LANDSCAPE, sketch by George Luks, 298
GERALDINE LEE, 184, 206
Gibson, Charles Dana, 24, 32, 100, 220, 288
Gillette, William, 66, 91
Glackens, William, 12, 44, 45, 47, 53, 58, 71, 81, 82, 96, 102, 103, 105, 108, 115, 122, 131, 147, 152, 245, 269, 284, 288, 294
Goldman, Emma, 123, 169, 199, 206
Good Housekeeping, 264
Gorky, Maxim, 74

Goya, Francisco, 39, 68, 86, 98, 197, 218, 259, 264, 269

GRAMERCY PARK, 236-237, *354*

Grand Central Galleries, 293

GRANDMA BELLOWS, 228

Grant, Charles, 26, 89, 91

Grisby, Lloyd, 68

Gruen, John, 300-301

Haggin, Ben Ali, 101, 147

Haggin, Mrs., 122, 157, 171

Hale, Philip, 159

Hallgarten Prizes, 83, 124, 168

Hals, Franz, 39, 174

Hambidge, Jay, 12, 216-217, 218, 238, 272

HARE, MEREDITH, 245-246

Hare, Mrs. Montgomery, 245-246, 294

Harper's Weekly, 152

Harris Prizes, 45, 195, 251

HARRY'S EYE, cartoon, *80*

Hartley, Marsden, 105, 131, 171

Harvard Club of New York, 189, 190, 192-194

Hassam, Childe, 70, 96

Hayward, "Big Bill," 74, 154

Hearst's International Magazine, 240, 258, 264

Henri, Marjorie, 86, 203, 207, 238, 261, 289

Henri, Robert, 12, 13, 37, 39, 40, 41, 42, 44, 45, 46, 47, 51, 52, 57, 58, 66, 68, 69, 70, 71, 72, 73, 74, 75, 78, 81, 82, 85, 86, 88, 90-91, 94, 95, 100, 103, 105, 107, 108, 110, 113, 115, 117, 122, 127, 128-129, 130, 131, 132, 135, 136, 137, 142, 149, 150, 153, 154, 156, 162-163, 168, 170, 172, 174, 180, 185, 191, 196, 199, 200, 201, 203, 206, 207, 208, 213, 214, 215, 226, 230, 232, 234, 237, 239, 249, 261, 263, 264, 265, 266, 267, 268, 269, 271, 272, 275, 278, 284, 288, 289, 290, 293

Herrick, Griffin, 278, 280, 281, 284

Hobson, Bishop Henry W., 264

Homer, Winslow, 29, 82, 83, 125, 152, 171, 172, 243, 269, 272, 294, 297, 299

Hopkinson, Charles, 192

Hopper, Edward, 42, 43, 57, 82

Huneker, James, 148, 149

Ibsen, Henrik Johan, 38, 254

IN A ROWBOAT, 201, *341*

Independent Artists' Exhibition, 107-110, 117, 130, 150

Inness, George, 51

IN THE WOODS, WATERFALL, (Zion), *317*

INTRODUCING GEORGES CARPENTIER, 247

INTRODUCING JOHN L. SULLIVAN, 260-261

INVERNIZZI, PROSPER, 77-78

IN VIRGINIA, 201

Ireland, Ted, 101

Isador Medal, 206

I.W.W., 154, 211

JABBERWOCK, THE, 147

JEAN, ANNE AND JOSEPH, 281, 291, *365*

JEAN IN THE PINK DRESS, 249, 251, *357*
Jefferies, Jim, 69, 260

Kalman, Leila, 275, 291
Keefe, Edward R., 42, 43, 44, 47, 51, 56, 60, 63, 65, 69, 82, 86, 91, 92, 93, 95, 97, 101
Keller, Helen, 207
Kent, Rockwell, 42, 43, 68, 82, 110, 130-131, 150, 153, 203, 215
Keppel Gallery, 219, 226, 241, 247, 292, 296
Ketchum, Arthur, 118-120
KIDS, 52, 69
King, Moses, 69
Kipling, Rudyard, 149
Knoedler Gallery, 201, 224, 226, 233
KNOPF, SAMUEL, 254
Kraushaar Gallery, 226
Kroll, Leon, 8, 123, 171, 172, 191, 200, 201, 203, 206, 214-215, 216, 230, 237, 245, 247, 265, 267, 268, 272, 279, 282, 288, 289, 293, 294
Kroll, Viette, 268, 272
Kuhn, Walt, 107, 150, 157, 162

LADY JEAN, 276, 291, *368*
Lakeside, Ohio, 25
Lauder, Harry, 42
LAUGHING BOY, 103, 104
Lawrence Mill Strike, 153-154
Lawson, Ernest, 73, 82, 108, 110, 288
Lenbach, Franz von, 93
Lindsay, Vachel, 113

Lithography, 197-198
LITTLEFIELD, WALTER, 195
LITTLE GIRL IN WHITE, 75, 104, 127, 166, 167, 168
Logan Purchase Prize, 230, 266
LOVE OF WINTER, 177, 195
Luks, George, 12, 45, 71, 81, 103, 108, 130, 215, 269, 294, 298
Lusitania, 191
Luxembourg Committee, 226-227, 228, 232-233, 236
Luxembourg Museum, 39, 45

Macbeth Gallery, 72, 80, 226
Macbeth, William, 72, 149
MacDonald, Ramsay, 154
MacDowell Club, 103, 122, 155, 210
Macgowan, Kenneth, 282
Madison Gallery, 126-127, 150
Makio, The, 27, 29, 32, *33*, 40, 152
Manet, Édouard, 39, 60, 215
MANSHIP, PAUL, 187-188
Maratta, Hardesty, 12, 65, 160, 174
MARDI GRAS AT CONEY, 129
Marées, Hans von, 159
MARGARET, 234
Marin, John, 13, 105, 131
Masses, The, 149, 169, 176-177, 208, 209
Masters School, The, 267
Matinicus, see Mattinicus
Matisse, Henri, 104, 105, 159, 227, 278
Mattinicus (Bellows' spelling), 172, 201-202

Maurer, Alfred, 13, 105, 131, 232
Maxim's, 122
Maynard Price, 178
McBride, Henry, 233-234, 268-269, 292, 293, 300
McCallip, Wright ("Bud"), 8, 67, 87
McFee, Henry, 203, 232
McGlannigan, Thomas, 57, 90
McHenry, Kathleen, 123
McIntyre, Robert G., 8, 149
McRae, Elmer, 150
MENDENTHALE, DR. T. C., 169-170
MEN LIKE GODS, 258, 259, 260, 269
MEN OF THE DOCKS, 148, *329*
Mencken, H. L., 241
Metropolitan Museum of Art, 41, 132, 293-295, 299
Middletown, R. I., 219-220, 224-228
Miller, George, 218
Miller, Kenneth Hayes, 90
MILLER, MRS. ALFRED, 160
Miss Dow's School, 254
Monet, Claude, 110, 175
Monett, Benjamin, 18, 34, 156, 157
Monett, Howard, 58, 64, 157, 219, 231, 237, 261, 280
Monett, Laura, 18, 34, 58, 64, 87, 97, 98, 100, 231, 237, 262, 272, 279, 280, 281
Monhegan, Maine, 68, 133-142, 156, 170-173, 180-181, 183-184, 191, 199
Montauk, N. Y., 120
Montross Gallery, 177, 226

Mooney, Tom, 201, 212
MORNING SNOW, 105
Morse, Samuel F. B., 71
MRS. STORY AT THE TELEPHONE, 271
MRS. T. IN CREAM SILK, 231, 233-234, *356*
MRS. T. IN WINE SILK, 231, 296
Murphy, J. Francis, 70
MUSICAL ORGANIZATIONS, *33*
MY BABY, 159
Myers, Jerome, 150, 151, 164, 168
MY FAMILY, 250
MY MOTHER, 13, 244, 266, 300, *359*

National Academy of Design, 13, 40, 42, 46, 47, 69-70, 71, 72, 74, 78, 82, 83, 94, 95, 105-107, 126, 130, 131, 148, 150, 166, 167-168, 169, 177, 178, 288
National Arts Club, 105, 110, 120, 226, 239, 241, 242
National Gallery of Art, 300
Nesbett, Evelyn, 54, 55
New Society of American Artists, 238, 239, 240, 268, 285, 291, 295
NEW YORK, 129, 132, *328*
New York School of Art, 13, 38, 39, 40, 43, 44, 48, 53, 60, 70, 90-91
Nicholson, Ben, 260
NORTH RIVER, 81-82, 83, 85, 88, 93, 96, 124-125, 131, *313*
Norton, Charles Eliot, 155, 193
NUDE, MISS BENTHAM, 66

NUDE ON A HEXAGON QUILT, 278
NUDE WITH A PARROT, 191, *338*
NUDE WITH BLUE OSTRICH FAN,
238, *355*

O'Brien, Cob, 118, 120
Ogunquit, Maine, 191-192, 199,
262
O'Henri, 67
Ohio State University, 25, 27,
32, 35, 90, 95, 152, 169, 177
Oldfield, Barney, 30
OLD LADY IN BLACK, see AUNT
FANNY
OLNEY, JUDGE PETER, 189-190,
192, *337*
O'Neill, Eugene, 91-92, 95, 101,
282-283
O'Neill, James, 91, 92
ON THE EAST SIDE, *62*
ON THE PORCH, 225, 237, 291, *349*
OUTSIDE THE BIG TENT, 156
Owl, The, 260

Pach, Walter, 158, 163
Paderewski, Ignaz, 276
PADRE, 211
Panama-Pacific Exposition, 185,
191
Patterson, Robert, 22, 157
Pennell, Joseph, 221, 266, 288
PENNSYLVANIA EXCAVATION, 68,
70, 78, 80
Pennsylvania Station, 68, 88, 93
Petitpas, 122, 126, 226
Photo-Secession Gallery, 105,
163
Picasso, Pablo, 159, 169, 278
Pierce, Waldo, 235

Players' Club, 226
POLO AT LAKEWOOD, 116, 126,
132, 164, *324*
POLO GAME, see POLO AT LAKE-
WOOD
Prendergast, Maurice, 73, 81,
105, 108, 110, 130, 164, 288
Preston, May Wilson, 80
PREZIOSSI, 47
Pyle, Howard, 73

Quinn, John, 165

RAIN ON THE RIVER, 88, 93, 103,
195
Raymond, "Sox," 67
RED-FACED BOY LAUGHING, 88
Redon, Odile, 163
Reed, John, 169, 186
Rehn Gallery, 259, 296
Reisinger, Hugo, 103-104, 105,
131, 132
Rembrandt, 39, 95, 159, 206, 245
Renoir, Auguste, 12, 215, 237,
263
RICHTER, MRS. WALTER, 255
Rickard, Tex, 246
RINGSIDE SEATS, 273, 275, 291,
363
Rivera, Diego, 149
RIVER FRONT I, 180, 185
RIVER FRONT II, 273, 291, *366*
RIVER RATS, 58, 60, 70, 76, 96,
104, 127, *308*
ROCK BOUND, 171
Roosevelt, President Theodore,
24, 74
Rosen, Charles, 278

ROSEN, KATHERINE, 247, 258, 259, 263, *352*

Ross, Denman, 175-176, 180, 184, 210

Rubens, Peter Paul, 174, 176, 180, 264

Ryder, Albert Pinkham, 243

Sag Harbor, N. Y., 17, 25, 58, 59, 87, 97, 121

Sandburg, Carl, 223

Sanger, Margaret, 199

San Mateo, Calif., 209, 211-212

Santa Fe, N. M., 213, 214-215

Sargent, John Singer, 29, 39, 75, 90, 161, 192, 221, 297

SCOTT, DR. WALTER QUINCY, 156

SELF PORTRAIT, watercolor, 179, lithograph, 286

Sesnan Medal, 149

Shadowland, 223

Sharkey's, 69, 76, 101

Shaw, George Bernard, 21, 27, 38, 197

Sheeler, Charles, 232

Shinn, Everett, 12, 45, 58, 71, 81, 102, 108, 131, 147, 151

SHIPYARD SOCIETY, 200

SHORE HOUSE, 125, 127, 283, *328*

Shotwell House, 236, 237, 245, 257

Slinkhard, Rex, 95-96, 98, 100, 101

Sloan, Dolly, 169, 207

Sloan, John, 12, 14, 44, 45, 47, 55, 57, 58, 71, 72, 80, 85, 102, 103, 107, 108, 110, 122, 128, 131, 149, 152, 197, 198-199,

200, 202, 206, 207, 214, 223, 242, 269, 271, 288, 294

Slyke, Judge Van, 275, 276

Smith, Elinor, see AUNT FANNY

Smith, Fanny, see AUNT FANNY

Smith, George Washington, 172

SNOW-CAPPED RIVER, 129

SNOW DUMPERS, 148, 177

Society of American Artists, 46, 47, 49, 71

Speicher, Elsie, 108, 289

Speicher, Eugene, 77, 108, 122, 189, 219, 224, 232, 235, 237, 238, 245, 249, 271, 272, 278, 284, 288, 293, 294

SPLINTER BEACH, 152

SPRING IDLERS, 116

Stafford, Scott, 107

STAG AT SHARKEY'S, 98, 101, 127, 198, 219, 220, 255, 292, *320*

STEAMING STREETS, 85, *316*

Stella, Joseph, 232

Sterner, Marie, 201, 255, 295

STERNER, OLIVIA, 199

Stieglitz, Alfred, 163; see Photo-Secession Gallery

Still's Restaurant, 226

Stokowski, Leopold, 244

Stone, Lucy, 48, 49

Story, Emma, see Bellows, Emma

Story, Lillian, 49, 50, 297

Story, William E., 48, 49, 50, 56, 64, 141, 143, 184, 287

Straight, Willard, 178-179

STRUGGLE WITH A DRUNK, 57

SUMMER CITY, 111

SUMMER NIGHT, 98-99, 104, *322*

Sunday, Billy, 177, 186-187

SUNDAY 1897, GOING TO CHURCH, *16*, 243, 244

Sweet, Frederick, 9, 299-300

Swope, Herbert Bayard, 246-247

Taylor, Professor Joseph, 27, 29, 34, 67, 79, 90, 95, 105, 108, 113, 115, 155, 157, 160, 169-170, 173, 177-178, 190, 191, 226, 253

Temple Award, 206

TENNIS AT NEWPORT, 222

Thaw, Harry K., 54, 55

Thayer, Abbott, 294

THE AFTER GLOW, 233

The Battleships, see THE WARSHIPS

THE BIG DORY (Monhegan), *335*

THE BLACK BULL, 227, *348*

THE BRIDGE, BLACKWELL'S ISLAND, 102, 104, 125, *319*

THE CIRCUS, 156, 224, *330*

THE CROSS-EYED BOY, 57, 60, 87, 124, *306*

THE CRUCIFIXION, 264-265, 268, 271, *362*

THE ENEMY ARRIVE, *182*, 218, 220

THE FISHERMAN, 210, 216, *343*

THE GOLF COURSE, 210, 224

THE HUDSON AT SAUGERTIES, 239

THE LIFE CLASS, *36*, 208

THE LONE TENEMENT, 102, *318*

THE MURDER OF EDITH CAVELL, 219, 220-221, 229, 252, *346*

THE PALISADES, 177

THE PICKET FENCE, 283, *367*

THE PICNIC, 273, 291, *364*

THE PIG IN HIS STY (Mattinicus), *342*

THE RED SUN, 227, 233

THE RETURN OF THE USELESS, 221, 229

THE RICH WOODS, 146

THE ROPE, see BUILDERS OF SHIPS

THE SAND TEAM, 210, *344*

THE SAWDUST TRAIL, 187, 207, *339*

THE SEA, 146

THE SKELETON, 200

THE STONE FENCE (Zion), 127

THE STUDIO, 205, 217, 224, *347*

THE TEAMSTER, 200

THE VIOLINIST, 275, 291

THE WARSHIPS, 118, *325*

THE WHITE HORSE, 258, *360*

THE WIDOW, 212

THE WIND BLOWETH, 254, 259, 269, 273

THE YOUNG HORSE GRAZING, 227

Thomas, Joseph B., 110, 115, 209, 211

THOMPSON, DR. WILLIAM OXLEY, 177-178, 253, *331*

THREE ROLLERS, 146

TINTORETTO, 264

Titanic, The, 153, 156

Titian, 174, 215, 244, 278

Tolstoi, Leon, 38, 67

TORSO OF A GIRL, 191

Touchstone Magazine, 208, 209, 210

Trumbull, John, 71

TWO WOMEN, 278, 290

Tyler, Mrs. Mary Brown, see MRS. T.

UP THE HUDSON, 85, 88, 131, *314*

Van Doren, Mark, 284
Van Gogh, Vincent, 159, 164, 172
Vanity Fair, 239, 240-241
Velásquez, Diego, 39, 60, 86, 95, 174
Virginia, University of, 86
Volstead Act, 223

WASE, MR. AND MRS. PHILIP, 278, 291
Watrous, Harry, *80,* 83, 94
Watson, Forbes, 191, 193-194
Waverly Place Players, 147
WEBB, CLIFTON, 48, 90, 113, *305*
Weber, Max, 13, 203, 226, 232
Weir, J. Alden, 150, 151, 185, 294
Wells, H. G., 64, 258, 260
WE WANT ANNE AND JEAN, 229
Whistler, James A. McNeill, 13, 38, 39, 131, 160, 191, 272, 294
WHITE HUDSON, 130

White, Stanford, 54, 55
Whitman, Walt, 27, 41, 149, 223, 299
Whitney, Gertrude Vanderbilt, 80, 123, 162, 178, 191, 271, 294
Willard, Jess, 198, 241
Wilson, Woodrow, 164, 183, 207, 208, 209
WINTER AFTERNOON, 105
WINTER ROAD, 148
Woodstock, N. Y., 235, 237-239, 245-249, 255, 258, 260-265, 275-279, 288, 296, 298

Yeats, John Butler, 226
Young, Mahonri, 169
Y. M. C. A., 23, 25, 37, 40, 41, 43, 77

Zion, N. Y., 92-93
Zorn, Anders, 29, 90
Zuloaga, 254, 281, 290-291, 293